Nutshell
Hornbook Series
and
Black Letter Series
of

WEST PUBLISHING COMPANY
P.O. Box 64526
St. Paul, Minnesota 55164–0526

Accounting
FARIS' ACCOUNTING AND LAW IN A NUTSHELL, 377 pages, 1984. Softcover. (Text)

Administrative Law
GELLHORN AND LEVIN'S ADMINISTRATIVE LAW AND PROCESS IN A NUTSHELL, Third Edition, approximately 420 pages, 1990. Softcover. (Text)

Admiralty
MARAIST'S ADMIRALTY IN A NUTSHELL, Second Edition, 379 pages, 1988. Softcover. (Text)

SCHOENBAUM'S HORNBOOK ON ADMIRALTY AND MARITIME LAW, Student Edition, 692 pages, 1987 with 1989 pocket part. (Text)

Agency—Partnership
REUSCHLEIN AND GREGORY'S HORNBOOK ON THE LAW OF AGENCY AND PARTNERSHIP, Second Edition, 683 pages, 1990. (Text)

STEFFEN'S AGENCY-PARTNERSHIP IN A NUTSHELL, 364 pages, 1977. Softcover. (Text)

American Indian Law
CANBY'S AMERICAN INDIAN LAW IN A NUTSHELL, Second Edition, 336 pages, 1988. Softcover. (Text)

Antitrust—see also Regulated Industries, Trade Regulation
GELLHORN'S ANTITRUST LAW AND ECONOMICS IN A NUTSHELL, Third Edition, 472

List current as of July, 1990

WITHDRAWN

HIEBERT LIBRARY
FRESNO PACIFIC UNIV.-M. B. SEMINARY
FRESNO, CA 93702

Antitrust—Continued

pages, 1986. Softcover. (Text)

HOVENKAMP'S BLACK LETTER ON ANTITRUST, 323 pages, 1986. Softcover. (Review)

HOVENKAMP'S HORNBOOK ON ECONOMICS AND FEDERAL ANTITRUST LAW, Student Edition, 414 pages, 1985. (Text)

SULLIVAN'S HORNBOOK OF THE LAW OF ANTITRUST, 886 pages, 1977. (Text)

Appellate Advocacy—see Trial and Appellate Advocacy

Art Law

DUBOFF'S ART LAW IN A NUTSHELL, 335 pages, 1984. Softcover. (Text)

Banking Law

LOVETT'S BANKING AND FINANCIAL INSTITUTIONS LAW IN A NUTSHELL, Second Edition, 464 pages, 1988. Softcover. (Text)

Civil Procedure—see also Federal Jurisdiction and Procedure

CLERMONT'S BLACK LETTER ON CIVIL PROCEDURE, Second Edition, 332 pages, 1988. Softcover. (Review)

FRIEDENTHAL, KANE AND MILLER'S HORNBOOK ON CIVIL PROCEDURE, 876 pages, 1985. (Text)

KANE'S CIVIL PROCEDURE IN A NUTSHELL, Second Edition, 306 pages, 1986. Softcover. (Text)

KOFFLER AND REPPY'S HORNBOOK ON COMMON LAW PLEADING, 663 pages, 1969. (Text)

SIEGEL'S HORNBOOK ON NEW YORK PRACTICE, 1011 pages, 1978, with 1987 pocket part. (Text)

Commercial Law

BAILEY AND HAGEDORN'S SECURED TRANSACTIONS IN A NUTSHELL, Third Edition, 390 pages, 1988. Softcover. (Text)

HENSON'S HORNBOOK ON SECURED TRANSACTIONS UNDER THE U.C.C., Second Edition, 504 pages, 1979, with 1979 pocket part. (Text)

NICKLES' BLACK LETTER ON COMMERCIAL PAPER, 450 pages, 1988. Softcover. (Review)

SPEIDEL'S BLACK LETTER ON SALES AND SALES FINANCING, 363 pages, 1984. Softcover. (Review)

STOCKTON'S SALES IN A NUT-

WITHDRAWN

GIBBERT LIBRARY
PUGGIO PACIFIC UNIV·M·R·SEMINARY
FRESNO, CA 93702

Commercial Law—Continued

SHELL, Second Edition, 370 pages, 1981. Softcover. (Text)

STONE'S UNIFORM COMMERCIAL CODE IN A NUTSHELL, Third Edition, 580 pages, 1989. Softcover. (Text)

WEBER AND SPEIDEL'S COMMERCIAL PAPER IN A NUTSHELL, Third Edition, 404 pages, 1982. Softcover. (Text)

WHITE AND SUMMERS' HORNBOOK ON THE UNIFORM COMMERCIAL CODE, Third Edition, Student Edition, 1386 pages, 1988. (Text)

Community Property

MENNELL AND BOYKOFF'S COMMUNITY PROPERTY IN A NUTSHELL, Second Edition, 432 pages, 1988. Softcover. (Text)

Comparative Law

GLENDON, GORDON AND OSAKWE'S COMPARATIVE LEGAL TRADITIONS IN A NUTSHELL. 402 pages, 1982. Softcover. (Text)

Conflict of Laws

HAY'S BLACK LETTER ON CONFLICT OF LAWS, 330 pages, 1989. Softcover. (Review)

SCOLES AND HAY'S HORNBOOK ON CONFLICT OF LAWS, Student Edition, 1085 pages, 1982, with 1988–89 pocket part. (Text)

SEIGEL'S CONFLICTS IN A NUTSHELL, 470 pages, 1982. Softcover. (Text)

Constitutional Law—Civil Rights

BARRON AND DIENES' BLACK LETTER ON CONSTITUTIONAL LAW, Second Edition, 310 pages, 1987. Softcover. (Review)

BARRON AND DIENES' CONSTITUTIONAL LAW IN A NUTSHELL, 389 pages, 1986. Softcover. (Text)

ENGDAHL'S CONSTITUTIONAL FEDERALISM IN A NUTSHELL, Second Edition, 411 pages, 1987. Softcover. (Text)

MARKS AND COOPER'S STATE CONSTITUTIONAL LAW IN A NUTSHELL, 329 pages, 1988. Softcover. (Text)

NOWAK, ROTUNDA AND YOUNG'S HORNBOOK ON CONSTITUTIONAL LAW, Third Edition, 1191 pages, 1986 with 1988 pocket part. (Text)

VIEIRA'S CONSTITUTIONAL CIVIL RIGHTS IN A NUTSHELL, Second Edition, 322 pages, 1990. Softcover. (Text)

Constitutional Law—Civil Rights—Continued

WILLIAMS' CONSTITUTIONAL ANALYSIS IN A NUTSHELL, 388 pages, 1979. Softcover. (Text)

Consumer Law—see also Commercial Law

EPSTEIN AND NICKLES' CONSUMER LAW IN A NUTSHELL, Second Edition, 418 pages, 1981. Softcover. (Text)

Contracts

CALAMARI AND PERILLO'S BLACK LETTER ON CONTRACTS, Second Edition, approximately 450 pages, 1990. Softcover. (Review)

CALAMARI AND PERILLO'S HORNBOOK ON CONTRACTS, Third Edition, 1049 pages, 1987. (Text)

CORBIN'S TEXT ON CONTRACTS, One Volume Student Edition, 1224 pages, 1952. (Text)

FRIEDMAN'S CONTRACT REMEDIES IN A NUTSHELL, 323 pages, 1981. Softcover. (Text)

KEYES' GOVERNMENT CONTRACTS IN A NUTSHELL, Second Edition, approximately 530 pages, 1990. Softcover. (Text)

SCHABER AND ROHWER'S CON-TRACTS IN A NUTSHELL, Third Edition, approximately 438 pages, 1990. Softcover. (Text)

Copyright—see Patent and Copyright Law

Corporations

HAMILTON'S BLACK LETTER ON CORPORATIONS, Second Edition, 513 pages, 1986. Softcover. (Review)

HAMILTON'S THE LAW OF CORPORATIONS IN A NUTSHELL, Second Edition, 515 pages, 1987. Softcover. (Text)

HENN AND ALEXANDER'S HORN-BOOK ON LAWS OF CORPORATIONS, Third Edition, Student Edition, 1371 pages, 1983, with 1986 pocket part. (Text)

Corrections

KRANTZ' THE LAW OF CORRECTIONS AND PRISONERS' RIGHTS IN A NUTSHELL, Third Edition, 407 pages, 1988. Softcover. (Text)

Creditors' Rights

EPSTEIN'S DEBTOR-CREDITOR RELATIONS IN A NUTSHELL, Third Edition, 383 pages, 1986. Softcover. (Text)

NICKLES AND EPSTEIN'S BLACK LETTER ON CREDITORS' RIGHTS AND BANKRUPTCY, 576 pages,

Environmental Law—Continued

pages, 1988. Softcover. (Text)

RODGERS' HORNBOOK ON ENVIRONMENTAL LAW, 956 pages, 1977, with 1984 pocket part. (Text)

Equity—see Remedies

Estate Planning—see also Trusts and Estates; Taxation—Estate and Gift

LYNN'S AN INTRODUCTION TO ESTATE PLANNING IN A NUTSHELL, Third Edition, 370 pages, 1983. Softcover. (Text)

Evidence

BROUN AND BLAKEY'S BLACK LETTER ON EVIDENCE, 269 pages, 1984. Softcover. (Review)

GRAHAM'S FEDERAL RULES OF EVIDENCE IN A NUTSHELL, Second Edition, 473 pages, 1987. Softcover. (Text)

LILLY'S AN INTRODUCTION TO THE LAW OF EVIDENCE, Second Edition, 585 pages, 1987. (Text)

McCORMICK'S HORNBOOK ON EVIDENCE, Third Edition, Student Edition, 1156 pages, 1984, with 1987 pocket part.

(Text)

ROTHSTEIN'S EVIDENCE IN A NUTSHELL: STATE AND FEDERAL RULES, Second Edition, 514 pages, 1981. Softcover. (Text)

Federal Jurisdiction and Procedure

CURRIE'S FEDERAL JURISDICTION IN A NUTSHELL, Third Edition, approximately 260 pages, 1990. Softcover. (Text)

REDISH'S BLACK LETTER ON FEDERAL JURISDICTION, 219 pages, 1985. Softcover. (Review)

WRIGHT'S HORNBOOK ON FEDERAL COURTS, Fourth Edition, Student Edition, 870 pages, 1983. (Text)

Future Interests—see Trusts and Estates

Health Law—see Medicine, Law and

Human Rights—see International Law

Immigration Law

IMMIGRATION AND NATIONALITY LAWS OF THE UNITED STATES: SELECTED STATUTES, REGULATIONS AND FORMS. Softcover. Approximately 400 pages, 1990.

Immigration Law—Continued

WEISSBRODT'S IMMIGRATION LAW AND PROCEDURE IN A NUT-SHELL, Second Edition, 438 pages, 1989, Softcover. (Text)

Indian Law—see American Indian Law

Insurance Law

DOBBYN'S INSURANCE LAW IN A NUTSHELL, Second Edition, 316 pages, 1989. Softcover. (Text)

KEETON'S COMPUTER-AIDED AND WORKBOOK EXERCISES ON INSURANCE LAW, 255 pages, 1990. Softcover. (Coursebook)

KEETON AND WIDISS' INSUR-ANCE LAW, Student Edition, 1359 pages, 1988. (Text)

International Law—see also Sea, Law of

BUERGENTHAL'S INTERNATIONAL HUMAN RIGHTS IN A NUTSHELL, 283 pages, 1988. Softcover. (Text)

BUERGENTHAL AND MAIER'S PUBLIC INTERNATIONAL LAW IN A NUTSHELL, Second Edition, 275 pages, 1990. Softcover. (Text)

FOLSOM, GORDON AND SPA-NOGLE'S INTERNATIONAL BUSI-NESS TRANSACTIONS IN A NUT-

SHELL, Third Edition, 509 pages, 1988. Softcover. (Text)

Interviewing and Counseling

BINDER, BERGMAN AND PRICE'S LAWYERS AS COUNSELORS: A CLIENT CENTERED APPROACH, Approximately 400 pages, October, 1990 Pub. Softcover. (Coursebook)

SHAFFER AND ELKINS' LEGAL INTERVIEWING AND COUNSELING IN A NUTSHELL, Second Edition, 487 pages, 1987. Softcover. (Text)

Introduction to Law—see Legal Method and Legal System

Introduction to Law Study

HEGLAND'S INTRODUCTION TO THE STUDY AND PRACTICE OF LAW IN A NUTSHELL, 418 pages, 1983. Softcover. (Text)

KINYON'S INTRODUCTION TO LAW STUDY AND LAW EXAMINA-TIONS IN A NUTSHELL, 389 pages, 1971. Softcover. (Text)

Judicial Process—see Legal Method and Legal System

Juvenile Justice

FOX'S JUVENILE COURTS IN A NUTSHELL, Third Edition, 291

Juvenile Justice—Continued pages, 1984. Softcover. (Text)

Labor and Employment Law— see also Employment Discrimination, Social Legislation

LESLIE'S LABOR LAW IN A NUT-SHELL, Second Edition, 397 pages, 1986. Softcover. (Text)

NOLAN'S LABOR ARBITRATION LAW AND PRACTICE IN A NUT-SHELL, 358 pages, 1979. Softcover. (Text)

Land Finance—Property Security—see Real Estate Transactions

Land Use

HAGMAN AND JUERGENS-MEYER'S HORNBOOK ON URBAN PLANNING AND LAND DEVELOPMENT CONTROL LAW, Second Edition, Student Edition, 680 pages, 1986. (Text)

WRIGHT AND WRIGHT'S LAND USE IN A NUTSHELL, Second Edition, 356 pages, 1985. Softcover. (Text)

Legal Method and Legal System—see also Legal Research, Legal Writing

KEMPIN'S HISTORICAL INTRODUCTION TO ANGLO-AMERICAN LAW IN A NUTSHELL, Third Edition, approximately 302 pages, 1990. Softcover. (Text)

REYNOLDS' JUDICIAL PROCESS IN A NUTSHELL, 292 pages, 1980. Softcover. (Text)

Legal Research

COHEN'S LEGAL RESEARCH IN A NUTSHELL, Fourth Edition, 452 pages, 1985. Softcover. (Text)

COHEN, BERRING AND OLSON'S HOW TO FIND THE LAW, Ninth Edition, 716 pages, 1989. (Text)

Legal Writing

SQUIRES AND ROMBAUER'S LEGAL WRITING IN A NUTSHELL, 294 pages, 1982. Softcover. (Text)

TEPLY'S LEGAL WRITING, ANALYSIS AND ORAL ARGUMENT, 576 pages, 1990. Softcover. Teacher's Manual available. (Coursebook)

Legislation

DAVIES' LEGISLATIVE LAW AND PROCESS IN A NUTSHELL, Second Edition, 346 pages, 1986. Softcover. (Text)

Local Government

MCCARTHY'S LOCAL GOVERNMENT LAW IN A NUTSHELL,

Local Government—Continued

Third Edition, approximately 400 pages, 1990. Softcover. (Text)

REYNOLDS' HORNBOOK ON LOCAL GOVERNMENT LAW, 860 pages, 1982, with 1990 pocket part. (Text)

Mass Communication Law

ZUCKMAN, GAYNES, CARTER AND DEE'S MASS COMMUNICATIONS LAW IN A NUTSHELL, Third Edition, 538 pages, 1988. Softcover. (Text)

Medicine, Law and

HALL AND ELLMAN'S HEALTH CARE LAW AND ETHICS IN A NUTSHELL, 401 pages, 1990. Softcover (Text)

KING'S THE LAW OF MEDICAL MALPRACTICE IN A NUTSHELL, Second Edition, 342 pages, 1986. Softcover. (Text)

Military Law

SHANOR AND TERRELL'S MILITARY LAW IN A NUTSHELL, 378 pages, 1980. Softcover. (Text)

Mortgages—see Real Estate Transactions

Natural Resources Law—see Energy and Natural Resources Law, Environmental Law

Office Practice—see also Computers and Law, Interviewing and Counseling, Negotiation

HEGLAND'S TRIAL AND PRACTICE SKILLS IN A NUTSHELL, 346 pages, 1978. Softcover (Text)

Oil and Gas—see also Energy and Natural Resources Law

HEMINGWAY'S HORNBOOK ON OIL AND GAS, Second Edition, Student Edition, 543 pages, 1983, with 1989 pocket part. (Text)

LOWE'S OIL AND GAS LAW IN A NUTSHELL, Second Edition, 465 pages, 1988. Softcover. (Text)

Partnership—see Agency—Partnership

Patent and Copyright Law

MILLER AND DAVIS' INTELLECTUAL PROPERTY—PATENTS, TRADEMARKS AND COPYRIGHT IN A NUTSHELL, Second Edition, approximately 440 pages, 1990. Softcover. (Text)

Products Liability

PHILLIPS' PRODUCTS LIABILITY IN A NUTSHELL, Third Edition, 307 pages, 1988. Softcover. (Text)

Professional Responsibility

ARONSON AND WECKSTEIN'S PROFESSIONAL RESPONSIBILITY IN A NUTSHELL, 399 pages, 1980. Softcover. (Text)

ROTUNDA'S BLACK LETTER ON PROFESSIONAL RESPONSIBILITY, Second Edition, 414 pages, 1988. Softcover. (Review)

WOLFRAM'S HORNBOOK ON MODERN LEGAL ETHICS, Student Edition, 1120 pages, 1986. (Text)

Property—see also Real Estate Transactions, Land Use, Trusts and Estates

BERNHARDT'S BLACK LETTER ON PROPERTY, 318 pages, 1983. Softcover. (Review)

BERNHARDT'S REAL PROPERTY IN A NUTSHELL, Second Edition, 448 pages, 1981. Softcover. (Text)

BURKE'S PERSONAL PROPERTY IN A NUTSHELL, 322 pages, 1983. Softcover. (Text)

CUNNINGHAM, STOEBUCK AND WHITMAN'S HORNBOOK ON THE LAW OF PROPERTY, Student

Edition, 916 pages, 1984, with 1987 pocket part. (Text)

HILL'S LANDLORD AND TENANT LAW IN A NUTSHELL, Second Edition, 311 pages, 1986. Softcover. (Text)

Real Estate Transactions

BRUCE'S REAL ESTATE FINANCE IN A NUTSHELL, Second Edition, 262 pages, 1985. Softcover. (Text)

NELSON AND WHITMAN'S BLACK LETTER ON LAND TRANSACTIONS AND FINANCE, Second Edition, 466 pages, 1988. Softcover. (Review)

NELSON AND WHITMAN'S HORNBOOK ON REAL ESTATE FINANCE LAW, Second Edition, 941 pages, 1985 with 1989 pocket part. (Text)

Regulated Industries—see also Mass Communication Law, Banking Law

GELLHORN AND PIERCE'S REGULATED INDUSTRIES IN A NUTSHELL, Second Edition, 389 pages, 1987. Softcover. (Text)

Remedies

DOBBS' HORNBOOK ON REMEDIES, 1067 pages, 1973. (Text)

DOBBYN'S INJUNCTIONS IN A NUTSHELL, 264 pages, 1974.

Remedies—Continued

Softcover. (Text)

FRIEDMAN'S CONTRACT REMEDIES IN A NUTSHELL, 323 pages, 1981. Softcover. (Text)

McCORMICK'S HORNBOOK ON DAMAGES, 811 pages, 1935. (Text)

O'CONNELL'S REMEDIES IN A NUTSHELL, Second Edition, 320 pages, 1985. Softcover. (Text)

Sea, Law of

SOHN AND GUSTAFSON'S THE LAW OF THE SEA IN A NUTSHELL, 264 pages, 1984. Softcover. (Text)

Securities Regulation

HAZEN'S HORNBOOK ON THE LAW OF SECURITIES REGULATION, Second Edition, Student Edition, approximately 1000 pages, 1990. (Text)

RATNER'S SECURITIES REGULATION IN A NUTSHELL, Third Edition, 316 pages, 1988. Softcover. (Text)

Social Legislation

HOOD, HARDY AND LEWIS' WORKERS' COMPENSATION AND EMPLOYEE PROTECTION LAWS IN A NUTSHELL, Second Edition, 361 pages, 1990. Softcover. (Text)

LAFRANCE'S WELFARE LAW: STRUCTURE AND ENTITLEMENT IN A NUTSHELL, 455 pages, 1979. Softcover. (Text)

Sports Law

SCHUBERT, SMITH AND TRENTADUE'S SPORTS LAW, 395 pages, 1986. (Text)

Tax Practice and Procedure

MORGAN'S TAX PROCEDURE AND TAX FRAUD IN A NUTSHELL, Approximately 382 pages, 1990. Softcover. (Text)

Taxation—Corporate

WEIDENBRUCH AND BURKE'S FEDERAL INCOME TAXATION OF CORPORATIONS AND STOCKHOLDERS IN A NUTSHELL, Third Edition, 309 pages, 1989. Softcover. (Text)

Taxation—Estate & Gift—see also Estate Planning, Trusts and Estates

McNULTY'S FEDERAL ESTATE AND GIFT TAXATION IN A NUTSHELL, Fourth Edition, 496 pages, 1989. Softcover. (Text)

Taxation—Individual

HUDSON AND LIND'S BLACK LETTER ON FEDERAL INCOME TAXATION, Third Edition, approximately 390 pages, 1990. Softcover. (Review)

Advisory Board

JOHN A. BAUMAN
Professor of Law, University of California, Los Angeles

CURTIS J. BERGER
Professor of Law, Columbia University

JESSE H. CHOPER
Dean and Professor of Law,
University of California, Berkeley

DAVID P. CURRIE
Professor of Law, University of Chicago

YALE KAMISAR
Professor of Law, University of Michigan

MARY KAY KANE
Professor of Law, University of California,
Hastings College of the Law

WAYNE R. LaFAVE
Professor of Law, University of Illinois

RICHARD C. MAXWELL
Professor of Law, Duke University

ARTHUR R. MILLER
Professor of Law, Harvard University

ROBERT A. STEIN
Dean and Professor of Law, University of Minnesota

JAMES J. WHITE
Professor of Law, University of Michigan

CHARLES ALAN WRIGHT
Professor of Law, University of Texas

COMPARATIVE LEGAL TRADITIONS
IN A NUTSHELL

By

MARY ANN GLENDON
Professor of Law
Boston College

MICHAEL WALLACE GORDON
Professor of Law
University of Florida

CHRISTOPHER OSAKWE
Eason-Weinmann Professor of
Comparative Law
Tulane University

St. Paul, Minn.
WEST PUBLISHING CO.
1982

Nutshell Series, In a Nutshell, the Nutshell Logo and the West
Publishing Co. Logo are registered trademarks of West Publishing Co.
Registered in U.S. Patent and Trademark Office.

COPYRIGHT © 1982 By WEST PUBLISHING CO.
50 West Kellogg Boulevard
P. O. Box 3526
St. Paul, Minnesota 55165

All rights reserved
Printed in the United States of America

Library of Congress Cataloging in Publication Data

Glendon, Mary Ann   1938–
  Comparative Legal Traditions in a Nutshell.

  (Nutshell series)
  Includes bibliographies and index.
  1. Comparative law I. Gordon, Michael W.
II. Osakwe, Chris. III. Title. IV. Series.
K560.G43   340.'2   82–2022
                      AACR2

ISBN 0–314–65175–6

      Glendon, Gordon, Osakwe
      3rd Reprint—1990

PREFACE

The purpose of this Nutshell is to provide, in a comparatively brief format, a discussion of several important areas in each of the three major legal traditions of the West. This approach has been undertaken recently by several European writers. Their works, however, have tended to focus on elements of the three legal traditions viewed from the perspective of a civil law scholar. Our attempt, contrastingly, has been to write from the viewpoint of the American trained lawyer, resulting in a concentration on elements of the three traditions notable from the viewpoint of the American lawyer, rather than the European civil law lawyer.

This form of presentation of the materials has been used over the past few years by the authors of this volume for teaching Comparative Law courses at the law schools of Boston College, the University of Florida and Tulane University. This work is the product of over forty years of cumulative teaching experience by its three co-authors. We hope this Nutshell will provide a useful outline to anyone interested in a basic foundation in these three major legal traditions. It should serve as an appropriate introductory volume for use with additional prepared materials, or with any of the current casebooks on Comparative Law. We have organized the subjects in much the same way one would do for classroom discussion.

One important function of teaching Comparative Law is to raise challenging problems and questions for the future and, in this context, to discuss the important considerations which go into the process of reaching answers which will stand the test of time. The main functions of this Nutshell, however, are to set forth as many as possible of the settled resolutions to problems which have arisen during the development of these three legal traditions, to describe the state of currently perplexing issues in these traditions and to be a source book of the working premises which underlie the course in Comparative Law. Naturally, not all issues in this field are settled, nor should they be, because the quest for understanding is and will always remain an ongoing process.

In writing this Nutshell we owe much to our colleagues and to generations of students, and in particular to those foreign colleagues and students with whom we have worked here and abroad, and with whom we have discussed many questions and problems relating to the legal systems covered here.

MARY ANN GLENDON
Newton, Massachusetts

MICHAEL WALLACE GORDON
Gainesville, Florida

CHRISTOPHER OSAKWE
New Orleans, Louisiana

OUTLINE

OUTLINE

PART TWO: THE COMMON LAW TRADITION

OUTLINE

PART THREE: THE SOCIALIST LAW TRADITION

OUTLINE

*

COMPARATIVE LEGAL TRADITIONS
IN A NUTSHELL

*

INTRODUCTORY MATTERS

§ 1. Scope

An increasing number of American law schools are offering courses rather consistently labeled Comparative Law. This trend has been noticeable particularly in the past fifteen years. It is a tendency generated by both internal and external forces acting on law schools. As law schools grow and faculties become more diverse, there is an increasing likelihood that there will be more law faculty members with some training in legal traditions other than the common law. While they may limit the use of that training to occasional comparative references in traditional courses, their presence often leads to the introduction of a course in Comparative Law. Externally, the greater interdependence of the United States and other nations of the world suggests to law schools' curricular planners that students are best equipped to deal with this interdependence if they have some basic training in international and comparative law. This is reflected both by the addition of Comparative Law in the J.D. curriculum, and the development of international and comparative law graduate programs at many law schools in the United States.

Despite this trend, traditionalists among law professors still express doubts as to whether a course in Comparative Law properly belongs in a law school three-year curriculum. Such traditionalists manifest their skepticism by asking such questions as: What is the scope or purpose of your comparison? What legal systems are you comparing? What is the methodology of your comparison? This introduction will attempt to offer some answers to these three traditional questions.

We would prefer at the outset not to refer to the course as "Comparative Law". The term really has little meaning. The French term *droit comparé* (meaning *law compared*) is somewhat better, but we prefer to focus our attention, for reasons explained below, on the study and comparison of legal systems rather than substantive law. We consequently prefer to use the title "Comparative Legal Systems" or "Comparative Legal Traditions".

Among comparativists there are two principal schools of thought on where the focus should be in an introductory course in Comparative Legal Systems. Some believe that the subject matter of the comparison should be substantive law; others hold that the proper focus of the comparison should be the legal infrastructure. We have chosen the latter approach, believing that the students' understanding of legal systems will be enhanced if they are first introduced to the different legal systems as systems, with their distinctive components and internal relations. The study of the substantive law of a foreign legal system cannot be undertaken without some grasp of the infrastructure of that system. Serious study of the substantive law of foreign legal systems, consequently, should be left to more advanced courses. The basic course in Comparative Legal Systems should provide an outline of the infrastructure of the systems treated, which we believe consists of the following component parts: history, culture and distribution of the system; legal structures or institutions; roles and actors; procedure; and divisions and sources of law. In the course of our discussion, reference obviously must be made to substantive rules. But this will be done only for illustrative purposes.

§ 2. Purpose

Among comparativists there are basically three approaches to the threshold question of the main purpose of an introductory course in Comparative Legal Traditions. The first treats the course as serving primarily a professional purpose, *i. e.*, to help a lawyer or judge in one jurisdiction who needs to know what the law is in another jurisdiction, or a legislator who wants to learn from the experience of legislators in other jurisdictions. The second approach treats the course as serving a cultural purpose, *i. e.*, to widen the perspectives of the students and to make it possible for them to better appreciate and function within their own legal system. The third approach views a course in Comparative Legal Traditions as serving a scientific purpose, *i. e.*, to compare the rules of law in the different legal systems in an effort to discern the general principles of law of all the systems. The purpose of such scientific investigation, according to this last school of thought, is to find a basis for a universal rule of law or a scientific truth or, possibly, to seek a harmonization of legal rules or even a unification of different legal systems.

Quite naturally if one were to give a few lectures on comparative law to an audience consisting of practicing lawyers or judges or legislators, one might seek to pursue the first goal in order to make the lectures professionally relevant to that audience. Similarly, if the course was directed to a group of persons who believe that there ought to be a common law of mankind, one would seek to show how comparative law might be used for the purpose of harmonization of the legal systems of the world. We believe however that the purpose of this course in a law school curriculum, should be the second, *i. e.*, it should seek to enrich students' minds and to broaden their horizons. Accordingly, the materials that are presented here are designed to enable students to appreciate better their own legal system by giving them a broader perspective and comparative insights into other courses in the law school curriculum.

§ 3. Major Legal Systems and Traditions

Even though no two nations' laws are exactly alike, some national legal systems are sufficiently similar in certain critical respects to permit classification of national legal systems into major families of law. Comparativists believe that the grouping of legal systems into legal traditions or families is possible because within every national legal system there are certain constants as well as certain variables. In grouping laws into legal traditions comparativists look for the constants. Those legal systems that have the same recurrent constants fall into the same legal tradition. There is no unanimity among comparativists as to what denominators should be used in grouping legal systems into traditions of law. Among the criteria that are often used for this purpose, however, are the following: historical background and development of the legal system, theories and hierarchy of sources of law, the working methodology of jurists within the legal system, the characteristic legal concepts employed by that system, the legal institutions of that system, and the divisions of law employed within that system.

Using these criteria most comparativists are of the opinion that there are three major legal traditions in the modern Western world. These are those of the Anglo-American common law tradition, the Romano-Germanic civil law tradition and the socialist law tradition. One might wish to move immediately from these legal traditions to national legal systems, such as the Canadian legal system or the French legal system or the Yugoslav legal system, within the three above traditions respectively. Indeed, in attempting to identify characteristics of legal traditions, one *must* at some point look at the traits of specific national legal systems. But between legal traditions and legal systems one may also identify major subtraditions, or branches, of the main tradition. For example within the Romano-Germanic civil law tradition one may identify Romanist, Germanic or Latin American legal subcultures.

But one cannot chart a "family tree" of legal traditions and systems which will illustrate three separate traditions without inter-relationships. A number of legal systems are hybrids, possessing elements of more than one legal tradition. For example, the South African legal system possesses elements of both the common law and civil law traditions. The subtraditions of which we speak above exist also within the socialist law tradition, for example that of Eastern Europe and that of the Far East. But the latter branch opens an entirely new idea, because it moves beyond the bounds of the three major legal traditions in the West and includes elements of still other major legal traditions in the world, Far Eastern (or Oriental) legal traditions and religious legal traditions. We must indeed emphasize that there are other important legal traditions existing beyond those which we discuss in this volume.

In addition to the three major legal traditions in the modern Western World, comparativists also identify a group of religious legal traditions, *i. e.*, Muslim law, Hindu law, Jewish law and canon law. Also, among comparativists there is an identifiable notion of African (and other indigenous) customary law. A traditional American introductory course in Comparative Legal Traditions does not deal with these traditions.

Of the three major legal traditions in the modern Western world the Romano-Germanic legal tradition is the oldest, the most influential and the most widely distributed. Historically this system dates to 450 B.C. (the supposed date of the Twelve Tables in Rome). However, the crucial event, so far as the development of the civil law tradition is concerned, was the Justinian compilation of Roman law around 534 A.D. The civil law is regarded as the most influential legal tradition not only because of its influence on national legal systems, but also because it has had more impact on international law thinking than any other system. To most civilians the civil law tradition is more civilized than, and culturally superior to, the other two legal families. Typically, the civilian jurist regards the common law tradition as relatively crude, uncultured and highly unorganized. (Comparativists, however, gener-

[*6*]

ally consider the question of whether any of the three systems is inferior or superior to the other to have little meaning). To a considerable degree, the development of the Romano-Germanic legal tradition was guided and shaped by legal scholars. But the leading role of legal scholars within this system since has yielded ground to the presently dominant notion of legislative positivism.

The common law tradition is the next oldest of the three traditions. The fact is not widely recognized that the common law system is younger today than the Romano-Germanic system was at the time of the founding of the common law itself. Historically, the origins of the common law are traced back to 1066—the date of the Norman Conquest of England. English common law evolved from necessity and was rooted in the centralized administration of William the Conqueror. The impact of legal scholarship on the development of the English common law historically has been negligible. It is a tradition that originally was designed by judges, for judges and as such was deeply rooted in the practices of judges. Over the years, however, the preeminence of the judge within the common law tradition has suffered considerable diminution. In terms of the number of persons who live within countries of the common law tradition, this system is the least distributed of the three major legal traditions.

The youngest of the three legal families is the socialist legal system. The formation of this system dates to 1917—the victory of the Bolshevik revolution in Russia. This new system, however, did not mature into an identifiably different legal tradition until the mid 1930s. Unlike the other two legal traditions, the early development of socialist law was guided and shaped by the legislator. Legislative influence within this legal tradition remains very strong even today; it shows no signs of suffering any abatement. This new legal tradition was influenced to a considerable extent by the civil law tradition, but virtually not at all by the common law tradition.

§ 4. Methodology

Among comparative law scholars there are two principal techniques of comparison, *i. e.*, description and analytical comparison of the legal systems. The descriptive approach merely presents the different legal systems without attempting to relate one to the other. This approach is unsatisfactory because it is only through "relating back" that the students' understanding of the different legal systems can be deepened. For example, it makes no sense to a continental European motorist when you tell him that the highway speed limit in most American states is 55 miles per hour. It will be more helpful to him, however, if you tell him the speed limit in the United States is 90 kilometers per hour. The second method goes beyond mere description and actually converts the United States speed limit into continental terminology. But such transpositions are not always so easily made. The comparative analysis technique attempts to go further and to draw functional comparisons between different legal institutions operating within the different legal systems. For example, the role of the jurors in the common law tradition is compared with that of lay judges in the civil law and socialist law traditions. Similarly, the role and functions of the French *avocat* are compared with those of the English barrister or solicitor, as well as with those of the Soviet *advokat*. In the discussions which follow we will employ, as our limited space permits, the comparative analysis methodology. Since our readers will be familiar with the United States legal system, United States law will serve as the constant point of reference of our comparison.

For ease and clarity of analysis, however, we have elected to treat the three legal traditions in three separate parts of this Nutshell. To facilitate comparison among the traditions we have employed the same main structural subdivisions in the three parts. For example, a student who wishes to compare the Roles and Actors in each of the three traditions can readily turn to the appropriately designated Chapter in each of the three parts. Similarly, a discussion of the Divisions of Law and Sources of Law in each of the three traditions may be readily found in each of the three parts.

§ 5. Advice to Aspiring Comparativists

For most students, a course in Comparative Legal Traditions may be their first exposure to foreign law. That being the case, the student is likely to undertake such study with some preconceptions, based on United States law, about what law is or ought to be. A student may have the attitude that United States law is prototypical of all civilized legal systems, or even that any law that differs from United States law is presumptively deficient. To prevent such attitudes from impeding the progress of students in a course in Comparative Legal Traditions we would like to leave our reader with the following basic advice:

First, try to bear in mind that law is a concentrated expression of the history, culture, social values and the general consciousness and perceptions of a given people. No two national legal systems are exactly alike. Law is a form of cultural expression and is not readily transplantable from one culture to another without going through some process of indigenization. French law is as much a reflection of the French culture as Russian law is a reflection of Russian culture. For the same reason, it has been said that England and the United States are two countries separated by a common law. Viewed from a historical perspective, law is a normative expression of the conflicts and sufferings, as well as a reflection of the hopes and aspirations of the given people. It is a reflection of the country's experience. To the ordinary citizen law is not merely a collection of legal rules, but often part of a way of life. To understand any national law one must know what that law has been and what it tends to become. Accordingly, any meaningful study of any national legal system must begin with a backward glance at the origins of that law. Anyone who wishes to study a foreign legal system must first put aside ethnocentric biases and attempt to see that foreign legal system through the eyes of lawyers who operate within that system.

Second, strive for that scholarly objectivity, which is the first sign of a mature student of comparative legal traditions. Try to be emotionally removed from the legal systems that you are studying. Some of you may harbor hatred for Germany because of its National Socialist history. Others may dislike France and the French for whatever reasons. Others may detest the Russians as well as the Soviet political and economic systems. Others may be Anglophiles or Anglophobes. To the extent possible you must not let such attitudes color your study of the laws of these countries. When it comes to studying foreign legal systems your mental posture towards the particular system that you are studying makes a great difference in your understanding of that system.

Third, develop a dialectical approach to the study of foreign legal systems. Start off with the mental attitude that no legal system is absolutely bad or is so bad as not to have certain redeeming features. By the same token, begin with the presumption that no legal system is so good as not to be in a position to borrow new ideas from other legal systems. As you move along in this course you will begin to notice that even American law has a lot to learn from other legal systems. Do not close your mind to new ideas.

Finally, always remember that the goal of a course in Comparative Legal Traditions is not to condemn or praise any particular legal system. Comparative lawyers are not in the business of arranging legal traditions and systems into those that are good or bad. Our task as comparativists is to attempt to understand why a particular country has the laws that it has. Try to understand why some say that every country has the legal system that it deserves.

[*11*]

By comparing the different legal traditions it is hoped that students will gain valuable insight into the legal cultures of the different countries as well as understand the different national legal systems. To understand a foreign legal system is to understand an important part of that society, and to acquire a valuable perspective on one's own legal and social system.

PART ONE

THE CIVIL LAW TRADITION

CHAPTER 1

HISTORY, CULTURE AND DISTRIBUTION

§ 1. What Is the Civil Law Tradition?

When we refer to some of the world's legal systems with a common name, such as "Romanist", "Romano-Germanic", or "civil law" systems, we are calling attention to the fact that, despite profound national differences, these systems are grounded in a common legal tradition. The shared tradition of the civil law is, like that of the common law, a sub-tradition of a mode of legal thought that has come to be known as "Western". The Western legal tradition is rooted in the law of the Romans, whose preoccupation with order, administration, law and procedure was unique in the ancient world and has cast a long shadow into the modern one. Within the Western legal tradition, the subtradition of the civil law is characterized by a particular interaction in its early formative period among Roman law, Germanic and local customs, canon law, the international law merchant, and, later, by a distinctive response to the break with feudalism and the rise of nation states, as well as by the peculiar role it has accorded to legal science.

§ 2. Roman Law

To use the term Roman law to describe the entire Roman legal output of nearly a millenium stretching from the Twelve Tables (c. 450 B.C.) to the Justinian compilations (c. 534 A.D.) is about as helpful as describing the product of English legal minds from 1066 A.D. to the present as "common law." Thus, specialists in ancient Roman law usually subdivide their subject into various periods. It was as early as the third century B.C., during the Republic, that there appeared a class of men known as Jurisconsults, who made law their specialty. By the end of the Late Republic in the first century B.C., the Jurisconsults had acquired a monopoly of technical information and legal experience, and it can be said that they had become the first professional lawyers. In difficult cases, the lay judges began to turn to them for advice. Through this advisory role, the Jurisconsults stayed close to the practice of law and remained in constant contact with actual disputes. What we know as Roman law evolved through the accretion of the opinions they rendered case-by-case. Eventually the principles thus developed by the Jurisconsults were taught and expounded in treatises, all in a distinctive vocabulary and style.

At first rather formal, rigid and concrete, Roman law eventually moved away from fixed rules to flexible standards and from concrete to abstract modes of thought. It became characterized by attention to practical details, and by terms of art which caught on and endured. The law of the Classical period (which began around 117 A.D. and came to an end with the period of anarchy, invasions, plague and civil war that commenced in 235 A.D.), represents the fullest development of ancient Roman law. Of the great Jurisconsults of this period, Ulpian, Papinian and Gaius are chiefly remembered. At its height classical Roman law constituted a body of practical wisdom of a kind the world had not seen before. It was therefore of the highest interest to the Justinian compilers after the fall of the Western empire, and, through them, of great significance to the development of the civil law systems.

Centuries later, Roman law would be called "written reason" by the medieval scholars who "rediscovered" it as the Western world began to emerge from what the French legal scholar Jean Carbonnier calls the "customary thicket" of the Middle Ages. The Roman law that was "rediscovered", however, when Western society began to be ready for law to play a prominent role once again among the norms that govern human activity, was not the law of the Classical period in its original form. Most of the ancient sources by that time had been lost. What had survived was the monumental compilation of Roman law that was made at the direction of the Byzantine Emperor Justinian in the sixth century. By this time, the Roman Empire in the West had been breaking up for more than a century, its fall symbolized by the sack of Rome in 410 A.D. The significance of the work of the Byzantine jurists would be hard to exaggerate. From Justinian's times to the present, Roman law, except to specialists, generally has meant the sixth century Corpus Juris Civilis of Justinian.

The Corpus Juris Civilis included four parts: the Institutes, the Digest, the Code and the Novels. The *Digest* was by far the most important in terms of its influence on the civil law tradition, particularly in the areas of personal status, torts, unjust enrichment, contracts and remedies. The Digest was a treatise representing the distillation of what, in the judgment of Justinian's jurists, was most valuable from the best Roman legal writings from all previous periods. Since virtually all of the books they used in composing the Digest have been lost, the Digest itself became the principal source of knowledge about what the Roman law of earlier periods had been like. The *Institutes* were simply a short introductory text for students, the *Code* was a systematic collection of Roman legislation, and the *Novels* were the imperial legislation enacted after the Code and the Digest were completed. Together, the Digest and the Code were meant to be a complete and authoritative restatement of Roman law.

Byzantine Roman law did not reproduce exactly the law of earlier periods. The Corpus Juris was after all the product of a careful process of selection and rejection. In general outlook, as well as in matters of detail, it differed from the law of the Classical period. It continued the movement away from formalism, but this move was accompanied by a decline in technique. Equity, which in the Classical period was regarded as a principle of justice animating the whole of the law, degenerated into mere impatience with legal subtleties. Byzantine legislation was "humanitarian", in the sense of protecting "those whom it considers weak against those whom it considers strong," but Jolowicz says this tendency coincided with an "almost pathetic confidence in the power of law to do away with evils of an economic character . . . and a taste for excessive regulation by statute of matters to which fixed rules can hardly, by their nature, be applied with success." After the Lombard, Slav and Arab invasions that followed the reign of Justinian, the Corpus Juris Civilis fell into disuse for centuries.

§ 3. The "Customary Thicket" and Roman Law Survival

The fact that Roman law and legal science were left stranded by the collapse of the way of life that had produced them did not mean that Romanist legal influences disappeared altogether during the Middle Ages. Certainly the sophistication and technical perfection to which ancient Roman law had been brought over the centuries was not maintained during the legal and political disorder that followed the disintegration of the Roman Empire. For five centuries after the fall of Rome a series of raiders and settlers overran the areas that had once been Roman. There were no strong, centralized states. Kingdoms rose and fell. The condition of the people sank into local self-sufficiency. It would be centuries before scholars again would be capable of picking up and putting to use the technical instruments left behind by the Classical Roman and Byzantine jurists. When a reawakening of interest in Roman law did occur and when attention turned to the

Corpus Juris in the 11th century, the process became known as the "revival" of Roman law.

It is quite proper to speak, nevertheless, as the legal historian Franz Wieacker does, of a "survival" of Roman law from the fifth to the tenth centuries. Roman conquerors once had been all over Europe, and many of the Germanic settlers, legionnaires and migrating peoples who eventually overran the Empire had been, to a certain extent, "Romanized." As conquerors and conquered changed places, Germanic rulers used Roman law to govern their Roman subjects, while applying their own law to their own peoples. Over time it gradually became impossible to tell which group a particular person was in and the distinctions between groups disappeared. By the end of the tenth century, the rules were the same for all persons within a given territory. Crude versions of Roman legal rules had become intermingled in varying degrees with the customary rules of the Germanic invaders to the point where one can speak of the laws during this period as either "Romanized customary laws" or "barbarized Roman laws". Thus, though Roman legal science and Classical Roman law disappeared in the welter, diversity and localism of Carbonnier's "customary thicket", a Romanist element survived and served both as a strand of continuity and a latent, potential universalizing factor in what we now think of as the civil law tradition.

The Germanic customary laws that began to be written down as early as the fifth century A.D., (as well as particular local customs), formed part of this tradition too, particularly influencing aspects of marital property and inheritance law. Many of the most ingenious and useful legal devices of the modern civil law of property and commercial law derive not from Roman, but from medieval origins, and thus remind us that the legal confusion of the Middle Ages had its fruitful and creative, as well as its fragmented and disorganized, side. The Germanic element evolved through the Middle Ages, as tribal laws became territorial laws, to the point where it had produced the beginnings of a legal literature and a new legal culture that was quite different from the Roman. But its further development was arrested because of its essentially lay character, and because the crudeness of its procedures (*e. g.*, trial by ordeal) limited its potential for adaptation to the social and economic changes that were beginning to transform feudal society.

§ 4. Canon Law

With the break-up of the far-flung system of Roman administration, the Church took over some of the functions of government. Indeed, after the fall of the Roman Empire, and until the revival of Roman law in the 11th century, the single most important universalizing factor in the diverse and localized legal systems of the civil law tradition was canon law. But canon law itself was a hybrid of sorts. It had been produced by Christian notions interacting reciprocally with Roman law after the Christianization of the Empire, a process during which the reign of Constantine (d. 337 A.D.) was an important marker. The Justinian Corpus, in particular, was profoundly affected by Christian ideas, but the Church, for its part, had borrowed freely from the structure, principles and detailed rules of ancient Roman law. Furthermore, just as there was some degree of amalgamation everywhere of Germanic customs, indigenous customs and debased Roman law, there was a certain penetration by canon law into the codes promulgated by German rulers and, later, into the legislation of the Carolingian (c. 800 A.D.) and Holy Roman Empires (c. 962 A.D.). During the Middle Ages, the Church sought and won jurisdiction for its own tribunals over matrimonial causes, and over certain aspects of criminal law and succession to personal property. Many of the rules and procedures it developed in these matters were accepted in secular tribunals long after the Church had lost its civil jurisdiction.

§ 5. Revival of Roman Law

Europe entered a period of political, economic and cultural transformation from about 1050 A.D. onward. The gradual return of political order established conditions that facilitated speculative learning. Economic expansion, too, with its requirements for predictability and on-going dispute resolution, led to a renewed interest in law. Like scholars in other fields, jurists began to turn, with the excitement of discovery, to the accomplishments of antiquity. The revival of Roman law that took place in northern Italy towards the end of the 11th century was a rediscovery, through the Justinian legacy, of Roman legal science.

The University of Bologna became the principal legal center to which students flocked from all over Europe to hear learned teachers (including some nuns who were the first women law professors) lecture on the Corpus Juris Civilis. Irnerius, who is said to have given the first lectures on the Justinian Digest, proclaimed its intellectual superiority over the legal inheritance of the Middle Ages. But the ancient text dealt with so many institutions and problems that were no longer known, that it was difficult to understand. The first generations of scholars to study the Digest therefore made it their task to try to accurately reconstruct and explain its text. They became known as the Glossators because of their annotations (glosses) on the Digest. But their approach to interpretation in time gave way to the new methods of the Commentators (or Post-Glossators) of the 13th century, who saw their work as adapting the law of Roman society to the problems of their own day. The methods of the Commentators were much influenced by the new spirit of rational inquiry and speculative dialectic that would be brought to its highest form in the work of Thomas Aquinas (d. 1274). This way of thinking liberated them from the literalism of the Glossators and led them to search for the rationale and underlying principles of various Roman legal rules. Bartolus (d. 1357) is remembered as the greatest of the Commentators.

The thousands of European students who had come to the Italian universities carried back to their own nations and universities, not only the law of the Corpus Juris Civilis but also the methods and ideas of their teachers. They and their own students became the new profession of lawyers who found places not only in universities, but in the "administrations" of princes, cities and the Church. Their work was influenced at least as much by the Bolognese method of decision making by bringing a case within the terms of an abstractly formulated authoritative text, as it was by the substantive norms of Roman law. In Paris and Oxford, Prague and Heidelburg, Cracow and Copenhagen, a fusion took place between the medieval Romano-Germanic law and the learning based on the revived Roman law. In different ways and to varying degrees this new amalgam formed the base on which future variations and modifications would take place in all the civil law systems. The new learning, common to all those trained in Northern Italy, furnished the common methodology for the further development of national laws.

It was the shared background of the influential torch bearers of the new legal science that consolidated the civil law tradition. The Roman civil law, together with the immense literature generated by the Glossators and Commentators, came to be the *jus commune*, the common law, of Europe. As Merryman has said, "There was a common body of law and of writing about law, a common legal language, and a common method of teaching and scholarship." Canon law continued to play a role in this shared tradition, but in a new, more refined and "Romanized" form, as Bolognese scholars systematically compiled and digested some 700 years of ecclesiastical enactments and decrees. Gratian in the 12th century is generally credited with having transformed canon law into an independent "system" which then began to be taught alongside Roman civil law in the universities.

§ 6. Commercial Law

In addition to Roman civil law and canon law, commercial law furnished another universalizing tendency as Europe emerged from the relative economic stagnation of the Middle Ages. With the rise of towns, the birth of markets, fairs and banks, the rapid expansion of maritime and overland trade, and the eventual development of large flourishing commercial centers, there appeared the need for a body of law to govern business transactions. Since several features of Roman law proved unsuitable for this purpose, guilds and merchants' associations established their own rules and their own tribunals. The merchants' courts worked out informal rules and expeditious procedures that were practical, fair, and grounded in the usages of businessmen. These rules in time came to be recognized and applied as customary law by secular and ecclesiastical authorities. Eventually the "law merchant" became international, a body of generally accepted commercial rules that transcended political boundaries. It also proved stronger than legal traditions, spreading even into England where the Roman law, brought back from Italy, had met with resistance outside the walls of the universities.

§ 7. Reception of Roman Law

The Middle Ages were an era of numerous overlapping and competing jurisdictions and sources of law. In the absence of strong central states, the notion of law as command of the sovereign had no meaning. Ecclesiastical courts were apt to apply canon law; the courts of a guild would apply the law merchant; while other judges in cities and towns would tend to search for an appropriate rule, first, in local custom or statute, then, with the help of university scholars, filling the gaps with the *jus commune*. Aided by the expansion of economic activity, the enthusiasm of legal scholars, and by the idea of the "continued" Holy Roman Empire, the *jus commune* became the basic law of a great part of continental Europe. It proved capable of dealing with many of the new problems posed by a more complex economy; yet as part of a not entirely forgotten past, it had a certain familiarity. Through the process that civil law lawyers call *reception*, the revived Roman private law (including the writings of the Italian jurists and the canon law) moved from the universities into the courts. (It should be noted, however, that Roman *public* law, itself relatively undeveloped, was not similarly received. There was no place for public law so long as no strong central governments existed.)

The formality and the extent of reception in a given country and the type of interaction that occurred between the *jus commune* and the medieval Romano-Germanic base varied considerably. In certain parts of Italy, the influence of Roman law had remained so strong that it is perhaps not quite accurate to speak of a "reception" there. In Spain, however, the *jus commune* was always in tension with various vigorous local customary traditions. In the regions of France south of the Loire (known as the *pays de droit écrit*) where Roman law influence had been strong, the local customary law was already heavily romanized. Thus, there was a more extensive reception there than in the northern regions of France (known as the *pays de droit coutumier*) where the various local customs had always been of greater importance than Roman law.

The *jus commune* infiltrated the law of the various regions of the Holy Roman Empire of the Germanic nation to the point that it came to be regarded as the common law of the empire. In 1495, when a central imperial court was established, its judges were obliged to decide cases according to this common law, unless a conflicting local custom or statute could be proved. The difficulty of proving a controlling German rule meant in practice that the received Roman law became the basic law of all the regions of Germany. The reception of Roman law on such a large scale in Germany is usually explained by a combination of factors. Roman law met no resistance from a strong national legal profession, court system or from the existence of a common body of "German" law. Both the weakness of the imperial power and its claim to being the successor to the Roman Empire facilitated the reception. Finally, and probably most importantly, Roman law met the increasingly urgent need to deal with the inconvenience that the variety of local customs posed for intercourse among the many small independent territories that formed the German confederation.

The wide-scale Roman law reception in Germany was a crucial event for the later development of German legal science, producing a much more extensive systematization of law than occurred elsewhere. From the beginning, judges relied heavily on legal scholars for information and guidance concerning the local law as well as the received Roman law. Indeed, by 1600, it was a common practice for judges to send out the record of a difficult case to a university law faculty and to adopt the faculty's collective opinion on questions of law. This practice of *Aktenversendung*, which continued until the 19th century, resulted in the accumulation of an extensive body of common doctrine that transcended the borders of the various German political entities. Systematized in reports and essays, distillations from scholarly opinions rendered in actual controversies became, as Dawson has said, " a kind of case-law, secreted in the interstices of learned writings."

In Europe generally, the *jus commune*, like the Latin language and the universal Church, was an aspect of the unity of the West at a time when there were no strong centralized political administrations and no unified legal systems, but rather a continuous struggle among the competing and overlapping jurisdictions of local, manorial, ecclesiastical, mercantile and royal authorities. From the 15th century on, however, the relationship between the received *jus commune* and the diverse local and regional customary laws began to be affected, in varying degrees, by the rise of nationalism and the increasing consolidation of royal power.

§ 8. Nation States and National Law

Gradual political unification in Europe did not immediately bring about national legal unification, but it did arouse interest in customary law as "national" law. The way for this development had been prepared, in a sense, by the 14th century Commentators who had turned scholarly attention from textual exegesis of the

Digest to a consideration of the adaptability of Roman legal rules to contemporary conditions. In the 16th and 17th centuries, as the center of legal scholarship shifted to France and Holland, the methods of the Bolognese Commentators were replaced by those of the French Legal Humanists and the Dutch Natural Law School. The Humanists used the techniques of history and philology to study Roman law. Their view of Roman law as a historical phenomenon and of the Corpus Juris Civilis as merely an ancient text (rather than as "living law" or "written reason") marked a step toward eventual displacement of the *jus commune*. This indirect challenge to the authority of Roman law was continued by the 17th century Dutch Natural Law School, whose members developed a systematic theory of law grounded in what they conceived to be the universal law of nature. The comprehensive legal system-building of these Dutch jurists was the prelude to modern codification.

The awakening of interest in national law was only one of several parallel developments that marked the end of the unity of the West and the rise of modern nation states. National literatures began to appear. The vernacular languages began to be used in universities. The differences widened between national churches and Rome. In the legal area, so long as the state had been non-existent or minimal, there was no public, administrative or constitutional law in the modern sense. However, as political power became sufficiently centralized, at different times in different parts of Europe, both public law and national law developed rapidly.

§ 9. Codification

In many parts of Europe, legal nationalism early took the form of codification. The first of these national codes appeared in the Scandinavian countries in the 17th and 18th centuries. Then, a second generation of codes not only aspired to bring about legal unity within one kingdom, but also attempted a synthesis of the political and philosophical thought of the 18th century. These codes were the product of "enlightened" monarchs, like Voltaire's friend Frederick II of Prussia, and Joseph II of Austria, and their bureaucratic administrators. They were founded on the creed of the Enlightenment that a rational, clear and comprehensive legal system could be devised by intelligent human beings. It was taken for granted that such a system would be an improvement on traditional law. An inevitable consequence of the unification of national law in these early codes was that the *jus commune* was displaced as the basic source of law. To be sure, the draftsmen of the national codes drew heavily upon the *jus commune* as well as on national law, but the authority of the law from then on was derived from the state and not from any idea of the inherent reasonableness or suitability of the legal norms themselves. The Prussian General Land Law of 1794 is chiefly remembered today as a monument of legal hubris. In its ambition to foresee all possible contingencies and to regulate the range of human conduct down to the most intimate details of family life, it was hampered in operation both by its excessive detail and its failure to acknowledge the limits of law.

Two national codes, however, have had such widespread and lasting influence that they and their accompanying ideologies can be said to have become part of the contemporary civil law tradition. The French Civil Code of 1804 and the German Civil Code of 1896 have served as models for most of the other modern civil codes. So different from each other, yet sharing a common tradition, they have both decisively affected the shape of civil law systems of today. French revolutionary ideas and German legal science not only gave a special stamp and flavor to their respective national codes but affected legal thought throughout and beyond the civil law world.

The consolidation of French royal power from the end of the 15th century to the Revolution of 1789 made France the first modern nation, a politically unified society under strong central rule. The *ancien régime* was not able, however, to achieve legal unification. A traveller in France changed laws, Voltaire once said, as often as he changed horses. It remained for Napoleon to provide France with a unified national body of law. Under his rule, five basic codes were promulgated: the Civil Code, the Penal Code, the Commercial Code and the Codes of Civil and Criminal Procedure.

The French Civil Code of 1804, drafted in a remarkably short period of time by a commission of four eminent jurists, has a just claim to being the first modern code. Although it hewed rather closely to the framework of Justinian's Institutes, it was not, as Justinian's Code basically was, a restatement of the law. Its substantive provisions incorporated the results of a profound intellectual, political and social revolution. Though it is often referred to as the "Code Napoleon", its original name was the *Code civil des français* (the civil code of the French people). In what its title represented, as in other ways, it was unlike all earlier efforts at codification. It represented a new way of thinking about man, law and government.

The three ideological pillars of the French civil code were private property, freedom of contract and the patriarchal family. In the first of these areas, the Code made an abrupt break with the feudal past. Through such private law devices as prohibitions on restraints on alienation and limitations on freedom of testation, the Code's architects consciously sought to break up the estates of the powerful landed aristocracy. By the very fact of claiming the areas of property, contract and family for private, civil law, the Code was performing what may be called a constitutional function. In these three spheres, the primary role of the State was to be to protect private property, to enforce legally formed contracts, and to secure the autonomy of the patriarchal family.

At the same time that the French Civil Code was introducing new elements into the civil law tradition in the field of private law, French revolutionary ideas were contributing in important ways to the newly developing field of public law. The French revolution and subsequent Napoleonic rule had furthered the processes of strengthening the central state and eliminating intermediate sources of power and allegiance. In this new political situation, there was little role for Roman or medieval law to play in the fashioning of the rules that henceforth would regulate the relationships of the branches and agencies of government with each other and with citizens. (We have already remarked that the Reception of Roman law had been a reception of Roman private, not public, law). In the 19th century, modern public law was emerging from a crucible where those ways of thinking about government associated with the American and French revolutions were interacting with older, royal, bureaucratic traditions. To varying degrees, in different parts of the world, French ideas about equality, democracy, representative government, the separation of powers, and natural rights to life, liberty and property were influential in forming systems of public law.

In spite of all that was new in the French legal revolution, there was still much continuity with the past. First, and most obviously, continuity was provided by the sources drawn upon by Napoleon's draftsmen. With a short period of time at their disposal and under much pressure from the First Consul, they could not, and did not try to, create a code out of whole cloth. Naturally they turned to the *jus commune*, the royal ordinances, the doctrinal writing, and customary law—particularly the influential Custom of Paris, which had been conveniently written down in the 16th century. Like the draftsmen of other Enlightenment codes, they thought of themselves as putting all this prior law through a "sieve of reason", retaining or rejecting it according to rational principles. But the formal tripartite structure of their end product (Persons, Things and the Different Modes of Acquiring Property) was virtually identical to that of the first three books of Justinian's Institutes. So far as the substantive rules of law were concerned, the draftsmen relied primarily, and in about equal measure, on both customary law and the *jus commune*.

A few provisions, such as those on divorce by mutual consent and adoption, are attributable to the influence of Napoleon. The great personal interest that Napoleon took in the Code was not so much in its substantive content, however, as it was in the fact of its existence. He wanted to be remembered as a great lawgiver. Because of the importance he accorded to the Code, he secured its adoption in France, and imposed it in his conquered territories—in Italy, Poland, the low countries and among the ruins of the Habsburg Empire. In exile on St. Helena, Napoleon referred to the Code as a greater achievement than all his victories: "One Waterloo wipes out their memory, but my civil code will live forever."

In form and style, the French Civil Code stands in marked contrast to the German Civil Code which appeared nearly a century later. The *Code civil des français* was meant to be read and understood by the citizen. With its clear, fertile and intentionally concise provisions, its style resembles that of the United States Constitution, more than it does the German Civil Code of 1896. The founding fathers of the French Civil Code, like those of the United States Constitution, recognized that a legislator cannot foresee all possible applications of basic principles. The draftsmen opted for the flexibility of general rules, rather than for detailed provisions. The words of one of the draftsmen, Portalis, are still frequently referred to in this connection:

> "We have equally avoided the dangerous ambition to regulate and foresee everything. . . . The function of law is to fix in broad outline the general maxims of justice, to establish principles rich in implications, and not to descend into the details of the questions that can arise in each subject."

§ 10.   German Legal Science

The German Civil Code (*Bürgerliches Gesetzbuch*) appeared at the end, and the French Civil Code at the beginning, of the turbulent century of the Industrial Revolution. The German Code came out of an intellectual and political background that differed in many ways from the French Enlightenment and revolutionary thought that endowed the *Code Civil*. It is thus not surprising that Germany and France have inspired somewhat different subtraditions in the civil law world. Unlike France, where political unification had been achieved long before legal unity, Germany had remained a loose confederation of kingdoms, duchies, principalities and independent city states until it was unified under Bismarck in 1871. Indeed, as we have seen, the lack of effective central government and the need for a common law to facilitate trade had set the stage for the large scale reception of the Romanist *jus commune* in 15th century Germany. However, as German scholars worked with the *jus commune*, a certain "renationalization" of German law had taken place, especially in the 17th and 18th centuries. Like the Bolognese Commentators, these German scholars were occupied with adapting the Romanist law to their own contemporary conditions. In the course of their work, which came to be known as the *usus modernus pandectarum* (Pandects was a name given to the Justinian Digest), they increasingly introduced Germanic legal content into what remained a basically Romanist structure. This was particularly so in the areas of property and associations.

In the 19th century, as the French Civil Code began to be widely admired and imitated, the idea of codification aroused interest in Germany. By this time, Germany was already a leading center of legal scholarship on the continent, and the issue of codification became embroiled in a famous scholarly dispute. In 1814, a Roman law professor, Thibaut, advocated prompt adoption of a code as a means of furthering the process of political unification of Germany. Thibaut claimed that the Prussian, French and Austrian codes could serve as helpful models. The Prussian and French codes were in fact already in force in parts of Germany. Thibaut's view was disputed by members of the so-called Historical School, whose leading spokesman was Friedrich Carl von Savigny. He maintained that law, like language, was part of the genius and culture of a people. It could not be derived by the method of reasoning from abstract principles of natural law. Rather, he claimed, a nation's law would be revealed by the methods of historical research. It followed that a German code should not be adopted without extensive preliminary study of the development of German legal institutions.

The point of view of Savigny and the Historical School prevailed. Under the influence of their ideas, 19th century German legal scholars by and large abandoned the ahistorical natural law approach of previous codes in favor of what they thought of as a science of law. They viewed Germanic, and classical and received Roman law as data, and regarded themselves as scientists formulating and systematizing concepts and principles from this data. Some put their principal energies into the historical investigation of indigenous law. Others, including Savigny himself, turned to Roman law—not, however, to the *jus commune*, but to ancient Roman law. There they encountered the fact that the Roman jurists had been rather pragmatic individuals. If the Romans at times reflected on the methods and underlying structure of their legal system, they did not leave records of their ideas on these matters. So it came about that in 19th century Germany, legal scholars investigated classical Roman law with the aim of discovering its "latent system", which they might adapt to the needs of their own society. In the process, they brought the study of the Digest to its highest and most systematic level, and thus became known as the Pandectists. Though the Pandectist School grew out of the Historical School, in the end it came to adopt a rather ahistorical stance toward law. Believing in the superiority and lasting validity of the institutions of the Romans, the Pandectists tended to exclude social, ethical, economic and practical considerations from their legal work. As at the time of the Reception, there was still no organized and powerful class of practicing lawyers in Germany to temper this movement. The methods and concepts developed by the Pandectists came to dominate legal scholarship in Germany just at the time the preparation of the German Civil Code began in 1874.

The work on a civil code for the new German nation turned out to be a massive project. It went through two drafts and took over 20 years to complete. It was finally promulgated in 1896, to go into effect four years later—on the first day of the new century. In the end, as Dawson has said, the Code was neither Romanist nor Germanic. It was Pandectist. It was constructed and worked out with a technical precision that had never been seen before in any legislation. A special language was developed and employed consistently and legal concepts were defined and then used in the same way throughout. Sentence construction indicated where the burden of proof lies. Through elaborate cross-references, all parts of the Code interlocked to form a logically closed system. The draftsmen avoided both the prolixity of the Prussian Code and the "epigrammatic brevity" of the French. Though they did not descend to regulation in detail, their system was refined to the point where the various parts of the Code could be made to articulate tightly about nearly any given problem falling within its scope. At the beginning of the Code is the "General Part", in which definitions, concepts and principles of great breadth are set forth. These pervade all the specific subject matter areas covered by the Code. Other pervasive general principles are established within and for particular areas of law. (See further, infra Chapter 6 at Section 2.c.) These general provisions are in turn often qualified or restricted by specific provisions within the various sections of the Code dealing with particular subjects. The result was not a handbook for the citizen, but a system for highly trained experts. Within the civil law world, German legal science and the German style of codification developed their own sphere of influence.

Though the German and French civil codes differ in form, style and mood, one must not lose sight of their similarities. In the first place, they both drew heavily on the *jus commune* as well as on their respective national law. In both codes, the influence of the Romanist *jus commune* predominated in the law of obligations and in the general structure of the system, while national law sources were more influential in property and succession law. Secondly, there is an ideological correspondence between the two codes. Both were grounded in 19th century liberalism. They were infused with then current notions of individual autonomy and laissez-faire economics. But over the course of the near-century that separated the two codes, society had been changing rapidly. Thus, while the German Civil Code still resembled the French in its solicitude for private property, freedom of contract and the traditional family, it also reflected a number of changes that had taken place since 1804. Several important provisions of the German Civil Code begin to recognize a social obligation inhering in certain private rights, as well as the idea that rights can be misused. In family law, the authority of husbands and fathers is slightly more qualified than in the French Code. Women have somewhat more power with respect to their own property, and the boundaries of the family are more narrowly drawn. Certain aspects of contract and tort law show the effects of the increasing complexity of commercial transactions as well as the advance of industrialization.

In the years immediately following the promulgation of the German Civil Code, German scholars were preoccupied with the task of making it applicable in practice by explaining its difficult text and developing its main principles. But gradually the process of interpreting the Code "out of itself" became less fruitful and the stage was set for a new phase of German legal science. A reaction against the extreme formalism of the *Pandektenrecht* had indeed already begun to set in in the late 19th century when Jhering, a product of the Pandectist School himself, began to question its methods and assumptions. In a devastating satire of the movement, he placed its leading practitioners in a "heaven of legal concepts" to which no one could be admitted unless he gave up all memory of the real world. But it was not until the years following World War I that German legal science generally began to turn from what had become an increasingly sterile exercise. Then, salvaging from the Pandects their genius for formulating generalizations, but joining this for the first time to an obsession with detailed facts and concrete applications, German legal science transcended itself. With its new direction, born of the ability to relate powerful abstract reasoning to irreducible and stubborn facts, German scholars began to develop the methods that came to be associated with jurisprudence of interests, legal realism and the sociological schools of legal thought. Through the American legal scholar and codifier, Karl Llewellyn, and through the many eminent German jurists who came to the United States during the National Socialist period, these new ways of thinking about law entered into the mainstream of American legal theory.

§ 11.   Distribution of the Civil Law

France and Germany probably have been less influenced by each other's law, legal institutions and scholarship than have other countries within the civil law world. The distinctive French and German codifications and styles of thought each had far-reaching influence, and to some extent their influences overlapped in other countries. Thus, it may be correct to say, as Merryman does, that the "typical" civil law systems today are not those of France or the Federal Republic of Germany, but rather those civil law systems which in modern times have undergone the combined influence of both. Nevertheless, in the post-codification era, French law and German legal science have both become the principal tributaries to the modern civil law tradition.

Just as ancient Roman law had been introduced into the conquered territories of a vast empire, the French Civil Code was brought by Napoleon and his armies to Belgium, the Netherlands, parts of Poland, Italy and the western regions of Germany. Then, in the colonial era, France extended her legal influence far beyond continental Europe to parts of the Near East, Northern and sub-Saharan Africa, Indochina, Oceania, French Guiana and the French Caribbean islands. The influence of French law both outlived and went beyond the Napoleonic conquests and French colonialism. The Code was widely admired for its own merits: its clarity and elegance of style and its consolidation of the results of a revolution which had abolished the old, unequal statuses and relations of feudalism. Thus, one can speak of a "reception" of the French Civil Code not only in countries which retained it after French armies and colonial governments withdrew, but also in countries that were untouched by French military or colonial power.

The Civil Code remains in effect to this day, with revisions, in Belgium and Luxembourg; and was a major influence on the Netherlands Civil Code of 1838 (now extensively revised), the Portuguese Civil Code of 1867 (replaced in 1967), the Spanish Civil Code of 1888, some of the Swiss cantonal codes, and on the legal institutions of 19th century Italy, as well as on those of some of the Eastern European countries. French law and legal theory remained important for the former colonies and possessions even after they gained independence in the 20th century. Furthermore, when the Spanish and Portuguese empires in Latin America dissolved in the 19th century, it was mainly to the French Civil Code that the lawmakers of the new nations of Central and South America looked for inspiration. French culture and the French revolutionary heritage were widely admired in the Latin American countries. It thus was natural for them to turn to French law as a model. The language and concepts of the French codes were clear, and were already familiar because of their affinities with the legal ideas and institutions that had been introduced in Latin America by the Spanish and the Portuguese.

It was another story in 19th century Germany, however. Though French law and legal ideas were influential in German procedural and administrative law, they had hardly any effect on the thinking that went into the late 19th century German private law codification. The German Civil Code of 1896 put before the world an entirely different model from the French and earlier codes, but one which appeared too late to be as widely imitated as the French. By the end of the 19th century, the more developed countries had already adopted codes. Apart from those that had been influenced in varying degrees by the French Civil Code, there was the Austrian General Civil Code of 1811, the product of several decades of drafting under an enlightened and authoritarian monarchy, which had in turn influenced the law of Liechtenstein and of some parts of Eastern Europe. The Nordic countries, where the earliest national civil codes had appeared, historically had been and remained relatively far removed from the composite of influences from which the civil law tradition was forged.

Even if the German Civil Code had not appeared relatively late, its highly technical and reticulated structure, in all likelihood would have rendered its direct transplantation to foreign soil problematic. Nevertheless, the German Civil Code did play a significant role in the preparation of the Italian Code of 1942, and was the major influence on the Greek Civil Code of 1940, effective in 1946. Although the German Code as a whole was not built to travel, the legal science that preceded and accompanied it has had an important influence on legal theory and doctrine in other countries, particularly in Austria, Czechoslovakia, Greece, Hungary, Italy, Switzerland and Yugoslavia. It was one of many influences on the eclectic Brazilian Code of 1916, and on the new Portuguese Code of 1967. The Japanese Civil Code drew heavily upon the first draft of the German Civil Code and, as a result, German civil law scholarship has remained important in Japan. Through Japan, the German civil law influence also spread to Korea. Since the end of World War II, however, American law, too, has had a substantial impact on the law of Japan and South Korea.

Switzerland, except for certain cantons, had remained aloof from the reception of the French Civil Code, and when Switzerland achieved legal unity through its Civil Code of 1907, and its Law of Obligations which went into effect together with the Civil Code of 1912, it did not follow either the French or the German model. A single scholarly draftsman, Eugen Huber, fashioned for the confederation a civil code that was inspired by Swiss traditions and adapted to Swiss circumstances. He drew upon German and, to a lesser extent, French sources but did not permit them to dominate. In 1926, the Swiss Civil Code (together with the Law of Obligations) was adopted, almost word for word, as the Civil Code of the newly formed Republic of Turkey.

After World War II, the civil law influence on the European continent began to diminish when the Eastern European countries adopted new civil codes. Though these codes retain many characteristic civil law features, they are generally thought of as belonging to the socialist family of laws. The Nordic legal systems, though touched by the Roman law revival and affected in important ways by their proximity to the modern civil law systems, are generally thought of as *sui generis*, set apart by several unique features both from the common law and the mainstream of the civil law. Central and South American countries in this century have looked increasingly to North American models, particularly in the areas of public, constitutional and business law. Still, the civil law system remains the dominant one there, as it is in many former French, Belgian, Spanish and Portuguese colonies in Africa.

Civil law also survives in certain "mixed" legal systems such as the civil and common law hybrid systems of Louisiana, Quebec, the Philippines and Puerto Rico. Japan and South Korea have added so much civil, especially German, law, to their indigenous law, that some would classify them as being Romano-Germanic, rather than Oriental, systems. However, in Japan and South Korea, as in Latin America, the law of the United States has had an important effect on the public law. French-inspired civil law and legal theory remain influential in West Africa, and, in combination with Islamic law, in most North African states as well as in many Near and Middle Eastern countries. Civil law is also one of many elements in the complex, pluralistic, legal systems of Israel and Lebanon. In Asia, civil law influence extended to, and combined with, other legal influences in Kampuchea (Cambodia), Indonesia, Laos, South Vietnam, Taiwan and Thailand. Finally, it should be noted that civil law and codification are not co-extensive. A few places in the civil law world were untouched by codification. Thus, for example, in Scotland and South Africa, the Roman *jus commune* survives in uncodified form, combined in the case of Scotland with common law, and in the Union of South Africa with common law and Dutch law.

As the civil law has spread and entered into combination with other legal elements, its influence has become attenuated. In the wake of codification and national law movements, each country tended to concentrate on the development of its own legal system. Legal actors turned less frequently for inspiration and ideas to the fund of sources once held in common all over Europe. As a result, it is difficult today to find a single "civil law rule" on any given legal problem. Indeed, there is probably as much diversity in the responses of civil law systems to various legal issues as there is between the civil and the common law traditions. This makes it appropriate to ask what now remains that sets the civil law tradition apart from other legal traditions in the late 20th century. Law reform has become innovative and eclectic. Searching for legal approaches to new social problems common to many different countries, legislatures have been less concerned with the provenance than with the promise of new techniques and ideas. Outside the continental European cradle of the civil law, the received European law never fully penetrated the mores anyway, nor did it ever completely displace customary and religious laws. Within the European continent, contemporary civil law systems are becoming in several important ways like the legal systems of other developed nations. What, then, if anything, besides history, links the civil law systems together?

The beginnings of an answer may lie in a closer examination of the various meanings of the term "civil law." Historically, the term *jus civile* (from *civis*: citizen) referred to the law applicable to Roman citizens, the law which was eventually compiled by Justinian's jurists into the Corpus Juris Civilis. Common law lawyers, and we in this book, use the phrase "civil law systems" to describe the legal systems of all those nations predominantly within the historical tradition described in the foregoing sections. But within those systems, the term "civil law" has acquired a narrower meaning and some such term as "Romanist" or "Romano-Germanic" is used to designate their historical connection. The meaning of "civil law" (*droit civil, Zivilrecht*) to continental European lawyers is very limited: the civil law is the law relating to those subject matter areas covered by the civil codes and their auxiliary statutes. Thus, it not only does not include the entire legal system, it does not even take in all of private law if, as is usually the case, part of the private law is contained in a commercial code and other codes and statutes. (See infra Chapter 5 at Section 3):

The continental terminology leads us closer to what it is that still links the civil law systems as they move further and further from their historical roots. At the same time, it reveals the extent to which these links are becoming looser. All the major civil codes deal with a body of substantive law within the same framework staked out by, and still similar in important respects to, Justinian's Institutes: law governing personal status, including family law; property; and obligations, which may either arise from contract or result from one's conduct. One of the great links among the "civil law systems" is that the "civil law" was for centuries, in fact, the most important and fundamental part of the legal system, and is still regarded so in theory. The great legal scholars from the Bolognese Roman law revival to the German Pandectists devoted their lives to the study and refinement of the civil law. Their characteristic techniques of analysis, their ways of thinking about legal problems and formulating legal propositions were all developed within and for the civil law. This was all in marked contrast to the way the common law developed, with its obsession with facts and concrete situations, and its disdain for generalization and systematization.

Even today, as the law of the civil codes becomes relatively less central in fact, the civil law remains for most continental lawyers the very heart of the legal system. In some countries it can even be said to have a quasi-constitutional character. Thus, in legal education, in practice and in the work of legal scholars, there is not only a common fund of inherited concepts, a shared passion for theory and systematization, but more importantly, there are distinctive modes of thinking and communication. Still, it is well to remember that the edges of any system of classification of human activity are bound to be indistinct. This is especially so of artificial legal constructs. The civil law systems of the late 20th century are in the midst of a process of change in which the centrality of private civil law is being constantly reduced and through which the distinctiveness of the systems is somewhat diminished.

§ 12. Contemporary Civil Law

The transition of 19th century civil law systems into the 20th century is closely tied to the transformation of liberal laissez-faire governments into modern social welfare states with planned or regulated economies. As noted, the classification of civil law systems proceeds as if the only law worth taking into account were the areas of law covered by the civil codes. In those areas, the 19th century codes established a large role for individual autonomy and foresaw a minimal role for governmental intervention. This scheme accorded well with then-prevailing views about individualism and the market economy. By the turn of the century, however, the forces that would transform the legal and social order were already at work. In the late 20th century, it has become clear that the gradual shift away from 19th century liberalism and the market economy has meant a shift in emphasis from private or civil law to public law (infra Chapter 5, Section 4). The legal order has begun increasingly to take on the characteristics of a bureaucratic, or administrative, order. The dynamics of the legal change have worked primarily through a double movement away from the civil codes (via special legislation and judicial construction), and to a lesser extent, through code revision, constitutional law and harmonization of law within the European Economic Community.

Over the 20th century, legislation, in response to social and economic change, has removed large areas from the coverage of the civil codes and has created entirely new areas of law outside the codes. These areas (for example: landlord-tenant law, employment law, insurance, contracts of carriage, competition and monopoly, agricultural holdings, urban housing) are governed by special statutes in which the unrestricted freedom of contract of the civil codes is replaced by a network of mandatory provisions, prohibitions on certain types of agreements, and requirements of controls, permits, licenses, and the like.

While the legislatures have been creating one body of civil law outside the civil codes, the courts have created another by interpretation or by developing new judge-made rules. Judicial adaptation of the codes to new conditions has brought into being a substantial body of "common law" in the form of a gloss on the legislative texts. In some systems, such as the French and those based on its model, this process has been facilitated by the structural features (gaps, ambiguities and incompleteness) of the code. Since the lawmakers of 1804 were innocent concerning such litigation-producing aspects of modern life as industrial and traffic accidents, photographic reproduction of images, and the mass circulation of publications, it is not surprising that modern French tort law is almost entirely judge-made. In later codes, such as the German and the Swiss, judicial adaptation to changing circumstances was facilitated by the so-called "general clauses", code provisions which deliberately leave a large measure of discretion to the judge (infra Chapter

6, Section 3).   Although traditional civil law dogma denies that judges "make" law and that judicial decisions can be a source of law, contemporary civil law systems are more and more openly acknowledging the inescapable dependence of legislation on the judges and administrators who interpret and apply it (infra Chapter 6, Section 4).

To some extent, the legislatures have kept the civil codes up to date by amending their texts.   The West German Civil Code in particular has been amended frequently in recent years.   But given the magnitude of social change since their original adoption, many civil codes have been revised less frequently and less extensively than might be expected.   Indeed, many civil law countries have changed governments and constitutions more readily than they have amended their civil codes, which, to the extent this has been the case, resemble the American Constitution more than they do American statutes.   Code revision has in general been more extensive in the area of family law than in other areas. Many of the family law reforms were either prompted or made necessary by post World War II constitutional provisions or international conventions promoting new ideals of equality and liberty that were at variance in several respects with the patriarchal family law of the civil codes.   In other areas, where the interests of organized economic groups are more affected, the legislatures have often found it hard to make necessary reforms within the structure of the hallowed civil codes. They have resorted instead to statutes outside the codes which are more easily amended as interests and power shift and as circumstances change.

Twentieth century legislation and code revision differ in several important respects from the earlier "classical" codifications. In the first place, law reform has tended to be marked by more *eclecticism*. This takes the form of using comparative law to investigate approaches and solutions to common social problems even if the country whose law is being studied does not happen to be a member of the civil law family. With the entry of non-civil law countries into the Common Market, it can be expected that the exchange of ideas among common law, civil law and Nordic systems will accelerate. This is not only because of the "harmonization of law" provisions of the 1957 Treaty of Rome, but simply as a result of increased communication, mobility and cooperation. Second, law reform in the 20th century tends to take account of *diversity* in society, in contrast to the civil codes which typically imposed one model of behavior on all. This tendency to leave more scope for diversity is in turn related to another modern trend in many important areas toward legal decentralization. Third, the modern lawmaker is more *realistic* than the draftsmen of the Enlightenment codes or the highly abstract German Civil Code. This probably reflects a decline in the belief that universally valid legal postulates can be found by the exercise of reason, and also a continuation of the reaction against abstraction and legal formalism. Thus, private law reform today is often preceded by considerable fact and opinion research. In this way, sociology has found a place with comparative law among the tools of the lawmaker. Finally, contemporary civil law shows an awareness of the *limits of law*, and has withdrawn from the attempt to control and regulate many kinds of human behavior.

Taken together, the shift from private to public law, the influence of new ideas about fundamental rights, the legislatures' eclecticism, realism and their senses of social diversity and the limits of law, tend in the long run to blur the distinctions between civil law systems and the legal systems of other developed states. Nevertheless, as the remainder of this chapter shows, significant differences remain. Often subtle, they are more in the area of mental processes, in styles of argumentation, and in the organization and methodology of law than in positive legal norms. Thus, the distinctive characteristics of the civil law systems will become more apparent as we take up the subjects of legal education, the role of scholars, ideas concerning the divisions of the law, the working of the codes, and the judicial process, as they exist in the contemporary civil law world.

CHAPTER 2

LEGAL STRUCTURES

§ 1. Parliamentary Government

As we have seen, the classification "civil law systems" has no necessary connection with public law and government. Nevertheless, if one were to categorize different countries according to the structure and relations of the organs of their governments, most of the civil law nations would be found to have governments of the type known as parliamentary. But, since many common law countries, Great Britain in particular, also have the parliamentary form of government, one cannot say this is a hallmark of civil law systems. Also, a number of civil law nations outside Western Europe, notably in Latin America, have adopted a presidential, rather than a parliamentary, model and France, since 1958, has also gone far in this direction.

Parliamentary government is the form of constitutional government in which the executive authority emerges from, and is responsible to, the democratically elected legislative authority. Thus, it differs from the presidential government of countries like the United States where the members of the executive branch and the legislature are elected independently of each other. It differs, too, from socialist governments in parliamentary form to the extent that these are not based on competitive elections. Within the essential union of the legislative and executive branches that characterizes the parliamentary form of government, the legislature is supreme. The chief executive, the prime minister, usually is appointed by the head of state (a constitutional monarch or a president chosen by the parliament to play the role of a monarch). The head of state must choose as prime minister a person whom a parliamentary majority would elect. Thus, in practice, the prime minister normally is the leader of the majority party. The prime minister chooses the executive heads of government departments, the most important of whom constitute the cabinet. Together, the prime minister and the cabinet are known in parliamentary systems as "the government."

The government holds office only so long as it commands majority support in the legislature. The importance of continuing parliamentary support for the government is evidenced by the fact that the government regularly submits its program and its record for parliamentary approval. An adverse legislative vote on an important issue indicates a lack of confidence which requires the government either to resign or to try to secure a new parliamentary majority by means of a general election. Thus, the familiar American phenomenon of stalemate between an executive of one party and a legislature of another is meant to be impossible. Technically, the decision to dissolve parliament and call for new elections, like the choice of prime minister, belongs to the head of state. But in practice the head of state exercises this power only on the advice of the prime minister.

The parliamentary system has taken different forms from country to country. Thus the foregoing description of its typical features will not apply in all respects to every country whose government is organized in this general form. (For Britain, see infra Part Two, Chapter 8). France, in particular, has become a special case. There, under the 1958 constitution of the Fifth French Republic, and the extraordinary personal authority of President de Gaulle, the powers of the head of state were increased to the point where the power of the executive is on an equal footing with that of parliament. The French president not only possesses substantial powers under the constitution (including that of dissolving parliament), but, since 1962, is chosen by direct universal suffrage. (See also infra Chapter 6, Section 2). Thus, the president may have a popular mandate independent of parliament. This has led many observers within and without France to consider that France has ceased to have a parliamentary system and has instead a hybrid system with features of both presidential and parliamentary types.

The parliamentary system has become the pattern in the 20th century for governments in many of the new nations that have emerged from colonial control in Africa and Asia. Japan, too, has followed this model. The former French colonies in Africa, however, have tended to follow France in receding from the parliamentary form. The student of comparative law should keep in mind that in civil law countries like West Germany and Switzerland the existence of a federal system introduces important local legal structures. As in the United States, federalism also involves levels of complexity in the legal system that are not present in unitary states like England and France.

§ 2. Separation of Powers

Separation of powers means something quite different in the European context from what it has come to mean in the United States. Historically, notions about the proper distribution of power among the organs of government were shaped in England and in Europe generally by the struggles of representative assemblies against the rule of monarchs. In France, the doctrine of separation of powers was further affected by the profound revolutionary reaction there against the rearguard role that the judiciary had played in the *ancien régime*. This background is in marked contrast to the United States where neither the fear of government by judges nor the dogma of legislative supremacy played much of a role in the formative period. Many of the framers of the American constitution did fear, however, the unprecedented power of relatively popular legislatures as a threat to property and commerce. Therefore, Chief Justice Marshall in *Marbury v. Madison* did not have to deal with deep-seated attitudes that in Europe have been powerful obstacles to the establishment of judicial review. Separation of powers to an American evokes the familiar system of checks and balances among the three coordinate branches of government—legislative, executive and judiciary—each with its independent constitutional basis. To a European, it is a more rigid doctrine and inseparable from the notion of legislative supremacy.

We have already seen the significance of the doctrine of legislative supremacy for the role of the executive in parliamentary governments. So far as the judiciary is concerned, the doctrine in its extreme not only has been thought to exclude judicial power to review the legality of legislative, executive and administrative action, but has even been invoked to deny the courts a "lawmaking" function via interpretation of legislative texts.   However, these "logical" implications of legislative supremacy have not prevented modern civil law systems from moving increasingly toward some form of judicial review (infra Section 3), nor have they diminished the growing de facto importance of case law (infra Chapter 6, Section 4).

The rigid European version of separation of powers has had long-lasting effects on the structure of the court systems in most civil law countries. The principle of legislative supremacy and, in France, the mistrust of the judiciary, seemed to rule out the possibility of judicial review of the legality of administrative action or of adjudication by ordinary courts of disputes between agencies of the government. Yet some institutional mechanism for dealing with these matters was clearly needed. In France this was made one of the responsibilities of the Council of State (*Conseil d'Etat*), the central organ of governmental administration. A number of nations including Belgium and Italy have followed the French model. In other nations, such as Austria and West Germany, such disputes are handled by the judiciary, but within a separate system of administrative courts. Thus, the typical civil law system contains at least two (and sometimes more) separate sets of courts for administrative and private law matters, each with its own supreme court, its own procedural and substantive rules, and its own jurisdiction (infra Sections 4 and 5). This is in striking contrast with the unified American system, where a single set of courts within each state and at the federal level hears both public and private law matters and even has authority to review the legality of the actions of the other branches of government.

§ 3. Judicial Review

Despite the difficulties that are perceived in the civil law countries as standing in the way of a system of judicial review of the constitutionality of legislation, there has been considerable movement in the years since World War II toward the establishment of some form of review of legislative action. This is especially so in those countries that have adopted constitutions containing guarantees of enumerated fundamental rights, and where the constitution can be amended only by a special procedure rather than simply by the ordinary legislative process. The gradual introduction of judicial review has taken various forms in the civil law systems. As is the case with parliamentary government, classifications of legal systems in this area do not always coincide with civil law—common law lines of demarcation. Indeed, so far as judicial review is concerned, France and England would appear to fall within one group of countries where its existence in a technical sense is denied, while Italy, West Germany and the United States come within another group where judicial power to review legislation not only exists but is actively exercised by the courts. In between are several countries which in varying degrees have admitted the principle, but where the courts have been relatively cautious in implementing it.

The peculiar history of the judiciary in France—its identification with feudal oppression, its role in retarding even moderate reforms in pre-revolutionary France, the post-revolutionary reaction against and the vestigial distrust of judges, plus the comparatively nonprestigious role of the modern civil-servant judge, —has militated against placing the power to review the constitutionality of legislation in the judiciary. The ordinary civil courts are not even permitted to review the legality of administrative action, this task being reserved to the administrative tribunals within the executive branch (infra Section 4). So, when France in 1958 instituted a system of constitutional review of laws passed by Parliament, it created a new governmental organ, the Constitutional Council. This body is authorized to review laws, but only at the request of the executive or the legislature, only *before* promulgation and only for the limited purpose of ascertaining whether the laws are in conformity with the constitutional division of powers between the executive and the legislature. As Cappelletti has written, the Constitutional Council was meant to be a "mere watchdog of the prerogatives of the executive." However, in 1971 the Council claimed for itself, and has since exercised, the power to review laws, prior to their taking effect, for conformity with the constitution generally, including the unwritten "fundamental principles" of the French republican tradition. This and other straws in the wind indicate that even France is moving away from the older, rigid view of legislative supremacy.

In Austria, Italy and West Germany, special constitutional courts were established after World War II as part of the judicial system. Like the German administrative law courts, these constitutional courts are separate institutions within the judiciary with their own jurisdiction and judges. In West Germany, when a party raises a constitutional objection to a statute involved in any civil, criminal or administrative case, the court hearing the case will refer the question to the Constitutional Court for decision if it thinks that the statute is unconstitutional. When the decision is issued, the original proceeding is resumed. In contrast to France, where the courts are not competent to sanction violations of individual constitutional rights, the West German Constitutional Court also hears complaints filed by individuals aggrieved by unconstitutional official actions, provided they have first exhausted their other remedies. In addition, certain governmental agencies or officials can test the validity of a statute in the Constitutional Court even though the statute is not involved in an existing dispute. The decisions of the Constitutional Court, unlike those of ordinary courts, are binding in future litigation (see infra Chapter 6, Section 4).

§ 4. Public Law Courts

In a typical civil law system, the various types of disputes that are handled by courts of general jurisdiction in the United States are entrusted to two or more separate hierarchies of specialized courts, each with its own supreme court. The jurisdiction of the ordinary courts (infra Section 5) typically is limited to criminal law and private law disputes. The tribunals which adjudicate most public law matters and most disputes in which the government is a party are separate from the ordinary courts. In some countries, as in France, the administrative courts are within the executive rather than the judicial branch, although care is taken to assure their independence from regular executive functions. In other countries, West Germany for example, the administrative courts are one of the two main court systems within the judiciary.

In either model, it is necessary to have some mechanism for resolving disputes about which court system has jurisdiction over a particular case. In France, a special Tribunal of Conflicts has been created to decide whether a case falls within the administrative or the ordinary jurisdiction. Nor is the problem free of controversy in the West German system, where there are a number of separate hierarchies of courts. But the basic rule is that the courts have power to determine their own jurisdiction. A final decision refusing jurisdiction is binding on the transferee court, which may, however, transfer the case to still another court system.

Although the French model was shaped by specifically French historical circumstances, it has been more widely imitated than the German system of separate judicial jurisdictions. Because administrative law was largely a creation of the 19th century, it was natural that the early French experience would be drawn on by many other countries as they searched for mechanisms to control their rapidly growing public administrations. As noted earlier, the French revolutionary doctrine of separation of powers seemed to require that the actions of administrative bodies and disputes among or involving them should not be decided by the judiciary. Thus the administrative dispute-settling mechanism had to be located elsewhere. In Napoleonic times this authority was vested in the Council of State, which began as a body of advisors to the king under the *ancien régime* and later developed into the central organ of governmental administration. The membership of the present Council of State is composed of professional public administrators, whose backgrounds and training are quite different from those of the ordinary judiciary. (In the terminology commonly used in Europe, the "administration" is the civil service, while the "government" consists of the prime minister and the cabinet).

To this day, the Council of State performs its dispute-settling function through a special section which is separate from its regular administrative functions. In the first instance, an administrative dispute normally is brought before one of several lower administrative courts. There is no intermediate court of appeal. The Council of State functions as the appellate court for all these lower courts, and also as the court of first and last instance for certain types of cases, such as where the constitutional status of an administrative act is challenged. It will be recalled that constitutional review by the Constitutional Council extends only to parliamentary legislation, not to other governmental actions. But under the 1958 French Constitution, the legislature has power to legislate only in enumerated areas, leaving an extensive residuary law-making power to the executive. (infra, Chapter 6, Section 2). In a landmark decision of 1959 (*Syndicat Général des In-*

genieurs-Conseils), the Council of State boldly asserted, and has since exercised, power to review this "executive legislation". Despite the independence and
prestige of the Council of State, some French observers have expressed concern that a court which is, at
least theoretically, part of the executive branch has
the exclusive power to review the legality or constitutionality of the acts of the executive.

Of the countries that have followed the French
model, Belgium and Italy have done so rather closely,
while most others have considerably varied and adapted it to suit their own circumstances over the years.
Some of the developing nations which have followed
French law in other respects, have adopted a unified
court system for want of a sufficient number of judges to staff a dual hierarchy of courts.

In Germany, unlike France, separation of powers
was not understood to require the administrative
courts to be outside the judicial system. Rather they
constitute one of a number of separate court systems
within the federal judiciary. In contrast to the United
States, where a single federal Supreme Court stands
at the apex of a pyramid of all lower and intermediate
federal courts (with considerable power over state judicial determinations), West Germany has several federal judicial pyramids, each with its own jurisdiction
and each headed by its own Supreme Court. The two
main hierarchies are the ordinary (civil and criminal)
courts and the administrative courts. But there are
also hierarchies of labor courts, tax courts and social
security courts. The Federal Constitutional Court is
yet another separate part of this system, not only ex-

ercising the power of judicial review (supra Section 3), but also hearing complaints about violations of constitutional rights and deciding disputes of a constitutional nature among the various governmental organs and entities. Besides these federal courts, the Federal Republic of Germany has an extensive system of state courts which will not be discussed here.

The West German administrative courts have jurisdiction over public law disputes generally, except for constitutional issues, and except for those administrative matters which have been assigned to the specialized tax and social security courts. There are three levels of administrative jurisdiction: the administrative tribunals, intermediate appellate courts, and the Federal Administrative Court which is the supreme administrative court.

§ 5. Ordinary Courts

Just as the civil law is the heart of the substantive law in civil law countries, the so-called "ordinary courts" which hear and decide the great range of civil and criminal litigation are the core of the judicial system. These courts are the modern-day successors to the various civil and criminal courts that existed in Europe during the long period of the *jus commune*, before the modern state with its panoply of public and administrative law came into being. In the post-codification era, the main concern of the ordinary courts became the interpretation and application of the basic codes, but today they also routinely apply a great deal of law that is not found within the civil, commercial and criminal codes. The ordinary courts of first instance may, as in France, include a number of specialized courts. Intermediate appellate courts, as well as the Supreme Court, usually sit in specialized panels or chambers.

In the French system and its variants, the ordinary law courts and the administrative law courts form two separate and independent hierarchies, the public law system headed by the administrative Council of State (*Conseil d'Etat*) on the one side, and the private and criminal law system headed by the Court of Cassation (*Cour de Cassation*) on the other. Technically, only the second system composes what is known as the "judicial order." The Tribunal of Conflicts stands between the two systems as a kind of traffic officer for jurisdictional disputes. At the first level of ordinary court jurisdiction, several specialized courts co-exist with the regular civil and criminal trial courts. Matters arising under the Commercial Code, for example, are first heard in one of France's many commercial courts where the part-time judges (sitting in panels of three) are businessmen elected by their colleagues. Disputes between employers and employees in the first instance are brought before one of the labor courts (*Conseils de Prud'hommes*) where two elected representatives each from labor and management sit together. These labor courts attempt to settle disputes first by conciliation. If the matter proceeds to adjudication, and the judges become deadlocked, a professional judge sits with the panel. There are also special courts for rural leases and social security disputes. Except where minor civil or criminal matters are involved, courts of the first instance are collegial.

An appeal from a court of first instance is heard in the Court of Appeal (*Cour d'Appel*) within whose territorial jurisdiction the lower court is situated. At the highest level, the Court of Cassation has jurisdiction over the ordinary courts of the entire country. It is composed of about 100 judges who sit in varying combinations on panels in six specialized chambers (five civil and one criminal), and, in certain situations, in mixed chambers or plenary assembly.

In the West German system, it will be recalled that there are not two, but several, independent court systems, each with its own supreme court. (supra Section 4). The "ordinary jurisdiction" there includes all criminal and civil (including commercial) cases which are handled within the regular courts, and labor cases which are handled in a separate Federal Labor Court system. Traditionally in Germany, as in most other civil law countries, the first-instance courts of general jurisdiction have sat in panels consisting of a presiding judge and two associate judges. However, legislation in 1974 and 1976 has made it possible for many types of cases to be decided by a single judge. In commercial matters, the judge of first instance sits with two lay judges who are specialists in this field. Appeals from the first instance are heard in an intermediate appellate court (*Oberlandesgericht*), with final review by the Federal Supreme Court (*Bundesgerichtshof*). In the labor court system, appeals from the lower courts are taken first to the Labor Court of the state where the lower court is located, and finally to the Federal Labor Court. At the first and second levels, the judge acts in consultation with labor and management representatives.

§ 6. European Institutions

Membership in transnational organizations such as the European Economic Community, the European Coal and Steel Community, the European Atomic Energy Community or the Council of Europe entails the addition of certain transnational structures to the total picture of each member nation's legal institutions. The most important of these structures at present are the political institutions of the European Economic Community, or Common Market, whose membership has been expanded from the original six (Belgium, France, Italy, Luxembourg, the Netherlands and West Germany) to include Britain, Denmark, Greece and Ireland. Portugal, Spain and Turkey have begun procedures that are expected to lead to their eventual membership. The functions of the European Economic Community are mainly economic, but the measure of political sovereignty that each member state has yielded to the Community has, at least potentially, far-reaching effects on the national legal systems.

Under the EEC Treaty of Rome of 1957, which functions like a Constitution for the Community, the member states have transferred powers to an autonomous legal order composed of four basic institutions: the Council of Ministers, the Commission, the European Parliament and the European Court of Justice. Legislative power is shared by the Council and the Commission, rather than belonging to the popularly elected Parliament which, at this stage, is merely an advisory and supervisory body. The principal decision-making power is vested in the Council whose members, one from each member state, are subject to national governmental control. However, the power of "initiative", that of investigating, deliberating on, and proposing measures in the general interest of the Community, belongs to the independent Commission whose members are appointed by the common accord of the governments of the member states from among persons of exceptional general competence and independence. The Commission also functions as the executive of the Community in matters of day-to-day administration.

The law of the EEC consists of the Treaty of Rome and certain acts adopted by the Council and the Commission. The law-making powers of these two bodies are limited to those enumerated in the Treaty. The implementation of community law is the task of the European Court of Justice and of the national courts within the member states. The 11-member European Court of Justice is composed of at least one judge from each of the member states. Until 1973, it was a court composed exclusively of judges from civil law countries. With the entry of Britain, Denmark and Ireland, however, this transnational court became a hybrid civil law-common law-Nordic institution whose work should be increasingly interesting to observe. The Court has two main responsibilities, the judicial review of the actions of Community institutions and the supervision of the manner in which Community law is applied by national courts and agencies.

The primary responsibility for the supervision of the implemention of Community law falls on the courts of each member state. This is because the Treaty, rather than establishing a system of "Community courts", leaves it to the national courts to apply Community law in the cases before them. Thus, Community law becomes a new "source of law" within each national legal system (infra Section 6). However, in order to supervise compliance with the Treaty by the member states and to assure legal uniformity within the Community, the European Court has jurisdiction over actions against member states for failure to fulfill their treaty obligations and also over requests from national courts for preliminary rulings on issues of Community law. In certain situations, national courts are obliged to request an authoritative ruling from the European Court on the interpretation or application of Community provisions involved in cases before them.

In an important 1964 case (*Costa v. ENEL*), the European Court announced that Community law took precedence over national law, including national constitutional law. This supremacy doctrine, proclaimed by a court with no support from a strong central government and little enforcement authority of its own, has been accepted by the original six member states. In effect, it brings about a form of supranational judicial review in these nations. It remains to be seen, however, whether or to what extent the newer members, Great Britain in particular, will accept this doctrine.

Besides the "little Europe" of the European Economic Community, mention should also be made of the "larger Europe" of the Council of Europe which has

21 member nations. The most important product of the Council of Europe has been the European Convention on Human Rights. This document has had significant effect on national law, particularly on the law of signatories whose constitutions do not include a bill of rights. Furthermore, the Council's European Court of Human Rights at Strasbourg (through publicity more than through direct sanctions) plays an increasingly important role in safeguarding the fundamental rights of individual citizens of member states.

Some scholars believe that the European Convention on Human Rights is in the process of becoming part of European "Community law." They point to the fact that, in the course of developing "general principles of Community law," the Court of Justice of the European Communities has been referring increasingly to the Convention on Human Rights. It is too soon to say, however, whether and to what extent this practice will result in the integration of the Convention into Community law, and thereby into the domestic law of even those member states, where, like Denmark, Ireland and the United Kingdom, the Convention is not directly applicable at present.

CHAPTER 3

ROLES AND ACTORS

§ 1. Legal Education

A legal system, like any other system, is a group of functionally related, interacting, interdependent elements, which together give the system its character. The formal legal structures just examined are but one set of such elements. None of these structures is a necessary feature of a civil law system. However, these institutions enter into a nation's legal culture, absorbing special characteristics from, and imparting them to, that underlying culture. We have already traced the historical evolution of the common legal culture of civil law systems in the first part of this chapter. Now it is appropriate to turn to the modern-day individuals who have inherited this tradition—the practicing lawyers, the judges, the attorneys in government service, the prosecutors and professors. It is they who give life and a special imprint to the legal structures. The way a society defines their legal "roles" and the status it accords to them is as revealing of its legal culture as is the composition and the relations of the organs of government. Of equal importance are the background and identity of the legal "actors" who are assigned or permitted to play these roles. Therefore, our next step into the legal culture of the civil law world takes us to law school.

What might first strike an American lawyer as a major difference between legal education in the civil law countries and in our own system is that civil law training is undergraduate university education. Like most college training everywhere, it tends to be general, rather than professional. But this way of organizing of legal studies is also found in England. What is really distinctive about civil law legal education grows out of its methodology, which perpetuates the tradition of scholar-made law, just as our "case method" emerged from and contributes to the maintenance of the common law tradition of judge-made law. In both cases, a discrepancy is appearing between the tradition and the reality. In fact, a good argument can be made that changes now occurring will in the long run diminish the differences between the civil and common law systems of legal education. At present, however, legal education in both systems still draws its basic approach from the historical circumstances in which it developed. In England, legal education from early times was in the hands of the bar (infra Part Two, Chapter 9). On the continent, from the time of the Roman law revival, it was the province of the universities.

Against this background, it is not surprising that one of the greatest differences between legal education in common law and civil law systems appears in the manner in which the student is initiated into the study of law. While an American law student typically spends the first days of law school reading cases and having his or her attention directed over and over again to their facts, a student of the civil law is provided at once with a systematic overview of the framework of the entire legal system. A typical introducto-

ry text (not a casebook) may even include a diagram
depicting "The Law" as a tree, with its two great divisions, public and private, branching off into all their
many subdivisions and categories which will become,
in turn, the subject of later study in a curriculum consisting predominantly of required courses in programmed series.   While the common law student is taught
to mistrust generalization and is expected to ferret out
individually whatever patterns and structure are there
to be found, the civil law beginner is kept at a certain
remove from the facts and starts out with a ready-
made version of the organization, methods and principles of the system.   The student is introduced to a particular style of legal reasoning and learns what Mirjan
Damaska has called "the grammar of law": a "network of precise interrelated concepts, broad principles
and classificatory ideas."   All this is, of course, in
keeping with the tradition of legal science so firmly in-
grained in the civil law culture.

The methods of civil law legal education are a natural outgrowth of its principles.   Teaching materials ordinarily consist of systematic treatises and, where appropriate, an annotated code.   Typically the professor
lectures rather than engaging in discussion with the
class.   It is not uncommon for one professor to have
several hundred students in traditional lecture
courses.   Lectures and treatises both are relatively
less concerned with practical application of legal theory and with concrete social problems than would be
the case in a common law system.   Much has happened in recent years, however, to lessen these contrasts.   Both common law and civil law schools are

seeking a better balance between theory and practice. American law professors increasingly consider the case method only one of several useful teaching methods, while civil law faculties have come to recognize the importance of practical work, tutorials and small classes where discussion is possible. In some West German universities, legal education has become less general and more professional. In Western Europe generally, where nearly all legal education is public and relatively easily accessible, there has been considerable pressure for change. Particularly since the student unrest of the late 1960s, a number of law faculties have instituted various reforms and experimental programs.

§ 2. Legal Professions

It is apparent that legal education of the kind just described does not produce graduates who are trained to embark immediately on the practice of law. In fact, many students who take their general university education in law in civil law countries do not do so as a prelude to a career in the legal professions. By graduation, a student will have acquired facility in the "grammar of law" and a knowledge of the basic principles of the most important fields of law, but only a limited ability to do legal research and a nodding familiarity with the practical aspects of law. In contrast, the American law graduate is supposed to be prepared to do any kind of legal work (although to be sure a kind of de facto apprenticeship is needed before a beginning lawyer is capable of handling many matters alone). If the civil law graduate wants to enter a legal profession, some further practical training is required.

The type and duration of such training varies from country to country and often depends in part on the kind of legal career the graduate wishes to pursue. The civil law graduate is faced upon graduation or shortly thereafter with a choice among the various branches of the profession, a choice which is likely to be final. In a fundamental way this puts the civil law graduate in a quite different position from that of a budding American lawyer. It is uncommon for a civil law lawyer to change, as American lawyers often do, from one kind of legal career to another, or to combine careers during one's professional life. Once trained to be a practicing lawyer, a judge, a civil servant or a scholar, the civil law lawyer is more apt to remain so than a common law lawyer, even though the latter often experiences a gradual reduction in mobility over time through increased specialization.

In France, the crucial choice is made early since different kinds of practical training are required for different branches of the profession. The West German *Referendar* system, which serves as an apprenticeship for several different legal careers, gives the law graduate more time and a better opportunity to make an informed choice of career. There, all law graduates must pass a "first state examination", somewhat similar to our bar examinations, in order to be eligible to enter a required practical training period (the *Referendarzeit*). This is a two-year internship spent in different "stations," each corresponding to a different branch of the profession. For example, one might divide the apprenticeship among a court, a legal aid bureau, a private firm, a government agency and the public prosecutor's office. The internship is then followed by a "second state examination," after which the young lawyer generally settles upon a career.

§ 3. Private Practice

In order to enter private practice, the law graduate must ordinarily prepare for and pass a special examination and serve a practical internship in a legal setting. The West German system has been described above. In France, there is no such multi-purpose training period. A French law student who wishes to become a practicing lawyer must first obtain the *licence en droit* (the university degree awarded after three years of law study); then a master's degree (after a year's further study); and then pass a bar examination. Upon passing the bar, the graduate becomes a probationary lawyer for at least three years, during which time there is further course work and practical training. When this training period is completed, the French law graduate becomes an *avocat*. The *avocat*, however, is only one of the types of practicing lawyer officially recognized in France. Thus, we must briefly consider here the various actors that in the United States would all be called "lawyers," but who in the civil law world are frequently divided into sub-groupings according to the roles they play.

In most civil law countries, the practicing legal profession is officially divided to some extent, at least between lawyers and notaries. The French system is the most complex, encompassing *avocats* and *avoués* (similar, respectively, in some ways but not identical to English barristers and solicitors); legal consultants (*conseils juridiques*); and notaries (*notaires*). By a law of 1971, the *avocats* and *avoués* were merged into a single profession of *avocats*. Members of this merged profession, which had traditionally been that of the litigators, may now give legal advice, prepare pleadings and argue in court. However, important exemptions from the coverage of the 1971 law left the *avoués* of the intermediate appellate courts and the *avocats* of the Court of Cassation and the Council of State in their old positions. Thus, the post-1971 *avocats* have their full powers only when practicing in the courts of first instance. In the intermediate appellate courts, the services of an *avoué* are required to handle procedural matters such as the preparation of pleadings. In the Court of Cassation and the Council of State, only a limited number of specially appointed advocates are admitted to practice.

Traditionally in France the mere giving of legal advice, as distinct from being admitted to practice before a particular court, has been unregulated. Anyone was free to set up shop as a legal consultant, with or without a law degree. But since the 1971 law, the *conseils juridiques* must be licensed. Unlicensed French nationals are still allowed to give legal advice but are not permitted to use a title that has any form of the word "law" in it.

The *notary* occupies a special position in civil law systems. Unlike the common law figure with the same name, the civil law notary is an important legal personage. The notary has three major functions:

drafting certain documents such as marriage contracts, wills, mortgages, and conveyances; certifying documents which then have a special evidentiary status in court proceedings; and serving as a depositary for the original copies of wills and the like. Part of the uniqueness of the notary's position comes from the fact that a notary is a public official with a state-protected monopoly over some of these functions (typically marriage contracts and mortgages) within a given region. There are a limited number of notarial offices established by law. A law graduate who wishes to be a notary must pass a special examination and then wait for a vacancy. Unlike the regular lawyer, a notary is supposed to be impartial and to instruct and advise all parties involved in the transactions he or she handles. Because of the nature of these transactions, the notary often becomes a trusted family legal advisor whose assistance is needed in connection with the property aspects of such major events as marriages, divorces and death of a family member.

Even in those civil law countries where, except for the notaries, the bar is unified, practice before the highest courts is usually restricted to a limited group of lawyers. And, whether or not the bar is officially divided, there tends to be in most places, as in the United States, a de facto division of labor between those lawyers who advise clients and those who appear and argue before courts, as well as among the various legal sub-specialties. In recent years, especially in the more developed countries, the practice of law has been profoundly affected by the types of legal services demanded by large enterprises. It is often observed that this kind of client requires planning and drafting more than it does litigation services, and that a certain bureaucratization of the private bar has resulted. The increase of lawyers engaged in serving large organizations has brought about an expansion of the roles of the legal consultant and the notary, and, although small law firms have been the rule in civil law countries, a certain trend toward larger-sized firms.

The various forms of the private practice of law comprise only one set of options for the aspiring civil law lawyer. If he or she wishes to become a judge, a prosecutor, a government attorney or a professor, other avenues must be taken.

§ 4. Judiciary

A law student in a common law country who gives any thought to becoming a judge one day is apt to consider even a lower court judgeship as something one might look forward to as a recognition of a long and distinguished career at the bar. In civil law systems, by contrast, a judicial career is just one of many options open to a beginner. A new law graduate who wishes to be a judge can expect to be sitting on the bench as soon as he or she completes a training period and successfully passes an examination. This is because the judiciary, except at the highest levels, is just another civil service hierarchy in civil law countries. A young judge enters at the lowest level and over time works up through a series of programmed promotions. Ordinarily, only positions on the highest courts are open to distinguished practitioners or professors as well as to career civil servants. Lateral entry into the judiciary at any level has been uncommon, but this may be altered by a 1980 law designed to relieve court congestion by recruiting permanent and temporary judges from other branches of the profession.

In some countries, such as France and Japan, there are special schools for training judges. In others, such as West Germany and the Nordic countries, judicial training is acquired in the post-law school practical internship period. In West Germany, for example, a law graduate may be appointed to a lower court after completing the *Referendarzeit* and passing the second state examination. After serving a three-year probationary period, the judge is eligible for an appointment for life. In France, the first step to becoming a judge is to pass an annual competitive examination for which students prepare by taking a special program in their last year of law studies. Successful candidates then must undergo 28 months of training consisting of a period of formal study at the National School of the Judiciary, followed by a series of short practical internships in such settings as police departments, law offices, prisons and the Ministry of Justice in Paris. This training culminates in a judicial apprenticeship, during which the future judge participates on a daily basis in all the activities of a variety of courts. Upon completion of their training period, the students are ranked on the basis of their grades and the evaluations of supervisors, and then assigned to their first positions in the judicial system. Since the administrative law courts in France are not part of the judiciary, but rather of the administration, judges for these courts are drawn, not from the lawyers trained in the National School of the Judiciary, but from the civil servants trained in the National School of Administration.

The advantages of the civil law systems of judicial recruitment are that they make the career more accessible to members of diverse groups in society and provide greater assurance that all judges will be able to perform in a competent manner. Thus, there are proportionately more women judges in Western European countries than in the United States and the likelihood of a person with no particular judicial qualifications becoming a judge is practically ruled out. On the debit side, however, it is frequently observed that civil law judges, because of their standardized training, tend to share a common outlook, and that their concerns about advancement promote a civil-service mentality which discourages initiative and independence. This has become less so in recent years in France since the formation by some of the newer judges of a union, the *Syndicat de la Magistrature*, which has taken bold positions in such areas as that of sentencing white collar criminals. Furthermore, the outstanding West German judiciary, recruited from among the best recent law graduates, does not conform to the stereotype of the civil servant judge.

The way the civil law judge conceives of the day-to-day work of the courts, as well as the way the role of judge is regarded in the society generally, has traditionally been different from the common law outlook on the judicial process. Though there are signs of change, the judge still has a relatively low profile in most civil law systems. As John Merryman has put it, the standard image of the judge is as "a civil servant who performs important but essentially uncreative functions." While the common law tradition reveres the names of the great judges who created the system and accords prestige and power to their modern successors, the names of civil law judges of the past are hardly remembered and their present-day successors work largely in obscurity. The tendency toward judicial anonymity is reinforced by the fact that civil law judges, even at the lowest levels, usually sit in panels and their decisions are presented per curiam. Except in a few courts, such as the West German Constitutional Court, any disagreement among the judges will not show, either in the form of a dissenting opinion, or in a notation of the judges' votes.

Today this area of contrast between the civil and common law systems is diminishing somewhat as proliferating lower court judgeships in the common law countries cease to attract the best candidates, while appointments to certain civil law high courts, such as the West German Constitutional Court, tend to be made from among outstanding jurists. It is also true that increased litigation and crowded dockets have made much of the work of American judges administrative in nature, at the same time that civil law judges and their societies are slowly becoming conscious of the real law-making power of the judiciary. Furthermore, the West German experience shows that prestige and civil service are not mutually exclusive. Nevertheless, in contemporary reality as well as in folklore, the common law judge remains a more powerful, creative and respected figure than his or her civil law counterpart.

One need not search far for the historical roots of the difference. From the time the administration of English justice was centralized in the King's Courts at Westminster by the end of the 13th century, the law was developed by judges and the practicing bar dominated legal education. Although there were moments in history when things might have gone differently, the existence of a powerful English legal profession was an important, perhaps the crucial, factor in preventing an English reception of the Roman law brought back by English scholars from Bologna, and in checking the influence and power of university legal scholars. In our historical survey of the civil law tradition, we have already seen that the central actors were not judges, but great law-givers, like Justinian and Napoleon, and the great scholars. Next to these towering figures, the judges are almost invisible. This was so even in the classical Roman times when the lay *judex* who decided cases and the *praetor* who gave him the formulae for decisions turned to the Jurisconsult for expert advice on the law. We have also seen how medieval judges depended on University law faculties for opinions on the law. The idea of the judge as a legal actor without inherent law-making power, who applies the will of the sovereign and looks outside for advice, is thus quite deeply rooted. When French judges, in support of the social order of the *ancien régime*, began to break out of this traditional judicial role and to behave more like English judges, making new rules and dealing creatively with the

[*82*]

sources of law, they became the targets of revolutionary fury and post-revolutionary reaction. Then, when French ideas, law and institutions spread to other countries in the 19th century, this reinforced the traditional civil law conception of the judicial function as a strictly limited one.

The narrow conception of the judge's role is nowhere so evident as in France. We have seen that the doctrine of legislative supremacy took an especially rigid form there, to the point of forbidding judges to announce general rules when deciding cases, and denying that law could be made by judges. Indeed, to this day, French legal writers say that the judiciary is not really a third "branch" of government. It seemed at first to follow, logically, that a court could not decide a case on the basis of its own or even a higher court's prior decision. The judge was merely to find and apply the law made by the legislative representatives of the people. Today, even France has long since retreated from the extremes of these positions (infra Chapter 6), but civil law judges in most countries still are far from exercising the kind of leadership that traditionally characterizes their American and English counterparts.

§ 5. Government Lawyers

As in common law countries, many civil law graduates enter government service after completing their training and examinations. In some places, West Germany for example, lawyers dominate the higher offices in the civil service, while in others, such as France, the various official bureaus and agencies are apt to be staffed by persons who have been trained in a special school of administration. In Italy and Spain, a central government agency serves as the "law firm of the state", providing legal advice and representation to other government departments.

The public prosecutor in civil law countries is a civil servant, too. Like a district attorney in the United States, the public prosecutor prepares and argues the government's case in criminal matters. But in this role he is much more an officer of the court than our prosecutor normally is (infra Chapter 4, Section 2). In most civil law systems, the prosecutor has an additional function—that of representing the public interest in certain ordinary civil cases. On the theory that the parties to such proceedings will not always provide the judge with a full presentation of the facts and law, and will never provide an impartial view, the prosecutor is permitted, and in some cases required, to intervene in civil cases. In this role, the prosecutor is supposed to represent the interest of "society" as distinct from the interest of the state. Some civil law systems, like the West German, are content to let the judge perform this function.

An interesting aspect of the position of the public prosecutor in Italy and France is that the prosecutor is a member of the judiciary. A prosecutor follows the same course of training as a judge, and they both may move from one role to the other in the course of their advancement in the civil service. In France, the judges are known as the *magistrature assise* (sitting judiciary) and the prosecutors as the *magistrature debout* (standing judiciary). In West Germany, although the prosecutor is not technically a member of the judiciary, he or she is not strictly separate from it either and prosecutors and judges move easily from one position to the other.

§ 6. Legal Scholars

When the reknowned sociologist Max Weber turned his attention to the study of the world's legal systems, he observed that each had been decisively shaped by a particular group of leaders to whom he gave the name *Rechtshonoratioren*, the honored men of the law. The religious legal systems of Islamic, Jewish and Hindu secular communities were fashioned by theologians. The English common law was the creation of those judges whom Blackstone called the "living oracles" of the law. And, as we have seen, European continental laws received their characteristic features through the work of learned jurists.

It is the names of scholars, not judges, that have come down to us over the centuries of the civil law tradition, as the centers of high legal learning shifted from ancient Rome, to fifth century A.D. Byzantium, to 13th century Bologna, to 16th century France and Germany, to 17th century Holland and back to Germany in the 19th century. The civil law world venerates such names as Gaius, Bartolus, Domat, Pothier, Grotius, Pufendorf, Savigny, Gény and Jhering, as the common law world does Coke, Mansfield, Marshall, Story, Holmes, Brandeis and Cardozo.

In the historical introduction to this chapter we traced the ascendancy of academic jurists in the civil law world through the 19th century. The long-standing practice of judges to ask professors for their opinions in difficult cases was, in some places, institutionalized so that binding decisions in lawsuits were rendered by university faculties. The absence, at crucial formative periods, of centralized government and unified legal systems assisted the university scholars in gaining and holding their dominant position. As the "law" in civil law systems increasingly became codified or statutory, and as the doctrine of legislative supremacy took hold, one might well wonder why the law-maker did not fully supplant the scholar as the central actor in the civil law tradition. The answer seems to be related to the fact that it was the scholars and the professors who were the architects of the doctrine of legislative supremacy and the draftsmen of the codes (or important influences on the draftsmen). After the codes appeared, reliance on pre-code authorities declined, but the need for interpretation intensified. Legal scholars became the authoritative expounders and interpreters of the codes. The law of the codes thus remained, in an important way, scholar-made law.

This is still largely the case today so far as the civil codes are concerned. When the family law provisions of the French Civil Code were extensively recast in the 1970s, the government turned the task over to the highly respected French civil law scholar and legal sociologist, Jean Carbonnier. And in the American state of Louisiana, the drafting work for civil code revision is carried on under the supervision of the Louisiana State Law Institute housed at Louisiana State

University. The situation is different, however, when we depart from the domain of the civil codes.

As civil law systems, like those of the common law, have become increasingly dominated by frequently amended public and regulatory statutes outside the codes, one may wonder whether this change in the law itself in time will affect the position of the civil law scholars. John P. Dawson has pointed out that it was important for the success of the 19th century German legal scholars (culminating in the adoption of the German Civil Code) that their activities were almost exclusively concentrated within the supposedly apolitical and relatively non-controversial area of private law. In the 20th century, legislation increasingly is perceived as the product of conflicts resolved by majority vote, rather than of reasoned elaboration and adaptation of fundamental principles. As law becomes more public and bureaucratic, will the university jurist remain a protagonist of the civil law tradition?

Thus far it seems that the role of the academic profession in the civil law systems is relatively secure. In the first place, all other actors in the system receive their training from the scholars who transmit to them a comprehensive and highly-ordered model of the legal system that to a great extent controls how they organize their knowledge, pose their questions and communicate with each other. This model is not only taught in the universities but constitutes the latent framework of the treatises and articles produced by the professors. Furthermore, legal periodicals, which in civil law countries are run by professors rather than students, play a much more important role there than in common law countries in bringing new legislation and court opinions to the attention of the profession. The official reports of cases do not necessarily report all court opinions, nor do they always set forth the opinions in full. The bar tends therefore to rely on the editors of the privately published legal journals who select and print what they consider to be the important cases. Typically each case is followed by an annotation written by an expert (not necesssarily a professor) who may amplify the facts of the case, relate the case to other decisions, and discuss its general significance. Such legal periodicals are an indispensable tool of legal research.

Though not a formal source of law, the weight of scholarly authority, known in civil law terminology as "the doctrine," is everywhere taken into account by legislators and judges when they frame, interpret or apply law (infra Chapter 6). Unlike in the United States, with its complex federal structure, the expert authors of this critical literature can concentrate on the relatively manageable output of a single legislature and, basically, of two sets of courts. The interaction between these legal institutions and the scholars who closely watch them tends to result overall in a more coherent and predictable body of national law than that generated by the legislatures and courts in the 50 states and the federal system in the United States. A critical case note by a leading author, is, in effect, like an important dissenting opinion, indicating where controversy exists and the possible future direction of the law.

Given the influence and prestige of the academic branch of the profession, it is not surprising that the career of a law professor is not one that is easily accessible to law graduates in civil law countries. The path to an academic career is long, arduous and risky. One who wishes to pursue this career must first, as a rule, obtain a doctorate in law which involves, at the least, producing a major piece of research and scholarship as a doctoral thesis. In West Germany, a second "qualifying" thesis called the *Habilitationschrift* is usually required as well. Then the aspiring professor must wait for a regular appointment to become available. Permanent academic positions are so few and so hard to get, that the candidate will often pursue some other branch of the profession while waiting for an appointment. At this juncture, the help and influence of the professor who has directed the candidate's graduate work may be decisive. The road to academe is so rocky that it is unusual for anyone to become a law professor before his or her early 30s, and the select group that eventually succeeds is not as diverse as, say, the judiciary.

It is easy to overstate the contrast with the role of legal academics in the United States. Especially in West Germany, the status and influence of civil law judges has reached the point where their relationship with legal scholars has become what John P. Dawson has termed "a close working partnership" that has greatly benefited the legal system as a whole. At the same time, in the United States, Max Rheinstein traced the rise of law teachers and scholars as a "new group of co-leaders of the law," and the tendency of

American law to assume some of the traits of "professorial" law, which, however, because of the active role of professors here in social reform, assumes a different character from European professorial law.

To summarize then, even in modern administrative states where scholar-made civil law is in decline, it is still the scholars who supply the vocabulary, concepts, and methodology of the system. Though the word of the legislator is accorded the supreme position among the sources of law, the word often issues from, and its ultimate meaning is often determined by, the academy.

CHAPTER 4

PROCEDURE

§ 1. Civil Procedure

In civil law countries, civil procedure occupies the same central position in procedural law that the civil law occupies within substantive law. The basic source of law in this area is typically a code of civil procedure. The more modern procedural codes stress that judicial proceedings must be public and that, in principle, the control of the allegations and proof belongs to the parties. This principle, however, tends to be tempered in practice by the civil law judge's extensive power to supervise and exercise initiative in the proceedings as well as by the role that the public prosecutor can play in private actions (supra Chapter 3, Sections 4 and 5).

In a typical civil action, after the pleadings are filed, a period of evidence taking begins. From the outset, several differences from common law civil procedure appear. These differences can be summed up by noting that on the one hand, there is no real counterpart to our pre-trial discovery and motion practice, while on the other hand there is no genuine "trial" in our sense of a single culminating event. Rather, a civil law action is a continuing series of meetings, hearings, and written communications during which evidence is introduced, testimony is taken, and motions are made and decided. During this process, the judge plays an active role in questioning witnesses, and in framing or reformulating the issues. Although the questioning is typically done by the judge, the questions are often submitted by the parties' counsel who sometimes are permitted to question a witness directly. As the action proceeds, the judge may inject new theories, and new legal and factual issues, thus reducing the disadvantage of the party with the less competent lawyer. In addition, the court may obtain certain types of evidence, such as expert opinions, on its own motion. There are no requirements that documents be formally admitted into evidence, nor are there any rules against hearsay and opinion evidence. Rather, the parties informally introduce documents after providing the other side with notice and an opportunity to inspect. The weight to be accorded the evidence is for the free evaluation of the court.

Except for minor matters which do not concern us here, the bench is usually collegial, but as a rule only one judge will preside over the evidence-taking stage of the proceedings. In some countries, it may happen that the case is decided by an entirely different judge or panel from the one or ones who heard the parties and took the evidence. The better practice, as exemplified by West Germany, requires the judge who conducted the proceedings to render the decision in the case. A judgment on the merits is generally executed out of the defeated party's property. As civil law courts traditionally had no contempt power, it is said that their decrees are *in rem* rather than *in personam*. However, today some civil law judges are authorized to hold persons in contempt of court and, in other jurisdictions, the judge may impose financial

sanctions (the French *astreinte*) on persons who refuse to comply with a court order. Costs of litigation
are taxed in such a way as to discourage severely
hopeless or frivolous causes: as a rule, the defeated
party bears the cost of litigation, including attorney's
fees. If each party wins and loses in part, costs are
allocated proportionately.

Many of the differences between the foregoing
model and the usual American trial seem attributable
to the absence of the civil jury in civil law countries
and its presence in our own system. The civil law
countries have never felt the need to bring the parties,
their witnesses, their lawyers and the judge all together on one occasion because they have not had to convene a group of ordinary citizens to hear all the evidence, to resolve factual issues, and to apply the law
to the facts. The absence of the civil jury also helps
to explain the relatively great number of exclusionary
rules in the common law of evidence and the relatively
few restrictions on admissibility in the civil law systems. However, recent developments in both systems
tend once again in the direction of a certain convergence. American discovery practice and pre-trial hearings bring us close to a situation where, as in the civil
law, there are few surprises at trial. Meanwhile, civil
law desire for efficiency and economy has led, notably
in West Germany, to experiments with and widespread
use of a single comprehensive hearing model that is
said to work well for the relatively simple cases that
form the great bulk of civil litigation.

§ 2. Criminal Procedure

There are three common misconceptions in the common law world about criminal procedure in the civil law countries: that the accused is presumed guilty until proved innocent, that there is no jury trial, and that the trial is conducted in an "inquisitorial" fashion (with connotations of Inquisition-like unfairness to the accused.) The first of these notions is simply false. The second is incorrect as to some systems and, as to others, overlooks the fact that lay judges who participate on mixed courts with professional judges are a functional analog to the jury. The third misapprehension has resulted from the fact that the usual mode of proceeding in criminal cases in civil law systems is quite different from that which evolved in the common law. The epithet "inquisitorial" apparently derives from the active role played by the judge in the conduct of the trial, and, often, in investigating the facts. A better word to describe this process would be nonadversary.

The first phase of a criminal proceeding is an extensive pre-trial investigation, conducted in some countries by a judge, in others by the public prosecutor. This official decides whether there is sufficient evidence to warrant formal charges, after interrogating the witnesses, collecting the other evidence, and questioning the suspect. Under modern codes of criminal procedure, the accused has the right to be represented by counsel during the interrogation and to remain silent.

[*94*]

If the examining magistrate or prosecutor determines that there is what we would call reasonable cause, the dossier compiled during the preliminary investigative phase is forwarded to the criminal court. There is considerable variation among systems as to the composition of this court. Typically, one or three professional judges sit with a number of lay judges. Both the professional and lay judges participate in the decision of all factual and legal issues relating to the determination of guilt, and also in the sentencing decision.

In contrast to the accused in an American criminal prosecution, the defendant in a civilian prosecution has an unlimited right to discovery of all the evidence assembled by the prosecution. During the trial, the presiding judge takes the lead in examining the witnesses and the defendant. Two major differences from the common law adversary model are that the judge is less a passive arbiter between the parties, while the prosecutor is less partisan. The system seems to elicit no such dissatisfaction and controversy in the major Western European democracies as have plagued the American criminal justice system. "Except for political cases, which no system handles well, . . . the task of detecting and punishing crime is generally perceived to be handled effectively and fairly," according to John Langbein, a leading American specialist in comparative criminal procedure.

A peculiarity of criminal procedure in the civil law systems is the role accorded to the victim. In some countries, if the same wrongful act gives rise to both criminal and civil liability, the injured person is permitted to intervene directly in the criminal action rather than bring a separate civil suit. If the victim chooses to become a party to the criminal suit, and is successful, the court may order civil damages to be paid to the victim at the termination of the proceedings. In France, this *action civile* is not uncommon. But in West Germany, procedural and practical difficulties have discouraged its use. However, West Germany like many other civil law countries, has another way of permitting the victim to join the prosecution. In recognition of the victim's interest in seeing justice done, a victim who does not seek damages may sometimes be allowed to intervene on the side of the prosecution. A guilty finding in such a case will then play an important role in any subsequent civil action by the victim. Also, in certain types of cases, if the prosecutor declines to bring charges, an injured person may be permitted to bring a criminal proceeding individually. However, in West Germany and some other countries, the prosecutor has no discretion not to prosecute (and therefore no power to plea bargain) if there is reasonable cause to believe that the defendant has committed a serious offense.

§ 3. Appellate Review

Decisions of the ordinary civil and criminal courts of first instance may as a rule be appealed to an intermediate appellate court. In criminal cases, the prosecution as well as the defense has the right to appeal. Unlike a common law appeal of a trial court's decision, the proceedings in this intermediate court may involve a full review *de novo* of the facts as well as the law of the case. The panel of appellate judges initially will make its independent determination of the facts on the basis of the original record. In addition, however, the appellate court may question the witnesses again, or even take new evidence or send out for expert opinions. A party dissatisfied with the results of the appeal may seek review by the highest court which, like a common law appellate court, in theory considers only questions of law. (It may be noted in passing that civil law high courts have not been more successful than common law appellate courts in distinguishing factual from legal issues). Some of these high courts follow the French system of "cassation", while others follow the West German system of "revision." (In some civil law countries, appellate procedure in *criminal* cases does not follow the above pattern of review *de novo* of both law and facts. In West Germany, for example, decisions of the courts which have first instance jurisdiction in cases of serious crime are subject to appeal only on points of law, and such appeals are heard, not by intermediate courts, but by a court of last resort. The right to appeal *de novo* does exist however for minor criminal offenses which are first heard before a single judge or a local court).

The French Court of Cassation has several peculiar features which can only be explained historically. The Court, as originally conceived, was to act on behalf of the legislature to supply authoritative interpretations of the law and to guarantee the obedience of the judicial system as a whole to the norms of legislatively-given law. Article 5 of the French Civil Code specifically forbids judges to decide cases submitted to them by way of pronouncing a general rule. They were supposed only to find and apply the law of the Code or other legislation. The Court of Cassation was supposed to see that lower courts did not exceed this role. Its own functions were narrowly drawn. When a case is appealed to it, the Court can decide only the question of law referred to it, not the case itself. This means that it has only the option to affirm, or to quash the decision and remand the case for reconsideration by a lower court in the light of the Court's opinion on the legal questions (hence its name, Court of Cassation, from *casser* : to break or quash). It may not substitute its own decision for that of the lower court. If it disagrees with the original lower court's decision, it sends the case, with its own interpretation of the law, to a different lower court. In France, the court to which the case is remanded theoretically is free to decide the case the same way as the previous lower court. If this happens, a second appeal may be made to the Court of Cassation, which will sit this time in a plenary session. If the lower court decision is again set aside, the case must still normally be remanded to a third lower court which, by an 1837 statute, is then required to give judgment as directed by the Court of Cassation. Legislation in 1967, and again in 1979, has expedited this archaic procedure somewhat, and has permitted the Court of Cassation to dispose of some cases without remand after the second appeal. The cassation system as practiced in Italy is simpler. There, the first time the Court of Cassation remands a case, the lower court is bound to follow the high court's views.

Under the system of revision as practiced in Austria, Switzerland and West Germany, the high court may, if it finds reversible error, either reverse and remand, or it may modify the decision and enter final judgment itself.

It will be recalled that the administrative courts in most civil law countries are in a separate hierarchy from the ordinary courts. The procedure in lower administrative courts, by comparison with civil procedure, from which it is to a certain extent derived, tends to be more informal, less expensive and more controlled by the administrative law judge. In France, as we have seen, the decisions of these lower courts are reviewed by the Council of State. The procedure of the Council of State differs in material respects from that of the Court of Cassation. In the first place, decisions of the Council of State are final. Second, the statutory rules of administrative procedure are supplemented by a number of judge-made rules. The bulk of substantive French administrative law, which is uncodified, consists mainly of the case law which has been built up by the Council of State. A number of civil law countries, including Belgium, Italy and several developing countries formerly within the French sphere of influence, have followed the French model.

In countries, like Austria and West Germany, where the administrative courts are part of the judiciary, the procedure for appellate review is essentially similar to that for civil cases in the ordinary courts. The lower court decision is reviewed *de novo* in an intermediate

level administrative court, and the supreme administrative court hears appeals only on questions of law.

CHAPTER 5

RULES

§ 1. Divisions of Law

Comparative law is a relatively simple matter when the jurisdictions being compared share common legal structures, procedural rules and similar ideas about how legal problems are to be classified. An American lawyer, for example, need hardly reflect on the everyday process of consulting the law of sister states for guidance on a difficult or controverted legal question. The mere comparison of legal rules can be dangerously misleading, however, when it takes place between systems with different legal institutions, different procedural settings and different systems for classification of legal rules. Varying rules of procedure, for example, may produce substantially different outcomes in cases in two legal systems with identical substantive rules governing the type of case. Apparent diversity in rules, on the other hand, may be erased when the rules are seen in their proper institutional and procedural context. Classification systems, in particular, with their distinctive ways of identifying and dealing with legal problems, may pose obstacles for the comparatist. Consider, for example, the continuing importance of the historic distinction between legal and equitable rules and remedies in the common law, and the difficulties it poses for comparatists from civil law countries where the division between law and equity is unknown. The categories according to which civil law lawyers are accustomed to arrange their legal rules are similar enough from country to country to greatly aid transnational communication within the civil law orbit. But they are sufficiently different from common law categories to constitute an obstacle to civil law-common law comparisons.

The fundamental division in all civil law systems is that between public and private law. This classification, which is only latent or implicit in the common law, is basic to an understanding of the civil law. We have already seen how closely it is tied to the organization of the court systems of civil law countries (supra Chapter 2, Sections 4 and 5). As public law disputes became justiciable in the 19th century, separate court systems were created to handle them. The jurisdiction of the ordinary courts is limited to disputes governed by private law, with the one major exception of criminal matters. Besides these jurisdictional consequences, the public-private law distinction also describes a division of labor within the legal profession. The members of law faculties tend to be either "publicists" or "privatists." Courses and treatises tend to be in one or the other area, despite the fact that today any given subject matter is apt to have public law aspects (infra Section 4).

Despite the universal recognition of the distinction within the civil law world, there is no agreement among civil law lawyers on its theoretical basis or justification, and no uniformity among countries as to its scope and effects. Generally speaking, however, public law includes at least constitutional law, administrative law and criminal law; while private law includes at least civil law and commercial law. The proper classification of several other areas is the subject of dispute. Civil procedure, for example, is included by some systems within the private group of subjects, and treated by others as public law. Labor law, agricultural law, social security, as well as a number of other modern, highly regulated areas, are sometimes said to be "mixed" public and private areas, and sometimes described as sui generis.

§ 2. Public Law

Although the public-private law distinction has roots in Roman law, public law remained a relatively undeveloped category until modern times. It was the preserve of the sovereign, prudently left aside by jurists. As we noted in the historical introduction to this chapter, nearly all the Roman legal literature that has come down to us is concerned with private law, and legal science traditionally has concentrated on private law. We observed too, that in the localism and legal diversity of the Middle Ages, there was no place for public law. But when the centralized state and its administrative organs began to emerge on the continent (coinciding with the appearance of legally trained professionals), conditions were favorable to the development of administrative law. In the 19th century, as administrative law began to flourish, it seemed to civil law lawyers that the ordinary private law rules that applied to disputes involving private individuals or associations could not simply be carried over to relationships in which the state was a party. In France it seemed, too, that the ordinary courts could not be entrusted with the task of resolving disputes involving the state. The French view of the separation of powers led, as we have seen, to the establishment of a separate set of public law courts within the administration. In Germany, however, concern about administrative oppression was more prevalent than mistrust of the judiciary. So, to avoid having disputes between citizen and administration adjudicated by the latter, Germany created a separate system of administrative law courts within the judiciary. Today, as the French Council of State has established its own independence from the administration proper, advanced the protection of individual rights, and extended its own control over the administrative process, the fact that it is technically not a court is of diminished importance. In modern civil law states, whether on the French or German model, the tendency has been toward increasingly effective review of the legality of administrative action.

Today, when one speaks of public law in the civil law systems, what is meant is often merely administrative law. Constitutional law, as it pertains to the form and structure of the state and its organs, is still thought of as being akin to political science. As we have seen, it is only in relatively recent times that courts or other institutions have acquired the power to review the constitutionality of the acts of government. As for criminal law, though technically classified as public law, it has traditionally been the concern of the "privatists" and everywhere falls within the jurisdiction of the ordinary courts. Thus, the bulk of public law in civil law countries in fact consists of administrative law.

It is hard to define precisely what is included within the concept of administrative law, even within a single country. Generally speaking, it consists of the norms which regulate the organization, functions, and inter-relations of public authorities other than the political and judicial authorities, and the norms which govern the relationships between the administrative authorities and citizens. Tax law has become a major specialty within this field. Administrative law does not completely coincide with the jurisdiction of the administrative courts, because, in all civil law countries, certain administrative matters are relegated by special legislation to the jurisdiction of the ordinary courts.

It is primarily in the field of administrative law that the distinctive characteristics have developed which are thought to set public law apart from private law in the civil law systems. The most obvious of these is the uncodified state of administrative law. The fact that the great codifications left public law (except for penal law) untouched accentuated the division between private and public law. The separation deepened as the courts assumed a large role in establishing the general principles and rules of administrative law, a role formally denied them in the area of the civil law. At the present time, administrative law in civil law systems tends to be scattered among various statutes, with case law playing a major role. The relative importance of the case law is greater in France; that of enacted law is greater in West Germany and Austria.

As might be expected, public and private law will not necessarily arrive at different solutions to similar legal problems. Nevertheless, the student of comparative law must always be aware of the possibility that the classification of a dispute as private or public will bring into play a quite different substantive rule or a different method of interpretation. For example, in France during the severe inflations after World War I, the private law courts refused to grant relief to creditors whose fixed contractual claims had become practically worthless, while the Council of State developed a doctrine of unforeseeability to come to the aid of obligees in contracts governed by public law. Administrative law is said, too, to be set apart from private law by its susceptibility to frequent change; by the wider scope it allows for official discretion and the little room it leaves to the discretion of the parties; and by its more vague and fluid legal concepts. However, it should be noted that the general principles of private law are often carried over to supplement or to fill gaps in administrative law.

§ 3. Private Law

Just as the term "public law" is commonly used to designate administrative law, "private law" is often used interchangeably with civil law. In civil law systems, however, private law comprises two grand divisions of its own: civil law and commercial law. Civil law, in principle, applies to everyone and its basic provisions are found in the civil codes, supplemented by auxiliary statutes. Commercial law, which concerns specific groups of persons and/or specific types of activities, is in most civil law countries arranged in a separate commercial code. In Italy and Switzerland, there are no commercial codes, but commercial law nevertheless is considered and taught as a separate private law subject. Besides commercial law, there are a number of other fields which are usually classified as separate from civil law, but within the domain of private law: literary and artistic property, maritime law, insurance and industrial property. Labor law developed from the civil law of the individual employment contract. However, today it is variously classified as a special category of private law; as mixed public and private law; or as *sui generis*, neither public nor private.

a. Civil Law

Civil law (*droit civil, Bürgerliches- or Zivilrecht*) is traditionally arranged in treatises and for teaching purposes under the following major headings: the law of persons; family law; marital property law; property law; succession law and the law of obligations. These categories are not exhaustive, nor do they precisely correspond with the way the subjects are distributed within the civil codes of various countries. In Switzerland, for example, there is a separate Code of Obligations, and in France, family law is included within the law of persons.

The law of persons consists of all the norms concerning the status of the individuals and legal entities which are the subjects of the law. It includes the legal rules relating to such matters as names, domicile, civil status, capacity and protection of persons under legal incapacities of various sorts. Most legal entities have long been subjected to special regulation by administrative, commercial and labor law, so that only a few associations are now left within the domain of the civil codes.

Family law covers marriage formation; the legal effects of marriage; marriage termination by divorce, separation, and annulment; filiation; and family support obligations. In the first of these areas, which has remained quite stable, the civil law systems have taken from the French the requirement of a civil ceremony for the formation of a valid marriage. In all the other parts of family law, extensive code revision has taken place under the influence of three major trends: the liberalization of divorce; the equalization of the position of women in the areas of family decision-making and property rights; and the assimilation of the status of children born outside legal marriage to that of legitimate children.

Marital property law, with close links to family law, property law and succession law, is traditionally treated as a separate area of civil law. The civil codes establish and regulate a "legal regime", the system that governs the property relations of all spouses who do not choose an alternative regime by marriage contract. The legal regime is typically a form of community property, usually with pre-marital property and property acquired through gift or inheritance kept separate if it can be identified as such. The modern trend favors forms of the so-called "deferred community" in which the spouses are treated as separate owners of whatever they respectively acquire during the marriage, but property acquired during the marriage is divided equally upon its termination by divorce or death. In addition to establishing the legal regime, the marital property provisions of the civil codes typically establish and regulate a number of alternative regimes which may be chosen by contract, as well as the procedures for entering and altering marriage contracts.

Property law in civil law systems recognizes a distinction between movable and immovable property, which roughly corresponds to the common law distinction between personal and real property. Historically, as in the common law, land was considered to be of greater importance than chattels, and the law of the older codes, especially, reflects this. In the liberal tradition, the right of ownership was considered absolute, and the protection of private property was regarded as an important function of the state. In fact, the absoluteness of the property right as described in the civil codes has long since been extensively limited by public law legislation.

Another traditional attribute of civil law ownership, not found in the common law, is its unitary character. Although the civil law recognizes certain forms of co-ownership, it is hard for a civil law lawyer to conceive of ownership as divided over time as is the case with common law present and future interests; and the distinction between legal and equitable title is unknown. Property is thought of as having one owner (or at least one set of concurrent owners) and other interests affecting it are generally thought of as restrictions or encumbrances on the title of the owner. Leases of real estate are not considered property at all, but fall within the contractual area of the law of obligations. In modern civil law, however, the idea of unitary ownership seems to be eroding somewhat as new forms of shared ownership gain in popularity.

Succession law covers the disposition of property upon death by will or by intestate inheritance. Freedom of testation in civil law systems is typically limited in favor of the testator's children who are entitled to a "reserved share" of their parent's estate. Unlike American law, civil law systems do not traditionally accord such a forced share to the surviving spouse, whose economic interests are thought to be sufficiently protected by the division of marital property upon death. The modern trend everywhere, however, has been to improve gradually the successoral position of the surviving spouse and in some countries, West Germany for example, this has brought about a reserved share in his or her favor. Two typical aspects of civil law succession have attracted considerable attention in the United States in recent years. The first is the practice of having a will authenticated before a notary during the lifetime of the testator, a procedure which dispenses with the need for probate. The second is the fact that, in the normal situation, there is nothing corresponding to our period of administration of a decedent's estate. An inheritance simply vests upon death in the persons designated by the will or the laws of intestate succession, subject to their right of renunciation. Another idea from the civil law of succession has already been incorporated into many American probate law reforms. This is the subjection of certain types of inter vivos gifts to the same restrictions in favor of family members that apply to gifts made by will.

The law of obligations is the most technical, abstract and (at first sight) stable part of the civil law. It covers all acts or situations which can give rise to rights or claims and is customarily divided into three parts: the law of contracts, the law of tort (delict), and the law of unjust enrichment. The contract law sections of the codes typically begin with rules which are applicable to all contracts, and then set forth special rules for particular sorts of contracts: sales, leases, agency, loans, etc. The civil law conception of tort liability is a unified one: in contrast to the common law which developed separate pigeonholes for different kinds of harms, it is a law of *tort* rather than torts. The civil law of unjust enrichment has been built up from general principles with a heavy component of case law.

The distinction between contractual and delictual (tort) responsibility has been treated as fundamental in civil law theory, even though both contract and delict are regarded as parts of the single field of obligations. As with other legal classifications, however, a great deal of literature has been devoted to the distinction without successfully clarifying its precise nature. And, as with other legal categories, there is no uniformity among systems as to which acts fall within which domain. The French tort specialist André Tunc has stated, in a comparative survey, that there is a trend in modern practice toward the decline, but not the disappearance, of the distinction, as contractual and tort liability become increasingly intertwined and

[*111*]

as the underlying unified principles of the law of obligations (including unjust enrichment) come more prominently into view.

Chief among the unifying factors within the law of obligations are the expanded range of facts that modern courts consider legally relevant, the movement away from formalism, and trends toward protecting reasonable reliance and expectations. However, at the very time that contractual and delictual responsibility appear to be converging, the scope of the field of obligations appears to be diminishing. At the outset of this section it was stated that the law of obligations is at first sight the most stable area of the civil law. If one looks only at the civil codes, the parts containing the law of obligations have been little changed, and they are recognizably related to the oldest parts of the civil law tradition. Legislation outside the codes, however, has altered both the substance and the underlying philosophy of the law of obligations. (See infra Section 4).

b. *Commercial Law*

Commercial law (*droit commercial, Handelsrecht*) generally includes corporations and other business associations, securities, banking, and negotiable instruments, as well as other commercial transactions. We have seen in our historical introduction how commercial law had developed from mercantile customs and the practice of merchants' courts into a well-established separate branch of private law even before the codification period. The dichotomy between civil and commercial law survived both codification and the centralization of justice, thanks mainly to France, which adopted the *Code de Commerce* in 1807 and established separate commercial courts within the first level of jurisdiction. Most other civil law countries followed suit.

The division between civil and commercial law is not, however, absolute or clear-cut. First, all systems have found the concepts of "merchant" or "commercial act" difficult to define for purposes of determining whether a transaction is governed by civil or commercial law. Second, the commercial codes lack the general principles and internal coherence of the civil codes. Thus, civil law is frequently brought in to fill the gaps in the commercial codes and their supplementary laws. This is so much the case that some writers now speak of the "civilization of commercial law", by which they mean that commercial law is now becoming just a special field within the civil law. Third, the differences are further diminished by a countertrend toward "commercialization of the civil law." This takes the form of reducing unnecessary formality, increasing protection of reliance by third parties, and a tendency to view transactions as parts of on-going relationships, rather than as isolated legal events. Finally, in Switzerland, Italy, and in the draft code of the Netherlands, the decision has been made to dispense with a separate commercial code, a development which may represent the wave of the future.

However, at the same time that civil and commercial law, through mutual enrichment, are coming to resemble parts of a unified field within private law, another legal trend is operating to remove much of commercial law from private law altogether. Originally based on custom, then codified on the liberal principle of individual freedom, commercial law has increasingly become a body of legislation regulating commercial and corporate activity. As state economic planning replaces the market economy, it becomes hard to distinguish commercial law from administrative law. This process has continued to the point where French and West German writers have renamed the classification. Instead of "commercial law", they refer to the field of "commercial and economic law," economic law being the regulatory law of the administrative state.

c. Labor Law

If commercial law now lies somewhere along the border between public and private law, it is clear that labor law, for most practical purposes, has escaped the private law domain entirely. The employment contract, once a civil law relation, has now been organized by legislation as a group relation heavily regulated by rules which are of a public law nature. The "labor codes" which exist in some countries are not true codes, but rather collections of diverse statutes pertaining to employment relationships. With general statutory protection against discharge without cause in most civil law countries, and with mandatory employee participation in shop-floor decision-making as well as in the actual control of the enterprise, the role of private autonomy is reduced mainly to the decision whether or not to become an employer or an employee. The question then arises whether labor law is, as is often said, an autonomous field, or whether it is in fact the archetype of all law in modern administrative states. This question of course challenges the public-private law distinction which has always been vulnerable and is now increasingly difficult to maintain.

§ 4. Merger or Desuetude of Divisions

Legal classifications, being artificial constructs, can never completely contain the fluctuating variety of human activity upon which they are imposed. However, it does not necessarily diminish their utility that there will always be definitional problems about where they begin and end, about what is included or excluded. The distinctions between public and private law, civil and commercial law, contractual and delictual responsibility, need not be shown to be impermeable or to have an inherent logic in order to be functional for various purposes, not the least of which is pedagogical. Thus, it is likely that, however much some parts of contract may merge with certain areas of delict, there will still be, as the English scholar, Weir, has put it, a distinction to be made between "transactions and collisions." Similarly, though civil and commercial law have fused in many ways, it is probable that commercial law will continue to be studied as a separate subject and that it will tend to be practiced mainly by specialists. The civil law classification that is most eroded by time and events is the "fundamental dichotomy" between public and private law, but that too survives, in the court systems and in the minds of civil law lawyers.

As we have observed throughout this section, intervention by the state in areas once reserved to private activity increasingly blurs the public-private law distinction. Yet the French comparatist René David wrote in the 1970s that, in contrast to public law, which he described as subject to the vicissitudes of change and political crises, the Civil Code seems to French lawyers to be "the most lasting and the only true constitution of France." There is indeed a sense in which the Civil Code is constitutional: the law of the Civil Code is the area of the law in which the function of government is limited to the recognition and enforcement of private rights. Especially in the field of contracts, the civil codes impose few rules in the name of public policy. Most of the law of contracts is of the type that civilians call dispositive, suppletive or directory, as opposed to compulsory. Dispositive rules apply only if they have not been expressly or impliedly excluded by the parties. However, one can maintain this "constitutional" view of the civil codes only if one ignores the effect that statutory law has had upon them. Special legislation has been an institutional bypass through which the codes have been left intact but emptied of much important content.

Legislation outside the civil codes has, first and foremost, undermined the constitutional function of the codes by establishing a new and competing set of premises. While freedom of contract still appears to be a fundamental principle of the civil codes, a variety of mandatory provisions and prohibitions have been introduced by statutes in the name of public policy—which in some cases means protection of the weaker party, and in other cases means the effectuation of economic planning. In the area of property, the codes still promote the notion that the role of government is to protect private property, while special legislation qualifies the property right by subtracting elements in the public interest, or modifies it by adding social obligations. With the development of public and private insurance schemes, delictual liability is no longer the main source of compensation for personal injuries; there is now a wide overlap between private tort law and public social security law. The stability which is so characteristically associated with the civil codes appears as an illusion when one takes into account that all this legislation is frequently amended. Indeed, the volatility of the special legislation is often cited as a reason why the civil law cannot be re-integrated into the codes.

The contraction of the area which is left for regulation by the civil codes is not the only manifestation of the expansion of public law. Administrative law, the child of the 19th century, came into its own in the 20th century. Not only did new areas come under regulation, but government's role in providing social services increased. The public agencies that were created to perform these services have often appropriated private law means and institutions to do so. In the process, the distinction between public and private is further blurred. Also, the state's increased role in the economy not only modified the civil law of contract, tort and property, but has led to new kinds of "economic law" regulating competition, the structure and activities of enterprises, and employer-employee relations. As more areas of public concern are identified, such as protection of the environment, or protection of health and safety in the workplace, the scope of administrative law continues to expand.

Still, in the final analysis, as David's characterization of the French Civil Code shows, the distinction between public and private law has a firm hold on the minds of civil law lawyers. For that reason, even if it is vague or dissolving, it remains important to the understanding of the civil law tradition.

CHAPTER 6

SOURCES OF LAW

§ 1. In General

In the civil law theory of sources of law a fundamental distinction is made between primary sources, which are *binding* on the judge, and secondary sources, sometimes called *authorities*. The primary sources in all civil law systems are enacted law and custom, with the former overwhelmingly more important. Sometimes "general principles of law" are also listed as a primary source. Authorities may have weight when the primary sources are absent, unclear or incomplete, but their use is not binding, and they are neither necessary nor sufficient as the basis for a judicial decision. Case law and the writings of legal scholars are such secondary sources, and in the Netherlands, the draft of the proposed new civil code is treated as such.

In theory, enacted law is the pre-eminent source of law; court decisions are not binding in subsequent cases, either on the courts that issue them or on lower courts in the same hierarchy. A study of the process of *interpretation* of enacted law, however, reveals a considerable gap between theory and practice. For purposes of comparison, it is essential to supplement the formal theory, not only with an examination of what happens to the primary sources through interpretation, but also with a functional analysis of the mechanisms which promote the values of certainty and predictability while permitting growth and adaptation within the system. Finally, it must be cautioned that the significance of the sources of law within civil law systems, and the range of judicial behavior with respect to them, varies from country to country, and, even within a country, from time to time and from subject matter to subject matter.

§ 2. Binding Sources

a. *Enacted Law*

The concept of enacted law includes not only those legal rules adopted by the legislature, but those issued by the executive and by administrative agencies, or adopted by popular referendum. The various types of enacted law form a hierarchy with the constitution at the pinnacle, followed by legislation (which, in France, as we shall see, may issue from the executive as well as from the parliament), then by executive decrees pursuant to delegated legislative power, then by administrative regulations, and finally by local ordinances. In federal states, this hierarchy must be supplemented by the rules concerning the relationship of state to federal law. Account must also be taken of international treaties and conventions and the effect given to them under local law. Within the European Economic Community, for example, Community law has been accorded primacy over internal law, at least by the original six member states (supra Chapter 2, Section 6). In general it can be said that parliamentary legislation is today the most prevalent source of law in civil law countries. Within this category, the various codes, though still of central importance, now constitute only a small part of the total volume of existing legislation. The ever-growing body of separate statutes reinforces the traditional pre-eminence of enacted law within civil law systems.

Special mention should be made here of the role played in France since 1958 by executive legislation. It may be recalled that a cardinal tenet of the French revolution was that all law-making power was to be vested in a representative assembly. However, it soon became apparent in France, as elsewhere, that the complexity of modern government requires the legislature to delegate substantial power to the executive to implement legislation and to adopt administrative regulations. Such delegated power was not thought to derogate from the principle of separation of powers. But the 1958 Constitution of de Gaulle's Fifth Republic went a step further, by putting the law-making power of the executive on an autonomous non-delegated basis. In Article 34 of the Constitution, those matters falling within the parliamentary law-making domain are enumerated. Then, in Article 37, the Constitution states that matters other than those reserved for the legislative domain by Article 34 are of an executive character. Thus, the legislative law-making power, though it covers the most important matters, has become the exception and the executive-administrative jurisdiction the rule—a direct repudiation of the traditional French doctrine of legislative supremacy. This grant of autonomous law-making power to the executive is in addition to its continued delegated power to issue regulations in the course of executing parliamentary laws.

Two further aspects of the modern French development of the law-making power of the executive are noteworthy. The first is the treatment of the problem of the constitutionality of executive legislation. The Constitutional Council, it will be recalled, has power to review only parliamentary legislation for conformity to the Constitution. The concern that executive legislation might escape review altogether was allayed by the Council of State which promptly claimed and has continuously exercised constitutional control over it. The second aspect of the 1958 changes in the distribution of power between the executive and legislative branches is that these changes conferred upon the executive a privileged position in the parliamentary law-making process. As the French code reformer and civil law scholar, Jean Carbonnier, has put it: "Legislation has become to a great extent the work of the Ministry of Justice and other departments. It is something of a return, if not to the Justinian style, at least to that of the Jurisconsults."

b. *Custom*

In the civil law theory of sources of law, custom is regularly listed as a primary source, but routinely dismissed as of slight practical importance, except in Spain and some of the other Spanish-speaking countries. In certain provinces of Spain, notably Catalonia, the national Civil Code does not apply to matters covered by local customary laws (*fueros*). In such places, custom is an important, as well as a primary, source of law. In other civil law countries, where custom is less important but still considered to have binding force, there is an apparent difference between systems, such as the West German, which permit custom in certain cases to prevail over written law, and those systems which, like the French, permit custom to supplement, but not to abrogate, the written law. The real extent of this difference may be questioned, though, in view of the rigorous insistence of the former system on the establishment of a "true custom", and the relaxed attitude of the latter concerning the nicety of the distinction between "supplementation" and "abrogation." As might be expected, custom plays a greater role in commercial and labor law than it does in civil law generally. Some treatise writers have characterized settled case law as custom, but it is not officially recognized as such.

c. General Principles

It is sometimes said that general principles, derived either from norms of positive law or from the existence of the legal order itself, are a primary source of law. They are so characterized by some French writers, especially in connection with discussions of French administrative law, but also in discussions of the judicial doctrine of abuse of rights and the expansion of the notion of unjust enrichment. Such a characterization raises the question whether the source of law is really the general principle or the judge, a problem which will be discussed below in connection with interpretation.

§ 3. Interpretation

One of the many ways in which the classic codifications represented a break with the civil law past was in their transformation of the idea of sources of law. The *jus commune* and previous authorities of all sorts were displaced by codes that were supposed to be comprehensive within the areas they covered. In the post-codification era, scholarly attention and the judicial process has focussed on the codes,—their language, their structure, the interrelation of their parts, and their animating spirit. An enormous volume of literature on interpretation has been generated. Indeed, one may say that the technique of interpretation of enacted law has become as much of an art in civil law systems, as the manner of dealing with case law has in common law systems. Since it is in connection with the civil codes that these techniques have been refined, the discussion here will be concerned primarily with code interpretation. But it must be remembered that in modern civil law systems, a judge's everyday work is as much concerned with ordinary statutes, decrees and regulations as it is with the language of the codes, and that the theory and techniques of interpretation may be modified depending on the source of the legal norm involved.

Since the time of the codifications, there has been a considerable evolution in the way the relation of the judicial process to the written law has been perceived, an evolution which has taken somewhat different courses in different countries. We may begin our consideration of this by distinguishing four different types of intellectual operations that are often grouped together under the general heading of "interpretation." First, there is the kind of interpretation involved in every use of language: the ascertainment of the linguistically most plausible meaning to be ascribed to the words used. If one meaning is much more plausible than others, and it covers the case before the court, the judge applies that version. This process of ascertaining meaning may be so automatic and unconscious that the judge may think of it as "law finding", although modern linguistic theory would describe it as interpretation. The dream of the draftsmen of the Prussian Civil Code that all law could be so "found" and "applied" has long since proved to be an illusion. But the fact remains that many everyday legal questions can be and are resolved in just this way.

A second type of interpretation occurs when there is an ambiguous or unclear provision, or an apparent inconsistency between provisions in the text. A third type occurs when there is a gap in a legislative text. In these second and third situations, the process of interpretation becomes a conscious one. Here, all civil law systems are characterized by the presence of a number of methods devised to elucidate unclear or ambiguous texts and to help supply lacunae in a legal rule. All of these methods have in common the ultimate aim of applying the legal rule as clarified or completed.

A fourth, and entirely different set of intellectual operations is involved when the usual gap-filling or ambiguity-resolving methods fail to yield a solution; when the law is completely silent on a problem; or when an old law, because of changed circumstances, has become completely unsuitable to current conditions. Though the judge's activity in these situations is often disguised or characterized as interpretation, it is clear that whatever process he or she engages in is not interpretation in the sense of the search for the meaning of a legislative text. In this fourth group of situations, judges develop the law on their own, but there is great variation in the extent to which this is openly acknowledged and in the manner in which the judges proceed in modern civil law systems. In France, for reasons which are largely historical, the process of judicial development is largely hidden from view, in contrast to what the West German scholar Larenz has called the "open development of the law" in Germany.

In the early years after the adoption of the French and German civil codes, the codes were treated, not as complete, but as self-sufficient, in the sense that they contained a comprehensive body of rules and principles, and (the German more than the French) embodied a system for applying these norms to all cases arising within the areas they purported to cover. Interpretation was thought of as the process of "enlarging the code out of itself". No matter what type of problem arose, if the text failed to supply an answer, the judge would pretend that its solution could be derived from the code, from the relation of its parts, from its structure, or from its general principles. To be sure, this process resulted in the creation of new judge-made norms, but the activity of judges was almost universally disguised as the finding and application of legal rules consistent with legislative intent or purpose.

So long as interpretation was viewed as the process of discovering the express or implied will of the legislature, its principal techniques were exegetical. They involved grammatical analysis, and such logical operations as reasoning by analogy or *a contrario* from code provisions, or deriving an inclusive principle from a set of related sections. In this type of interpretation, legislative history, particularly of the type known in civil law terminology as "the preparatory work" on a statute or code, is an important aid to determining legislative purpose so as to choose between conflicting or competing views of the meaning of the text. In many cases, grammatical or logical interpretation, or the search for legislative intent on a specific problem will be fruitful and will lead to the assignment of a plausible meaning to the text. But even when these procedures lead to a dead end, the pretense that the judge is doing no more than carrying out the will of the legislature is facilitated by the so-called "general clauses", provisions of such breadth that, somewhat like common law equitable principles, they can be used to modify the effect of more rigid code provisions or to set the course of a new development.

General clauses may range in their application over the entire subject matter of the code. Of this type, for example, are Article 6 of the French Civil Code which forbids individuals to derogate in their private arrangements from those laws which concern public order and good morals (*bonnes moeurs*), and Article 138 of the German Civil Code which provides that a transaction that offends good morals (*guten Sitten*) is void. Other general clauses may be confined to specific sub-

[*127*]

ject matters, as are, for example, Article 242 of the German Civil Code and Article 1134 of the French Civil Code, both of which require good faith in the performance of obligations.

Gradually, it has become widely recognized and accepted in both France and Germany, as well as in other systems, that the courts, at least when they are dealing with situations of the fourth type mentioned above, are making law on their own. Because the response to this recognition has varied significantly in different civil law systems, we must consider separately the modern process of interpretation in France, Germany and in those civil law countries whose codes contain specific directions on what the judge is to do when the law is silent.

In France, a number of factors contributed to the firm establishment and long predominance of the exegetical school of interpretation. Not the least of these was the Civil Code itself. It may be recalled that the revolutionary reaction against the royal courts found expression in Article 5 of the French Civil Code of 1804, forbidding judges to lay down general rules in deciding cases, and that it importantly affected the organization of the court system. Article 4 of the Code forbids a judge, on pain of misdemeanor, to refuse to decide a case "on the pretext that the law is silent, unclear, or incomplete." It is worth noting, however, that the draftsmen of the Civil Code of 1804 had an expansive conception of the judge's role. The eloquent Portalis knew full well that the law in its generality required the cooperation of the judge to fill its gaps and adapt it to change. Portalis acknowledged that the legislature could not and should not try to foresee everything: "How can one hold back the action of time? How can the course of events be opposed, or the gradual improvement of mores?" Conceding that a great many things are necessarily left to be determined by the judges, he wrote: "[T]he science of the judge is to put the principles [of the law] into action, to develop them, to extend them, by a wise and reasoned application, to private relations; to study the spirit of the law when the letter killeth, and not to expose himself to the risk of being alternately slave and rebel. . . . "

The post-revolutionary judges, however, were eager to show their submissiveness to the new order. The Court of Cassation led the way by developing a cryptic opinion style which usually consists of a single long paragraph containing a recital of the applicable legal provisions, the briefest description of the facts, and a series of "whereas" clauses through which the decision is made to appear to emerge as though from a mechanical process of application of the enacted law to the facts. This style, an outward sign of deference to the legislature through literal obedience to Articles 4 and 5 of the Civil Code, has persisted to the present time in the Court of Cassation, while the opinions of lower courts are only somewhat more ample. Within this form, however, the judges have in fact been quite creative: the lower court judges through their power to find the facts, and the Court of Cassation aided by the very conciseness and generality of the French Civil Code. In legal scholarship, the school of literal interpretation held sway until nearly the end of the 19th century when François Gény, in a celebrated work on methods of interpretation and sources of law, pointed out that the judges had in fact been making law all along. Gény argued that, when the text is unclear or silent, the judge should be freed from the limitations inherent in the methods of textual exegesis and allowed to consider the entire social and economic context of each problem in order to find the most just solution.

The views of Gény and others were welcomed into French legal theory, but not—at least not visibly—into the practice of the courts where the form of judicial opinions continues to mask what Carbonnier has called "a tacit eclecticism in methods of interpretation." Observers of the French courts find it implicit in the judges' work that they interpret legislative texts so as to adapt them to current social and economic conditions. But this process is nowhere discussed in the brief and uninformative judicial opinions. Paradoxically, then, the system which imposes the most external restraints upon its judges leaves them most free to exercise disguised discretion.

Unlike the French Civil Code, but in consonance with the views of Portalis, some of the other 19th century codes openly acknowledged and dealt with the problem of the silence or insufficiency of the text. The Austrian Civil Code of 1811, which had been in preparation over the latter part of the 18th century and was strongly influenced by natural law ideas, directs the judge to look to the "principles of natural justice." The Spanish Civil Code of 1888 provides that deficiencies in the law shall be supplied by reference to "general principles of law", understood as those principles which can be derived from the rules of positive law. The draftsmen of the German Civil Code considered including some such general interpretive directions, but eventually rejected the idea because it was felt that the Code implicitly contained its own methods of interpretation. If the ordinary methods of exegesis inherent in the structure and system of the code yielded no answer, it was anticipated that the judge would resort to general principles, not limited to those discoverable in the positive law, however, but including those principles which arise from the spirit of the legal order. This concept was later made an explicit direction in Article 12 of the Italian law on interpretation of legislative texts.

The most famous of all such interpretive directions is contained in Article 1 of the Swiss Civil Code of 1907, which provides that if the judge can find no rule in the statute, he must decide in accordance with customary law, and failing that, "according to the rule which he as a legislator would adopt," having regard to approved legal doctrine and judicial tradition. This provision, with its unprecedented grant of authority to the judge, was regarded at the time by continental legal theorists as revolutionary. In fact, however, in the years since the Swiss Civil Code has been in force, Article 1 has been rarely used, Swiss judges almost always preferring to couch their decisions in the language of traditional methods of interpretation.

In Germany, after an initial period of exegesis, the judges began to exercise their authority to adapt and develop the law openly. They have developed an opinion style which resembles the American in its attention to the facts and its exposition of the reasoning process through which the court arrives at its decision. As anticipated by the draftsmen of the German Civil Code, the courts have not considered themselves to be tightly confined within the limits of statutory authority. They have, however, taken seriously the idea that they are bound by the legal order, the idea of law as a whole. Their care, when exercising what may be called their creative function, to incorporate new institutions into the framework of the legal order and to conform them to the basic principles of the legal order have been admired by many foreign observers. In general, the courts' authority to develop the law in this fashion is undisputed in present-day West Germany, although there is there, as elsewhere, disagreement as to the limits of such power.

In summary, it can be said that while modern theory of interpretation generally acknowledges that principles are hard to find and identify and that judges dealing with legislative texts are often making law, the extent to which the behavior of the courts reflects this perception varies. It varies, not so much in the results achieved (which lead one to suspect that most courts are doing the same thing most of the time), as it does in the degree to which the process is open or concealed. In France, where the process tends to be hidden, eminent scholars have pointed out that the absence of the reasoned opinion deprives the system of a valuable tool and an important mechanism for controlling the discretion of judges. In West Germany, where the process is more open, criticism tends to fo-

cus on the democratic problem: what limits should
there be on the legal and political decision-making
power of an official who is neither representative nor
politically accountable?

§ 4. Authorities

a. Case Law

It has been evident in our description of the role of
the judge in the civil law tradition that the judicial
function has, from ancient times, been regarded as
limited to deciding particular cases. The notion goes
back to Justinian that only the sovereign can make a
generally applicable rule. In modern nation states,
the judge's role remained the same, but the limitation
was justified on the ground that only a representative
legislature should be able to "make" law. We have
seen in the foregoing section the extent to which modern civil law systems have retreated from that principle.

As it became generally recognized that judges frequently do in fact make law, the question arises
whether and to what extent judicial decisions are a
source of law. Civil law theory does not recognize the
existence of a formal doctrine of *stare decisis*. Thus,
judicial pronouncements are not binding on lower
courts in subsequent cases, nor are they binding on
the same or coordinate courts. In the extreme French
situation, the decision of the highest civil court is not
even binding on a lower court in the *same* case until

the second remand, and then only by statute (supra Chapter 4, Section 3).

This formal civil law theory of the role of case law is, however, subject to a number of qualifications. Initially, it is not a simple matter for a high court to decide a particular case one way and later to decide a similar case another way. If a division of the high court wishes to deviate from a prior decision, the legal question involved will usually have to be referred to a super-panel of the court. This procedure has the obvious aim of assuring consistency in the output of the court charged with the ultimate responsibility for the uniformity of the application of the law within its own hierarchy. Second, in civil service judicial systems, the de facto influence of higher court decisions upon lower court judges (whose promotions may be affected by too many reversals) is considerable. Third, the decisions of the Constitutional Courts of West Germany and Italy on the compatibility of statutes with the constitution have the force of law. Fourth, a settled line of cases (*jurisprudence constante, ständige Rechtsprechung*) has great authority everywhere. In some parts of the Spanish-speaking world this settled case law is made binding by legislation. Some German legal theorists consider that, in rare instances, a line of cases can create a rule of customary law which is then binding as such. Fifth, it is observable that entire bodies of law in civil law systems have been built up by judicial decisions in a manner closely resembling the growth of anglo-American common law. This is markedly so, for example, in the case of French tort law, and also in the area of substantive administrative law which is largely uncodified.

As a practical matter it is generally recognized in civil law systems that judges do and should take heed of prior decisions, especially when the settled case law shows that a line of cases has developed. Where the case law has not become "settled", prior decisions of high courts have some weight. Even in France, where the force of precedent is weaker than in West Germany, the decisions of the Council of State are considered reliable precedent, and some writers say that a single decision of the Court of Cassation is important in settling the case law. Court decisions, then, are de facto legal rules whose authority varies according to the number of similar decisions, the importance of the court issuing them, and the way the opinion writer expresses himself or herself. The extent to which a court has relied on prior decisions, however, is not always easy to determine in a given case. In this respect, judicial opinions in German-speaking countries bear a certain resemblance to American decisions with their presentation of facts, reasoning and authorities. But the cryptic opinions of the French Court of Cassation summarize the facts only briefly and do not refer to prior cases. Lower court opinions in France sometimes do cite cases and provide more ample fact statements, but they are less informative than a typical West German or American opinion. When the courts are not forthcoming about their reasoning processes and the sources they have relied upon, it is only by reading a line of cases that one can make inferences about the influence of precedent.

Civil law decisions have weight for the same reasons that underlie the common law doctrine of *stare decisis*. The most important of these reasons go to the very heart of the legal system: the requirements of reasonable certainty and predictability; the elementary demand of fairness that like cases be treated alike; and the related, but distinct, consideration that justice should not only be done, but should appear to have been done. In addition to serving the values of predictability, fairness and legitimacy, continuity in the case law is itself in no small way promoted by such homely considerations as the conservation of mental energy and the fear of reversal.

In view of the importance of case law as a civil law authority, the sometimes asserted contrast between civil and common law systems in this area appears as more of a nuance than a major difference. This seems especially so when it is recalled that in the United States *stare decisis*, as a formal rule, only means that the decision of a higher court is binding on lower courts in the same jurisdiction in cases "on all fours" with each other. In all other situations, *stare decisis* in American common law is, as in the civil law, not a rule but merely an observable aspect of judicial behavior. In England, however, where a more rigid view of precedent prevails, it is only since 1966 that the House of Lords announced that it considered itself free to overrule its own decisions. Thus, one may say that the contrast in the weight accorded to case law is greatest between England and France, and least between the United States and West Germany.

b. *Doctrine*

The writings of legal scholars (*la doctrine, die Rechtslehre*), like the decisions of courts, are considered authorities in civil law systems. Their role is, however, quite different from that of the case law. As we have just seen, case law authority operates to settle the law and secure consistency within a judicial hierarchy. The doctrine, on the other hand, exerts its greatest direct influence when the law is unsettled or when there is no established law on a point. But the two types of authorities are related, in that civil law systems have left the task of organizing and analyzing the case law mainly to the learned writers. Thus, the doctrine indirectly controls, to a great extent, the judges' understanding of the case law.

The weight attached by judges to doctrinal writing varies according to a number of circumstances, including the reputation of the author and whether the view expressed is an isolated one or represents the consensus of the most respected writers. In general, it can be said that civil law judges pay close attention to scholarly opinions, as expressed in general and specialized treatises, commentaries on the codes, monographs (including the best doctoral theses), law review articles and case notes, and expert opinions rendered in connection with litigation. Persistent doctrinal criticism will often prompt re-examination of a holding, and will sometimes even lead to the abandonment of an established judicial position.

As we noted earlier in our discussion of the role of legal scholars in civil law systems, the importance of the academics' function in presenting analyses of cases and statutes to judges and lawyers cannot be overestimated (supra Chapter 3, Section 6). There is a circular chain of reinforcement among the civil law theory on the force of case law, the mechanics of law-finding, and the influence of legal writers. Since case law (theoretically) is not binding, civil law systems lack sophisticated and comprehensive citators for direct access to cases and for the coordination of cases with each other and with statutes. The absence of such tools in turn, would make it very difficult for a formal rule of *stare decisis* to operate. As things stand, periodicals and treatises which collect and analyze the most important cases become the main sources relied upon in research. But this means that one set of authorities is pre-selected and filtered by another. It will be extremely interesting to observe the effect on civil law practice and adjudication of the introduction of computerized law-finding devices of the type that are now common in the United States.

Once again, however, the apparent differences between the civil and common law systems should not be exaggerated. In the latter, certain kinds of legal writing and certain writers have become highly influential, as evidenced by the measurable increase in citations to doctrinal sources in contemporary judicial opinions. Judges and lawyers in common law systems also rely to some extent on treatises and articles to find, organize and analyze the case law. On the other hand, the introduction of American computerized law-finding devices in civil law systems will probably liberate civil law practitioners and judges somewhat from their traditional reliance on the academics. Nevertheless, differences are likely to persist in the degree of deference accorded to scholarly opinion, and, perhaps in the degree to which the care and responsibility exercised by the respective academic professions merit such deference.

§ 5. Stability and Growth

Every legal system, for optional functioning, needs mechanisms to promote certain important aims which are always in tension, if not in conflict, with each other: predictability and flexibility, stability and growth. Traditionally, in the common law, predictability and stability were provided by legal rules developed in cases and by the doctrine of *stare decisis*, while flexibility and growth were furnished by the rules of equity and the techniques for limiting and distinguishing precedent. In the code systems of the civil law tradition, predictability and stability were assured by the "written law" of the codes, while flexibility and growth were permitted, internally, by general clauses tempering rigid rules, and externally by interpretation, made more supple by the absence of a formal rule of *stare decisis*.

In both of these traditional systems, the present-day predominance of statutory law has diminished the role of the traditional mechanisms for maintaining equilibrium. Legislation and regulations, general or fragmentary in scope, have made case law less central to the common law and the codes less central to the civil law. In this new situation, it would seem at first that the civil law systems have an advantage, in that highly developed techniques for statutory interpretation are now of more utility than are case law techniques. But in both systems, relative certainty and predictability are adversely affected by the fact that modern statutory law, unlike the civil codes, generally is neither stable nor particularly rational (in the sense of being systematically organized). Its susceptibility to frequent amendment does not introduce much flexibility in the traditional sense either, since it is not in the nature of the political process to develop legal rules on a reasoned or principled basis. The courts, for their part, are increasingly called upon to rule not only on particular disputes, but also on problems of social conflict which often cannot be resolved by the reasoned elaboration of principle. Thus, both the civil and the common law, still living on their Roman inheritance of legalism and administration, share common problems of legitimation in modern administrative states.

SELECTED BIBLIOGRAPHY AND SUGGESTIONS FOR FURTHER READING

X. Blanc-Jouvan and Boulouis, *France*, in I Int'l Encyc. of Comp.Law, (National Reports) F–48 (V. Knapp ed.) (Tübingen, Mohr 1972).

M. Cappelletti, *The "Mighty Problem" of Judicial Review and the Contribution of Comparative Analysis*, 53 S.Cal.L.Rev. 409–45 (1980).

J. Carbonnier, *Droit Civil*, 4 vols. (Paris, P.U.F. 1972–75).

J. Carbonnier, *Essais sur les lois.* (Paris, Répertoire du notariat defrénois 1979).

J. Dainow ed., *The Role of Judicial Decisions and Doctrine in Civil Law and Mixed Jurisdictions.* (Louisiana State Univ. 1974).

J. Dawson, *The Oracles of the Law.* (Univ. of Michigan 1968).

S. Herman & D. Hoskins, *Perspectives on Code Structure: Historical Experience, Modern Formats, and Policy Considerations,* 54 Tulane L.Rev. 987–1051 (1980).

H. Jolowicz, *Historical Introduction to the Study of Roman Law,* (2d ed.) (Cambridge 1967).

J. Langbein, *Comparative Criminal Procedure: Germany.* (West 1977).

D. Medicus, *Federal Republic of Germany,* in I Int'l. Encyc. of Comp. Law, (National Reports) F–1 (V. Knapp ed.) (Tübingen, Mohr 1972).

J. Merryman, *The Civil Law Tradition.* (Stanford 1969).

J. Merryman & D. Clark, *Comparative Law: Western European and Latin American Legal Systems.* (Bobbs-Merrill 1978).

Palandt, *Bürgerliches Gesetzbuch* (37th ed., Munich, Beck 1978).

M. Rheinstein, *Einführung in die Rechtsvergleichung.* (Munich, Beck 1974).

R. Schlesinger, *Comparative Law* (4th ed.) (Foundation Press 1980).

E. Stein, P. Hay & M. Waelbroeck, *European Community Law and Institutions in Perspective.* Vol. 1. (Bobbs-Merrill 1976).

C. Szladits, *The Civil Law System,* in II Int'l Encyc. of Comp. Law 15–76 (R. David ed.) (Tübingen, Mohr 1974).

A. von Mehren & J. Gordley, *The Civil Law System.* (Little, Brown 1977).

F. Wieacker, *Privatrechtsgeschichte der Neuzeit* (2d ed.) (Göttingen, Vandenhoeck & Ruprecht 1967).

K. Zweigert & H. Kötz, *An Introduction to Comparative Law,* 2 vols. (Tony Weir, tr.) (Amsterdam, North-Holland 1977).

PART TWO

THE COMMON LAW TRADITION

CHAPTER 7

HISTORY, CULTURE AND DISTRIBUTION

§ 1. Introduction

English common law evolved from necessity, rooted in the centralized administration of William, conqueror at Hastings. A single event, the 1066 Norman Conquest, was the progenitor of this tradition, its foundation a unique, "unwritten" constitution and the recorded, but orally rendered decisions of an extraordinarily gifted and respected judiciary. The harmony of a homogeneous society, tested by internal stresses but free of foreign invasion for nearly a millennium, aided an orderly development of legal institutions. Focusing on the resolution of specific, current issues, English law developed insulated from the continental reception of Roman law, and the later emphasis on codification. As Pollock has said, English laws "grew in rugged exclusiveness, disdaining fellowship with the more polished learning of the civilians."

Comprehension of the rule of law in England today, and its litmus role in other common law systems, calls for an understanding of the cardinal incidents in English history which were generative of the slow but persistent development of institutions which comprise the common law tradition.

§ 2. Roman Occupation

English legal scholars trace the origins of English common law principally to the Norman Conquest. Legal institutions before that time made few lasting contributions. The early law was unwritten, handed down through generations by oral tradition. We know that over centuries the tribal laws changed to accord with the times, but we know little with exactitude of when the changes occurred or the precise forces impelling those changes.

Julius Caesar led exploratory expeditions in 55 and 54 B.C. to Southeast England. Disparate Celtic tribes, about whose legal structures Maine has commented, "One rude folk are much like another," supported periodic revolts in Britain against the Roman dominion. A century later Claudius, timidly seeking status as a conquering caesar, chose weak Britain to subdue. Romans ruled much of the island for nearly four centuries. Britain was marked indelibly with Roman culture—the rose, its road system, the Latin language and central heating—but the Romans did not bestow upon the inhabitants the Roman legal system. Britain had not been developed, it had been occupied. Roman law was an incident of occupation. It governed relations between Romans, but it began a decline in 410 A.D. when it appeared that the departing legions would not return. What Rome contributed to the English legal system was indirect, occurring through the survival of remnants of institutional structures of a civilized society.

§ 3. Roman-Norman Hiatus: The Anglo-Saxon Period

With the Romans departed, the Britons were left with little but a few Christian missionaries to face Angles, Danes, Jutes and Saxons—again society became dominated by diverse tribal communities, with law predominantly unwritten local custom. There was sufficient cohesion for Pope Gregory's missionary, St. Augustine, to establish Christianity in the late sixth century, giving English kings the imprimatur of the supreme source of justice, but less than the divine right of kings, the latter an important reservation in later centuries.

Anglo-Saxon law possessed elements of Teutonic tribal traditions and customs, but personal wealth began to replace "blood and kin" as the measure of political power. England developed feudal attitudes, but not in the continental sense. Landowners rather than the community or state provided protection to and drew loyalty from the dependent classes. Lords administered justice for their tenants and villani, and their lands provided the source of taxes to defend the nation.

§ 4. The Norman Conquest

The victory at Hastings by William was more a succession than a conquest. William's claim to the English throne was no less tenuous than Harold's. The law of England, an aggregate of disparate local customs, was left largely intact by the conqueror. But he confiscated all of the land and then apportioned possession among his most trustworthy followers, extracting pledges of loyalty and service. William allocated the land in a manner to prevent his barons from concentrating their power and challenging William's central authority. This limited holding of the land, with ownership remaining in the sovereign, is today largely theoretical.

William achieved his goal of kingly vestiture at Westminster, but duties in Normandy demanded his attention. Establishing centralized rule at Westminster permitted the governance of a large number of Saxons by comparatively few Normans. William's administrative efficiency produced the Domesday survey in 1086, an inventory of all property throughout England, which facilitated a much larger revenue collection.

William resolved matters of royal concern at Westminster; local issues remained in the courts of the shires and hundreds. Only judicial disputes of an extraordinary nature were brought before the king as chief justiciar. Administrative necessity rather than legislative design played the central role in fashioning the early structures of the common law. William's legacy was the creation of a highly centralized legal system.

§ 5. Royal Courts

No separation of government functions existed in early Norman England. The king, acting with close advisors in council, the *Curia Regis*, exercised judicial as well as executive and legislative powers. The council was as mobile as the king. But some functions of the *Curia Regis* later were delegated to newly created institutions. Judicial powers were assumed by the royal courts, beginning an important unification, the development of a law common throughout England. The three courts which were to develop over the ensuing two and a half centuries affirmed centralized judicial authority. They sat at Westminster even in the absence of the king.

The Court of Exchequer, a judicial offspring of the financial side of the *Curia Regis*, was the first common law court. It reflected the king's paramount interest in efficiently settling tax disputes. Exchequer's initial jurisdiction was more extensive, limited to resolving tax disputes only after the development of the Court of Common Pleas.

The Court of Common Pleas resolved issues between subjects which did not involve a direct interest of the king, thus the name *common pleas*. The disputes usually dealt with title to land, or personal actions of debt, covenant or detinue. It later developed an exceptional formality of procedure and became an expensive court for the litigants.

The third central court was King's Bench, established to hear issues with a direct royal interest, pleas of the Crown. It issued writs of mandamus, prohibition, certiorari and habeas corpus, to control question-ed actions of public officials. King's Bench later became an important check on the abuse of prerogative powers of the king. Its civil jurisdiction expanded, encroaching upon the Court of Common Pleas, encompassing most torts through the broadly interpreted writ of trespass and elaborate fictions, and later extending to contracts by the writ of assumpsit.

The English barons were on the verge of rebellion by the evolution of these common law courts. Although the king's courts did not replace directly the old local shire and hundred courts, if overlapping jurisdiction existed, litigants usually preferred the common law courts. Procedure was more progressive and fairer in the latter, and participants avoided the harsh proof by ordeal or oath of the local courts. This preference eroded the role of local courts and reduced revenue generated from court fees, revenue intensely coveted by both the king and the barons.

§ 6. Writ System

Jurisdiction of the common law courts was limited severely by a writ system. A civil action lay before one of the courts only where a specific writ was available from a high official ("where there is no writ, there is no right"). Issued in the name of and constituting a command from the king, writs were addressed to an official authorizing commencement of specific suits, later known as "forms of action." The system was rigid; selection of the wrong writ resulted in dismissal. The variety of writs, first including the writs of debt, detinue, covenant, replevin and account, later increased. The writ of trespass was added and expanded to encompass ejectment, trover and assumpsit, important to the development of contract and tort. But these nevertheless were limited in scope, and neither the judges nor the Chancellor could freely create new writs. The Statute of Westminster 1285, limited the invention of new writs to circumstances similar to those then affording protection.

To increase further the jurisdiction of the common law courts, fictions were invented to extend the circumscribed writs. An example is ejectment. It originated as an action available only to a wrongfully ejected leasehold tenant, and was unavailable to a freeholder. But a fiction was created. The freeholder alleged a fictitious lease to a fictitious person, usually John Doe. Doe then alleged that he had been wrongfully ejected by Richard Roe, an equally fictitious character. Doe, the nominal lessee, next sued the ejector. The court had to determine the origin of the alleged lease, raising the issue of who owned the freehold. Thus, the common law court would rule on the title, an issue otherwise reserved to the local courts. This early common law emphasis on procedure was not unlike the early Roman law concentration on forms of actions, on the facts of a case rather than the origination of substantive, abstract legal rules.

§ 7. Magna Carta

The progressive loss of jurisdiction of the local shire and hundred courts induced revolt among the English barons. Joined by a similarly aggrieved clergy the barons in 1215 extracted a charter from King John, later to become venerated as the Magna Carta. It was a self-serving document for the barons, who viewed the charter as a contract to halt their losses of various feudal privileges. But the charter also included a very few stipulations protecting ordinary citizens—provisions which much later endowed it with stature as a constitutional document of exceptional magnitude.

The Magna Carta contributed to the evolutionary demise of the rural courts, a process which continued for three centuries after the Conquest. The common law courts and the writ system were central to this demise, supported by the Crown assuming ownership of all land, and the diminished power of local sheriffs. The Magna Carta denied sheriffs the right to hear pleas of the Crown, and the Statute of Gloucester 1278, was interpreted to severely restrain civil jurisdiction of rural courts.

§ 8. Ecclesiastical Courts

Ecclesiastical courts persisted as rivals to the Royal Courts longer than the rural courts. The ecclesiastical courts applied canon law, the roots of which were firmly in the Roman law. The church vigorously defended its right to try "religious" offenses, including adultery, incest and less distinct offenses against morality. It also assumed civil jurisdiction over family issues, principally marriage and succession, as well as criminal jurisdiction over clergy. "Benefit of Clergy" allowed a convicted cleric to transfer the case from a temporal to an ecclesiastical court for sentencing. This unique doctrine persisted for several centuries, protecting persons with the most transient connection with the church, and ultimately even anyone who could prove literacy. The jurisdictional clash of church and state reached violent dimensions during the Plantagenet period, provoking the murder of Thomas à Becket in 1170 in Canterbury Cathedral. Although the church largely forfeited its judicial role, ecclesiastical jurisdiction over family and succession issues persisted until the mid-19th century, when it merged with other civil matters before the Royal Courts. But the imprint of canon law remains to this day on English family and inheritance law.

§ 9. Equity

Forms of actions developed a rigid inflexibility by the early 15th century. A plaintiff unable to obtain a proper writ was left with no remedy. John Austin said that English equity "arose from the sulkiness and obstinacy of the common law courts, which refused to suit themselves to the changes which took place in opinion, and in the circumstances of society." However obstinate it may have been, the common law was not rigid; it accepted new institutions. To counter the severity of the writ system and provide relief other than money damages, the king and later his Chancellor, the "keeper of the king's conscience," accepted petitions for equitable relief. Heard in an inquisitorial fashion modeled on canon and Roman law, these equitable proceedings focused on avoiding the strictures of the common law. It was successful, and a formal Court of Chancery soon assumed jurisdiction of pleas in equity.

If the addition of such equitable concepts as injunctive relief and specific performance to supplement the common law was equity's paramount general contribution, the origin of the trust was its most important conceptual addition. The common law did not recognize an interest in a party who was not the titleholder to land. The transfer of property to a party to hold either for benefit of the grantor, who may have been trying to avoid feudal obligations, or a third party, did not create legal rights enforceable by beneficiaries. The Court of Chancery, acting to fill this acknowledged void in the common law by using its powers to demand good conscience, would rule that the holder of the property must administer it for the benefit of the donor or third party, as specified in the initial grant. From this concept arose an equitable interest held by the beneficiary, the person in possession assuming the status of a trustee obligated to deal with the property considering the nature of the equitable interest of the third party.

The discretion exercised by early Chancellors—John Seldon remarked that equity varied "according to the length of the Chancellor's foot"—by the 18th century had evolved its own procedural rules, paradoxically as rigid as those which equity had been created to avoid.

§ 10. Justices of the Peace

The Crusades of the 12th century disrupted rural English life. Returning soldiers had tasted the fruits of conquest. Concern over the maintenance of order in England moved Richard I to name Keepers of the Peace, knights commissioned to maintain rural order.

Their authority was expanded by the Justices of the Peace Act 1361, granting to "knights, esquires or gentlemen" of the area authority to "pursue, arrest, take and chastise" those breaching the peace. Lesser offenses were tried directly by these lay Justices of the Peace; more serious crimes were referred to the king's judges who conducted County Quarter Sessions four times annually. For 600 years the judicial process for keeping the peace has been lodged principally in the hands of ordinary citizens, rather than a professional judiciary.

§ 11. Wars of the Roses

The Wars of the Roses (1455–1471) tested English constitutionalism with civil disturbance, inept domestic rule and factionalism. Englishmen tended to prefer public order over freedom, accepting a firm rule which would have been unacceptable in the absence of the domestic disturbances. Common law institutions were strained, and later subordinated to sovereign decree during the Tudor and Stuart reigns, but they survived this single serious challenge to the common law in English history.

§ 12. The Tudors

Henry VII (1485–1509), the first of the Tudor kings, created the Court of Star Chamber. Evolving from the judicial remnants of the King's Council, the Star Chamber was vested with extensive criminal jurisdiction, including conspiracies, forgeries and perjury. Its history of coercion to extract confessions and the names of accomplices has identified it with unreasoned judicial harshness, but it was not at the time considered particularly repressive. Its fines and punishments were not unduly severe, nor did it impose the death penalty.

The inquisitorial procedure of the Star Chamber had roots in canon and Roman law. It was staffed by lawyers with a civil law education at Oxford and Cambridge, who showed disdain for what they viewed as an overly formal common law system, preferring anything touched by the Renaissance, including the allegedly more understandable civil law. But there was to be no reception of civil law in England, its influences limited mainly to aspects of commerce affected by international trade, particularly mercantile and maritime law.

The establishment of Parliament as a legislative chamber separate from the king and his council, although still closely controlled by the king, was a more positive contribution of the Tudor period than the new judicial institutions. The strengthening of Parliament was backed by the proponents of the common law, who feared the gathering power being exercised by the king. A populace benefiting from an improving quality of life and concerned with the unsettling consequences of the abuse of royal power, began to limit the use of the royal prerogative; feudalism was on its deathbed. By the end of the Tudor period Parliament achieved status as the supreme law-making body; only its laws, not sovereign decrees, were binding on the courts.

§ 13. The Stuarts

The sovereign-parliamentary conflict again surfaced under James I (1603–1625), first of the Stuarts. The Star Chamber became an oppressive institution of royal power, giving credibility to its reputation of unjustness undeserved at its formation. James would not admit to the philosophy of common law lawyers that ancient royal prerogative powers were divisible, vesting foreign policy and the declaration of war with the king, but assigning other issues to Parliament.

English judges, unlike the common law lawyers, were divided on the issue of sovereign power. Judicial loyalty to the Stuart conception of royal power was attributable to the historical control by the king over the appointment and removal of judges. Edward Coke led the opposition from his position as Chief Justice, ruling persistently to preserve the autonomy of the common law courts.

This divisiveness swelled under Charles I (1625–1649). He convened and then dismissed Parliament with a frequency measured by its loyalty to the Crown. Parliament enacted the Petition of Right 1628, an impermanent attempt to reestablish due process concepts of the Magna Carta, and thus restrict sovereign power. Charles' response was eleven years of rule without a Parliament (1629–1640). When Parliament reconvened, it was hardly repentant. It purged the nation of the Star Chamber and made government ministers accountable to Parliament as well as to the king. The ensuing civil war was the final test of the separation of powers, a conflict which brought to Charles defeat and execution (1649), followed by several years of ineffectual rule and then Oliver Cromwell's self-appointment as Lord Protector of the Commonwealth. In 1660, eleven years after its demise, the monarchy was restored as the lesser evil.

The House of Lords, abolished after Charles' defeat, was reestablished, with the House of Commons reinforced as vested with greater initiation and authority. The king conceded to the grievances of Parliament, and confirmed its power over the process of legislation and control of taxation. A bloodless revolution in 1688 established an enduring Protestant royal succession and constitutional government. The Bill of Rights 1689, joined the Magna Carta as foundations of English constitutionalism. The Bill mandated parliamentary consent for a peacetime standing army, free election of Parliament, parliamentary approval of the suspension of law or levying of taxes, regular parliamentary sessons and limitations on bail, fines and cruel and unusual punishment. The Act of Settlement 1700, created an independent judiciary, members removable only by Parliament. The Act confirmed what Coke had said decades earlier, the sovereign may not dismiss judges.

The common law had survived the tumultuous Stuart era. English political and legal institutions had been altered, but the challenge to the Stuarts did not spring forth from opposition of the same nature as that in France in 1789, where a radical overhaul of the legal system was a consequence of the political revolution. The common law lawyers in England had successfully protected their turf, Coke even once suggesting that common law precepts could not be amended by statute. The threat of civil law notions imposed on English soil, of codification of the very heart of the common law, was for the time dormant.

Nearly as influential within England as Coke, William Blackstone, the Vinerian Professor of English Law at Oxford, wrote his Commentaries on the Laws of England in a readable style and concise form, which allowed them to be easily carried to outlying areas of the colonies. Had Blackstone's work not been available, American lawyers would have been left to Coke's confusing Institutes or the inaccessible and complex case reports, or they even might have turned to civil law codes. Blackstone's impact in America is immeasurable; no other legal book has so affected American legal practice as these published lectures of this once obscure lawyer.

§ 14. 19th Century Reforms

English law in the 19th century was altered by structural and social legislative reform. Jeremy Bentham and others who had little respect for tradition and the sanctity of precedent, viewed the common law as inordinately slow in responding to social needs. They urged codification to provide certainty and comprehension to the law, and to avoid a social revolution. The conservative judiciary and bar neither desired reform nor believed that legislation should be its source. Parliament became the progenitor of social change, however, enacting laws extending education, creating a competitive civil service exam, broadening House of Commons representation, reforming child labor laws and the Poor Law system, centralizing such government activities as road construction and adopting a freer trade policy by reducing protective tariffs. It did not codify rules, but adopted laws directed to more narrow issues which supplemented rather than replaced English precedent. Although Bentham's influence was apparent in the vast amount of new legislation, he found little support for codification of English law in the tradition of the civil law.

Parliament next turned to make some order out of the fragmented judicial structures. Overlapping jurisdiction and prolonged delays, ridiculed in prose, were reduced by the Judicature Acts 1873. It created a Supreme Court of Judicature consisting of the High Court of Justice and the Court of Appeal. The High Court brought together as its new divisions the former courts of Chancery, Queen's Bench, Common Pleas, Exchequer and Exchequer Chamber and Probate, Divorce and Admiralty (the last including some subjects with influences of Roman law). Less than a decade later Common Pleas and Exchequer were merged into the Queen's Bench Division.

At first abolished as an appellate court, the House of Lords soon was restored to its judicial role by the Appellate Jurisdiction Act 1876, restricting its appellate jurisdiction and professionalizing the chamber by limiting members sitting on appeal to the Lord Chancellor, peers who had held high judicial office and newly created judicial peers, named Lords of Appeal in Ordinary. No longer would lay members of the House of Lords sit on legal appeals.

The Judicature Acts hastened the fusion of law and equity. Each division of the High Court was required to apply rules both of law and equity. But equity, that historically infant sibling of law, was to prevail in the event of a conflict. Despite the fusion, the Chancery Division nevertheless has retained much of its original character as the equity court, and matters involving complex equity questions generally are there directed.

The rigid forms of action were abolished by the reforms; civil trials henceforth commenced with a general writ of summons. With the addition of a more unified procedure, the contemporary English trial presents far fewer technical obstacles to reaching the substantive issues than earlier existed.

§ 15. The Modern Period

Labor and Liberal election victories in the early years of the 20th century markedly altered the structure of English society. The Victorian era was in its finale. Working class dominance in the House of Commons aroused new conflicts with the House of Lords. When the Lords persisted in questioning proposed legislation which its members considered radical, the Commons responded by reducing the legislative power of the Lords, effectively limiting it to a right of delay, permitting neither amendment nor rejection.

The Supreme Court of Judicature was further refined in the Courts Act 1971. Courts of Assize and Quarter Sessions were abolished. The Crown Court assumed criminal jurisdiction and joined the High Court and Court of Appeal as part of the Supreme Court.

English legal institutions have survived centuries of stresses and constitutional crises. The system has shown a remarkable resiliency to adversity. Current issues involving the adoption of a bill of rights, the role of the House of Lords, the progressive fusion of barristers and solicitors and the consultative role of labor unions regarding general policies and proposed legislation will continue to generate stresses on the common law. Its adaptability is illustrated by the distribution of the common law throughout the world. Although some of the strength of English law must be attributable to the homogeneous population in which the law developed; it is a system of justice which has been received in heterogeneous societies with as much ease as the civil law.

§ 16. "English" Law

There is some definitional confusion with the term *English law*, additionally blurred by reference to Great Britain, the United Kingdom, or the Commonwealth. From its origins in Southern England, the common law became the principal basis of the procedure and/or substance of the legal systems for nearly a third of the world's population. It is inappropriate, nonetheless, to suggest that it is *English* law which exists in the United States or Australia or India or South Africa, or that there is a Commonwealth law applied in the Commonwealth, or a British law of Great Britain. English law applies in England and Wales.

Great Britain, the political geographic term for England, Wales and Scotland, has no common legal system. Many English statutes are applicable in Scotland, but the Scottish private law is based primarily on the civil law and principally on Roman law, the result of an alliance with the Continent in the 14th and 15th centuries intended to inhibit recurrent English expansion. After union with England in the Treaty of 1707, the development of Scottish law was influenced largely by the English common law. Parliamentary enactments in many areas of private law were applicable in both England and Scotland. Scottish law remains a curious mix of civil and common law, an appropriate focus for the study of the potential for interrelation between these two legal traditions.

Northern Ireland and Great Britain comprise the United Kingdom, the principal geographic area to which parliamentary expressions apply. But, as in the case of Great Britain, the United Kingdom is a larger area than one associates with English law.

English substantive law is not directly applicable outside of England and Wales, and, to a lesser extent, Scotland; however, it retains some authority in many independent nations which were formerly part of the British Empire. The remnant of authority of the House of Lords Judicial Committee of the Privy Council continues a slender connection between England and some former colonies, a role diminished by the independence of former Commonwealth nations and by the Statute of Westminster 1931, the latter granting to Commonwealth legislatures the right to abolish appeals to the Privy Council.

§ 17. Devolution

Nationalism in Scotland and Wales engendered a demand in the 1970s for a transfer of some government power from London to national assemblies. Included was additional law-making power. Devolution was promoted more strongly in Scotland than in Wales, the former possessing more distinct government institutions and its unique civil law based legal system. A 1978 devolution bill requiring a referendum vote was rejected by Welsh electors. The Scottish voters narrowly approved it, but not by the required forty percent of all registered electors. Devolution in a large measure ended with the referendum, but there will continue to be occasional transfers of government power to local authorities in Scotland and Wales.

§ 18. Distribution

The distribution of the common law throughout the British Empire was not due always to a voluntary reception of English law; it often was an imposition of the law as part of British territorial expansion. Dicey has divided the distribution into those nations "seeded," (*i. e.*, India, Hong Kong), those "settled" (*i. e.*, United States) and those "conquered" (*i. e.*, South Africa). In Calvin's Case in 1608 it was ruled that English law was effective when England colonized an area where there was no civilized local law. Common law distribution differs from that of the civil law. There was a direct linkage to England with each of the principal nations in which the common law developed —Australia, Canada, Eire, India, New Zealand and the United States. Although generally a direct linkage

[*161*]

with Rome existed in the reception of the civil law *within* Europe, expansion outside of Europe and the areas of the Eastern Roman Empire lacked any direct contact with Roman law. Distribution was a result of territorial expansions of European nations with civil law systems rooted in Roman law, but with specific national characteristics.

Civil law is also the more easily received tradition. The convenience of codes rather than a matrix of case law and statutes, the more complex language of the common law and the ability to accept a Roman based civil law which is private and little threat to a political system tend to favor the civil law system in a voluntary adoption process.

The world is not easily divided into an orderly pattern of countries which received a single legal tradition. Changes in territorial dominion by colonial powers created some systems possessing elements of more than one of the principal legal traditions. The most notable example is South Africa, where a civil law system (in the Transvaal) based on Roman-Dutch law partially acquiesced to the common law upon England's succession to power.

The distribution of English common law in the three largest areas where there was no well-established system of justice beyond tribal law, occurred in Australia, Canada and the United States. England confronted only a small, indigenous population in Australia, and colonized the continent without expansionist competition from other European nations. Parliament decreed in 1828 that the Australian colony's legal system was the common law, including English statutes.

Australia developed as a six member federation, each with a constitution and state government, including a parliament. Federal power is limited by the Australian Constitution more severely than in the United States. The Constitution does not protect fundamental, individual rights; the High Court thus may not nullify a federal or state statute as in violation of the rights of individual citizens. United States federalism has evolved over two centuries, its broadly stated Constitution the foundation of a continued and significant growth of central government over previously state controlled activities. Australia has been a federal system for only eighty years; an additional century may witness an increase in federal power not unlike that in the United States.

Both procedure and substantive private law in the several states of Australia are relatively uniform. English appellate decisions, although not binding authority, have remained the foundation for the development of Australian law, an emphasis which will diminish as the quantity of Australian precedent increases. The small population of Australia means a longer period for the development of a substantial body of Australian precedent, however, and the attention to English decisions may endure. Respect for English decisions further is understandable by the peaceful growth of Australia as an independent nation; separation occurred from England without the adversy of a revolution. Australian law remains the most closely identified to English law of all the major nations which trace their legal systems to England. There was no advanced cultural development within the indigenous Australian population, such as was confronted in India, nor was any Australian territory acquired from other European nations, as in the case of South Africa, parts of Canada and the United States.

Acquisition by Britain in 1763 of the French settled area of Canada did not lead to a fusion of the legal systems. The English Parliament divided Canada into English and French speaking sections, each with a parliament. It was an unsuccessful experiment terminated in 1840 by the establishment of a common parliament with equal representation. The British North American Act 1867, created the Dominion of Canada, composed of Nova Scotia, Ontario, Quebec and New Brunswick. The relative equality in number of French and English speaking persons was altered by the incorporation of the Northwest Territories acquired from the Hudson Bay Company in 1869, and the joining in the Union in 1871 by British Columbia. Canada thereafter was influenced largely by English government, economic and social structures, although Quebec preserved its civil law system. Unlike later federal constitutions granted by the English Parliament to Commonwealth countries, the 1867 Act gave Parliament authority to approve any constitutional amendments in Canada. This residual English authority has caused concern recently in Canada, where constitutional reform is being considered.

The Supreme Court of Canada, functioning as an appellate court for the provincial tribunals, must occasionally apply the Civil Code of Quebec. Its interpretations are influenced by common law methodology. Quebec has a disproportionate participation on the Court, three of the nine members, but it is a minority and there is no weighted voting for cases from Quebec provincial courts.

Important changes in the development of Canadian law have occurred since the 1949 termination of allowing appeals to the Judicial Committee of the Privy Council in England. Additionally, decisions of English appellate courts are no longer binding, although they are treated with respect. A Canadian jurisprudence has developed which includes influences external to the historical affiliation to English law; particular notice is given to legal developments in neighboring United States.

The contiguity of common and civil law systems in Canada and its Province of Quebec, and to a lesser degree in the United States and Louisiana, contrast with the more complex common-civil law relationships in the legal system in South Africa. South African law initially possessed a strong Roman law base, resulting from Dutch governance. Shortly before Napoleon abolished Roman-Dutch law in the Netherlands and replaced it with his famous Code in 1809, England took possession of the Cape and incorporated it into the Empire. English procedure was first imposed on the Roman-Dutch law of the Cape, followed by the adoption of numerous English statutes, principally affecting commerce. Where this mixture of English and Roman-Dutch law was unclear, South African jurists, nearly all of them English trained lawyers, tended to look for guidance to English case law Political independence for the Union of South Africa in 1910 generated a restoration of Dutch culture, including a resurgence of legal scholarship which concentrated notably on Dutch law. South African law thus is a hybrid system; it possesses Roman-Dutch law substantive elements and aspects of English law procedural methodology and structure.

English settlers in North America, Australia, New Zealand and South Africa did not encounter the highly developed indigenous culture which existed in India. Expansion to India was not by unchallenged settlement, but by permission of the Grand Mogul of India and local leaders. The penetration first consisted of establishing coastal, commercial centers. Internal disorder beset India in the 19th century. The English took advantage of this weakness, extending their influence through transactions with Indian princes, and finally dominating all of India.

Initial attempts to apply the common law in the early 18th century in Madras, Bombay and Calcutta, to both English and Indian parties, were unsuccessful. Hindu and Islamic law were substituted for common law in land, family and succession matters, a practice which continued in the interior as English governance coalesced. But, except in matters of family and succession law, and religious issues, English trained judges considered the best justice to require the application of English law.

Reform concepts promoted by Bentham found greater reception in India in the early 19th century than in England. Uncertainty existed in Indian law;

little truly Indian precedent had developed, and there was insubstantial consistency among Indian courts in determining sources of law. A Law Commission began to codify Indian law, influenced by European codes and by the British acceptance of reforms after the Great Mutiny in 1857. A civil procedure code was adopted in 1859, a criminal code in 1861, and the Indian Succession Act in 1865. The private law of India thus was codified at an early date.

The common law distribution in India, a nation with a strong cultural and religious tradition, illustrates that the expansion of English common law did not require a weak, indigenous population; it could contribute to the administration of justice in a diverse social system.

English law influence extends far beyond the major nations noted above. It has had substantial impact in former English territories in Africa, in some smaller colonies in Asia and in the Caribbean basin. In many of these locations, nevertheless, particularly in Africa, the English law affected a comparatively small percentage of the population. This is not an incident attributable to the nature of English law, but to the structure of the host societies. Such an impact is witnessed also in many areas where the civil law tradition has been received, particularly in nations of Latin America with widely dispersed native communities. Reception of a legal system depends upon the fusion of the local culture with that of the settling nation. Where a cultural assimilation has occurred, the English common law has shown remarkable capacity for adaptation.

CHAPTER 8

LEGAL STRUCTURES

§ 1. The British Government

In the two centuries prior to the Revolution of 1688, the English king exercised extensive power by use of the royal prerogative. The very existence of Parliament was challenged by the king, but after the Revolution, the Act of Settlement 1700 confirmed Parliament as the central lawmaking authority.

Contemporary parliamentary authority includes direct enactment of legislation and delegation of power to ministers to adopt provisional orders and regulations. There is little separation of legislative and executive institutions. The two are so closely identified that the Prime Minister survives only while retaining the favor of Parliament. Convention dictates that a vote of censure by Parliament of a Prime Minister's actions, or the failure of the government to promote successfully a major bill, will precipitate a call for the dissolution of Parliament and new eletions. The system does not support an executive and House of Commons majority from opposing parties.

The mutual dependency of the Prime Minister and the Commons should not suggest a fusion of the two. A philosophical policy schism often evolves after the Prime Minister is appointed. Additionally, the Prime Minister possesses considerable power in directing the executive branch free from direct parliamentary control.

However interrelated may be the executive and the House of Commons, there is a clear separation between the judiciary and the executive-Parliament linkage. Judicial appointments, other than the unique role of the Lord Chancellor, illustrate an absence of political patronage. The immutable requirement for judicial appointment, a long and successful career as a barrister (or a rare barrister/politician), has resulted in a judiciary nearly devoid of politicians. The English judiciary has evolved from its own highly sectarian source, preserving a clear detachment from the executive and Parliament, however parochial are the internal constraints within the institution of the bar itself.

§ 2. Parliament—House of Commons

Legislation is adopted in the House of Commons, considered by the House of Lords, and given royal assent by the sovereign. But the legislative role of the House of Lords has diminished, and the sovereign by convention since 1640 must grant royal assent. Legislative power thus is lodged in the House of Commons, although effectively the cabinet is the real base. Lack of an effective bicameral legislature has generated recent discussion of parliamentary reform.

House of Commons members are elected by a plurality rather than a majority vote, referred to as the "first-past-the-post" process. Consequently, quite minor changes in voting patterns of the principal parties in the electoral districts can result in meaningful changes of power in Commons. The system does provide a close tie between members of the House and the member's constituents.

Party organization and loyalty are essential to the survival of the parliamentary party (the party in power is the parliamentary party, the major party not currently in power generally is known as the opposition party). Any serious breach in loyalty may result in a House of Commons vote contrary to the interests of the government, although obviously to the wishful expectations of the opposition party, ever prepared to confront the parliamentary party in a new election at a time of the latter's weakness.

An elected House of Commons may endure for up to five years; an extension is allowed only in an emergency and requires the concurrence of the House of Lords. The Prime Minister may dissolve Parliament and call new elections before the five year limit expires. Dissolution of Parliament may follow adversity to the government, reflected by opinion polls, a vote of censure or the government's failure to obtain an affirmative vote on a major proposal. Moreover, the Prime Minister may call for new elections in a time of popularity, predicting voter affirmation of the government's success and granting it a new five year period.

Major legislation is initiated by rule in Commons. If successful in Commons, the bill proceeds to Lords. Any rejection by the Lords only delays the bill, a second passage in the next session will negate further action by the House of Lords. But on the second attempt Commons might not again pass the bill, the Lords delay thus is not unlike a United States presidential veto. The delaying role of the House of Lords therefore can be significant. The only authority of Lords to reject bills absolutely involves a bill to extend the duration of Parliament beyond five years, and they have initiation authority for private bills dealing with local matters or issues affecting individuals.

Public participation by approval or disapproval of actions of the House of Commons in the past decade has to a degree limited the power of Commons. The Industrial Relations Act 1971, was never implemented effectively, and consequently was repealed in 1974. A public referendum has been used for two important issues to obtain public support of parliamentary acts. The first confirmed membership in the European Communities by a significant majority in 1975, and the second resulted in the rejection of the 1978 devolution bills for Scotland and Wales. Further use of a referendum following important parliamentary acts may well develop into a form of restraint on the House of Commons.

§ 3. Parliament—House of Lords

The composition of the House of Lords partially explains its decline in power. Composed of Lords Spiritual (certain bishops), Lords Temporal (peers and peeresses), and the Law Lords, this aristocratic body is largely conservative, and also quite adventuresome. It has been criticized by the public and challenged by the House of Commons. Little change in its composition has occurred over the centuries, although the Life Peerages Act 1958, which allows peerages to be limited to the grantee's life, has resulted in the granting of very few hereditary peerages.

The most serious loss of power of the House of Lords resulted from two parliamentary acts, in 1911 and 1949, which limited the role of the House of Lords to its delaying power. That delaying power has been used primarily against major and usually controversial proposals of Labor governments seeking social reform, often not to defeat the bills, but to obtain amendments. These delaying actions by Lords have led to direct but unsuccessful attacks on the very existence of the upper chamber, including proposals for total abolition. The future of the House of Lords is precarious; some reform generally is viewed as a prerequisite to survival. That reform probably will include the introduction of elections for membership and a reduction in the number of member peers.

§ 4. The Prime Minister and the Sovereign

The Prime Minister is not elected directly by the public, an aspiring candidate must succeed in being chosen from among the leaders of the successful party in the national election for House of Commons seats, not from a public constituency. That choice is then confirmed by the sovereign, whose role is approval, not selection. The sovereign is a ceremonial figure who undertakes state visits, signs documents, receives foreign ambassadors, bestows recommended honors and performs other similar acts. England functions in the name of the sovereign, but the latter acts only upon the advice of ministers. A strong sovereign nevertheless may be influential. The survival of the English monarchy is due principally to its nature as a constitutional monarchy in which the sovereign assumes essentially a symbolic role. By convention the Prime Minister visits frequently with the sovereign to comment on actions taken at Cabinet meetings, offering an interested and astute sovereign an opportunity for discussion of developing policy and legislation, sometimes referred to as the power to advise, encourage and warn.

The structure of the monarchy and activities of the sovereign are governed by legislation and conventions. The sovereign does exercise the royal prerogative as the historical fountain of justice, but there is no effective remaining *independent* sovereign power. There are rare rumblings from Labor to abolish the monarchy, but they are not as threatening as the challenges to the other remnant of vested privilege, the House of Lords. Criticism of the monarchy usually is directed to its financial burden to the nation, or to the minor transgressions of subordinate members of the royal family. But on the whole the monarchy seems quite secure, providing the sovereign does not allow use of the royal prerogative to stray beyond the symbolic.

§ 5. The Judicial Structure

The English court system has been refined in the past century by the Supreme Court of Judicature Acts 1873, and the Courts Act 1971. The courts nevertheless retain characteristics associated with their structure as formed in the three centuries following the Norman Conquest. It remains essentially a unitary system; all courts, both civil and criminal, lead to the Court of Appeal and House of Lords. The principal exception, the division of equity under the jurisdiction of the Court of Chancery, was transitory. The fusion of law and equity unified this one errant vestige, although many traces of equity persist in the organization and practice of law. The unified English court system has been altered in part by participation in the European Communities. The European Court of Justice in Luxembourg is the final authority on issues of Community law.

The structures and jurisdiction of the English court system are less surprising to an American observer than several particular characteristics, such as the extensive use of lay judges for minor criminal matters in magistrates' courts, the active participation of judges in proceedings, the comparative minor use of juries in civil trials, the less adversary nature of proceedings, and the colorful ceremonial trappings of court dress.

The axial courts in the English system remain the ordinary courts, although in the last half century tribunals of special jurisdiction have proliferated. Vested with judicial and quasi-judicial authority, these institutions are evidence of an increasing government involvement in the lives of citizens. The special tribunals do provide a small measure of duality to the system, but no separate administrative hierarchy of courts exists in England such as is present in many civil law systems.

Concern regarding both the increasing number of special tribunals and their separation from the traditional judicial process, has led to special commissions to review their role. The Franks Committee report in 1957, the most extensive recent review, led to the

Tribunals and Inquiries Act 1958, which permitted judicial review by the law courts of decisions of a number of tribunals. Such review is not without some cost, often involving an extensive and costly delay in the establishment of government promoted services. But the involvement of the ordinary legal process through judicial review is thought better to protect the rights of individuals affected by the actions of the government.

Ordinary courts in England most generally are classified as superior or inferior. Inferior courts, the jurisdiction of which is limited both geographically and according to the nature of subject matter, include those civil and criminal courts which decide the vast majority of disputes, the county and magistrates' courts, respectively. Superior court jurisdiction is limited neither geographically nor by value, and exists in the Crown Court, High Court, Court of Appeal and House of Lords. The most important special courts include the Judicial Committee of the Privy Council and Restrictive Practices Court.

§ 6. County Courts

County courts resolve comparatively minor civil matters. A county court is the forum in which the English citizen is most likely to appear in civil litigation. Arranged in districts, they convene as courts of first instance with appeals directly to the Court of Appeal for most issues, but to a divisional court of the Chancery Division of the High Court for matters of bankruptcy.

The shire and hundreds courts, which developed before the Conquest and which largely had declined or perished for lack of use by the Middle Ages, were the historical predecessors of the county courts. The modern county court traces its origins to the County Court Act 1846, and notably differs from the superior courts by dispersions into every corner of England and Wales, thus providing a local forum for civil disputes. The County Court Act 1959, broadened the jurisdiction of these courts, extending it beyond simple matters of contract and tort to probate of small estates, equity jurisdiction and, in some courts, limited admiralty matters and undefended divorces. The county courts are also assigned jurisdiction of some social legislation, but a large amount is confined to special tribunals.

Procedure in the county courts is simplified in contrast to the High Court, and costs are lower. The county court judges are professional judges; they are experienced barristers appointed in the same manner as to the superior courts, by the sovereign at the recommendation of the Lord Chancellor. Assisting these courts is a Registrar, a solicitor who serves as administrative chief of the court, who has authority to hear and decide both pre-trial motions and small claims. The Registrar actually is a second judge for minor cases. Solicitors as well as barristers may appear as advocates before the county courts, an intrusion by the former into the usually well preserved barristers' domain.

The county court is a familiar court to an American observer. With its comparative informality, its single professional judge, and its broad jurisdiction over less complex civil disputes involving modest sums, the county court serves as the most important adjudicatory body for private, civil matters throughout England and Wales.

§ 7. Magistrates' Courts

If the structure and function of the county courts appear to differ little from methods of resolving comparatively minor civil matters in many common law systems, the structure of the magistrates' courts may seem most unique. Established throughout England and Wales, magistrates' courts primarily are staffed by ordinary but carefully chosen citizens. Part-time lay members sit in collegiate form without a jury to resolve in summary form the great bulk of minor criminal charges. Three magistrates usually sit, choosing their own chairman.

The use of lay as opposed to professional judges for less serious criminal matters has strong historical roots. The return of English soldiers nourished with plundering from the continental wars and the Crusades, and the loss of as much as one-half of the population from the Black Death, encouraged government control of both wages and the free movement of persons. A few of the most influential persons in each community were appointed to keep the peace under the Justices of the Peace Act 1361. Now nearly twenty thousand justices, or magistrates, serve throughout England and Wales. Appointed by the Lord Chancellor from nominations of local commissions, the magistrates accept office as a public duty, for the prestige of being a part of the judicial system and being per-

mitted to append to their names the initials J.P.   They
were compensated in earlier years, but the remuneration has been abolished.   The lay magistrates are assisted by a law trained clerk, in larger cities a full-time
position, but in smaller towns a part-time local solicitor.   The clerk advises on procedural and substantive
issues, but at the magistrates' request may participate
in the discussion leading to judgment.

Magistrates are often referred to as "the great un-
paid," or by critics as "the great unlearned," an oppro-
brium which applies only to the lay magistrates.   In
the larger cities, full-time, salaried, law trained stipendiary magistrates sit in the magistrates' courts.   The
stipendiary magistrates, who are usually solicitors, sit
not in collegiate form, but alone.

Criminal jurisdiction is the paramount role of the
magistrates' courts in the system of English justice.
Summary offenses, those generally of a minor character, are tried without a jury.   The benefit is speed and
the low cost of appearance, in contrast to a proceeding
before the Crown Court.   The disadvantage is a highly
probable conviction.   A large percentage of magistrates' cases are violations of the road traffic acts and
regulations, although most persons so charged plead
guilty and submit by mail specified fines without a
personal court appearance.   Certain indictable offenses may be tried before a magistrates' court, but
the more serious are tried in the Crown Court.

The magistrates' court plays an important role involving young persons.   When the court convenes to
hear juvenile offenses, it assumes a status separate

from the criminal environment of magistrates' court proceedings. The juvenile proceeding is closed to the public, press coverage is limited and at least one of the required three lay justices must be female. This special status carries through to any issue requiring detention, which usually will be in a community home rather than confinement with adult offenders.

Jurisdiction of the magistrates' courts extends beyond its principal criminal law responsibility to include minor civil issues involving the collection of specific debts, such as national insurance contributions and utility charges, licensing matters, and some juvenile and domestic issues.

The magistrate system involves an extraordinary use of lay persons to adjudicate the vast majority of minor offenses committed within a community. It has no parallel in the United States; but rather is more closely identified with various comrades' courts in socialist law systems, although it lacks the political function of such tribunals.

§ 8. High Court

When we speak of the Royal Courts of Justice, usually we mean the High Court and the Court of Appeal, housed in an imposing building on the Strand in London. The Supreme Court of Judicature Acts 1873, created the High Court by bringing together the Courts of civil jurisdiction which had been formed shortly after the Conquest. The High Court was constituted in five divisions—Chancery; Probate, Divorce and Admiralty ("wills, wives and wrecks"); Queen's

Bench; Common Pleas and Exchequer. Common Pleas and Exchequer were merged into the Queen's Bench Division in 1880. The Courts Act 1971, abolished the Probate, Divorce and Admiralty Division, dividing its responsibilities among Queen's Bench, Chancery and a newly created Family Division.

This divisional structure is partially illusory. Each of the three divisions theoretically has equal jurisdictional competency, although the Rules of the Supreme Court express an allocation of matters to separate divisions. Matrimonial cases in the High Court are heard in the Family Division, and Chancery is assigned numerous matters which have a traditional equity nature. A High Court judge assigned to any division, nevertheless, may exercise jurisdiction over an issue which under the Rules of the Supreme Court technically is allocated to another division.

The Chancery Division, presided over by the Lord Chancellor, almost always sits in London. Chancery judges are not noted for travelling on circuit, although the Courts Act permits sessions of any division to be held anywhere in England or Wales. Chancery tends to concentrate on issues of an equitable nature earlier assigned to its predecessor, the Court of Chancery, including estate administration, trusts, mortgages, certain interests in land, partnership dissolution and bankruptcy of companies and some revenue matters. It has a limited appellate jurisdiction, allowing a single judge to hear appeals from the Commissioner of Inland Revenue, or two judges to sit for appeals of bankruptcy decisions from county courts. By far the most are revenue appeals.

The Family Division—a President is its chief judge —has original jurisdiction of matrimony, legitimacy, adoption, guardianship and various disputes between spouses. Its limited appellate jurisdiction involves guardianship, adoption, matrimonial and affiliation appeals from magistrates' and county courts.

The broadest civil jurisdiction, original and appellate, is assigned to the Queen's Bench Division. It also is given limited criminal appeals. The Queen's Bench broader jurisdiction, encompassing many contract and tort actions, is attributable to its being the successor to three of the original divisions of the early High Court—Queen's Bench, Common Pleas and Exchequer. Additionally, it is charged with admiralty jurisdiction, a unique function evolving from the transfer of admiralty issues from the former Probate, Divorce and Admiralty Division to Queen's Bench in the 1971 reform.

By far the largest number of cases before the High Court are heard in London. Although the widely dispersed county courts dispose of most minor civil matters, the more complex cases of higher value tend to be tried in London, much due to the concentration of barristers in London. But the High Court judges in the Queen's Bench Division do sit throughout the country, often hearing High Court cases on a circuit which has scheduled additionally the same judge to sit for criminal matters in local Crown Courts.

Civil appellate jurisdiction of the Queen's Bench is limited, involving a single judge deciding certain appeals from tribunals and from interlocutory orders of

Queen's Bench Division masters. Two or more Queen's Bench Division judges may hear some civil appeals from magistrates' courts, or from the limited civil jurisdiction of the Crown Courts.

The Queen's Bench Division is the only division of the High Court with any criminal jurisdiction. Two or three judges may sit as an appellate court in limited appeals from the magistrates' courts or Crown Courts.

§ 9. Crown Courts

The Crown Court is a superior court of criminal jurisdiction on a level comparable to the civil jurisdiction of the High Court. The divisions of the High Court have evolved over centuries, however, while the Crown Court was created by the Courts Acts 1971. It is, nevertheless, part of an evolutionary process of criminal courts. Hearing indictable offenses, the more serious crimes, the Crown Court has replaced Quarter Sessions and Assizes. The latter were local courts, their organization and administration varying throughout the country. Special criminal courts convened in several of the larger cities. The Central Criminal Court Act 1834, created the famous Assize Court for Greater London, popularly known as the "Old Bailey."

The geographic distribution of the English population was altered when urbanization accelerated in the late 18th century, and the very different characteristics of local criminal courts became apparent. Uniformity was thought desirable and best achieved through a national system of criminal courts with some consistency in structure and administration.

The Courts Act 1971 established a single superior criminal court, made part of the Supreme Court of Judicature and designated the Crown Court. The Crown Court is convened throughout the year in contrast to the abolished Quarter Sessions.

There was no unification of judicial qualification when the court structure was changed; the Crown Court cannot be said to have its own judges. The judges rather consist of all the judges of the High Court, plus Circuit judges, Recorders and Justices of the Peace. They sit alone. It is possible for a collegiate form to convene, but it does not happen. A Justice of the Peace may serve if there is also a judge of the High Court present, but the former sit principally when there is a hearing on an appeal or an issue of committal for sentence.

Supplementary to the jurisdiction of the Crown Court over the principal indictable offenses, are its roles for appeals to the magistrates' courts and as a sentencing tribunal after conviction in a magistrates' court. A magistrates' court may transfer sentencing to the Crown Court if the magistrates believe that their own sentencing powers are inadequate considering the severity of the crime.

§ 10. Court of Appeal

The Court of Appeal is part of the Supreme Court of Judicature, and is exclusively a court of appellate jurisdiction. Its jurisdiction extends to both civil and criminal matters. Civil jurisdiction involves appeals from the High Court, county courts and certain administrative courts and tribunals. The criminal side primarily hears appeals from the Crown Courts. The court is thus the point at which nearly all disputes merge if further proceedings are intended, a feature characteristic of most common law systems, in contrast to having parallel levels of appeal for several judicial hierarchies.

The Lords Justices of Appeal are the principal judges of the Court of Appeals, the Master of the Rolls and the Lord Chief Justice are the administrative heads of civil and criminal matters, respectively. The Lord Chancellor, the Lord Chief Justice, the Master of the Rolls, the President of the Family Division of the High Court, former Lord Chancellor, and the Lords of Appeal in Ordinary are all ex-officio judges. During times of substantial caseload, the Lord Chancellor may temporarily add a judge of the High Court, illustrative of the absence of absolutes in the identification of certain judicial positions with a single, specific court.

Appellate decisions are rendered in collegiate form, by three judges, although in some limited circumstances one or two judges may appear, usually to determine application for leave to appeal. If a particularly important issue of law is before the court, five or more judges may sit, although the resulting decision possesses no greater authority than one emanating from the more common three judge court.

§ 11.   House of Lords

The judicial role of the House of Lords antedates its legislative role. But few of its early judicial functions as part of the Curia Regis survive. Its current role is chiefly as the senior appellate court.

Decisions of the House of Lords prior to the 19th century did not command considerable respect. They often were rendered by House of Lords members who were not lawyers. It remains possible in theory for the entire House of Lords to hear an appeal, including both its legislative and judicial members. But in practice decisions are now rendered by the Appellate Committee of the House of Lords, which includes only professional members. The judges include the presiding Lord Chancellor, and the Lords of Appeal in Ordinary, called Law Lords. The Law Lords are chosen either by direct appointment from among the most eminent barristers or by elevating a judge from a lower court. Almost always the appointments are made from the Court of Appeal. A benefit of such appointment is a life peerage, to a degree offsetting the rather modest salary. One or two of the Law Lords are from Scotland, and are assigned to appeals from the highest Scottish court of appeal, the Court of Session.

The Lord Chancellor, appointed by the Prime Minister to serve during the duration of the government, has multiple roles. He is an administrator; he rarely hears cases with the Law Lords. He presides both in the House of Lords in its judicial capacity and over the Judicial Committee of the Privy Council, heads the Chancery Division of the High Court, is an ex-officio member of the Court of Appeal, and is responsible for the county court system, all in addition to other judicial duties. But he is also a member of the executive, usually in service in the Prime Minister's cabinet.

And finally, the Lord Chancellor is a legislator; he sits as Speaker (chairman) of the House of Lords.

Unlike most other English courts, the House of Lords as a judicial body sits quite informally. The Law Lords hear appeals in a committee room rather than the chamber of the House, and they dispense with the formal judicial wigs and robes. Opinions of the Lords are actually speeches by the individual judges in support of their vote, currently written down rather than read aloud as was the early practice.

The jurisdiction of the House of Lords is predominantly appellate, and is almost exclusively related to matters from the Court of Appeal in England, although it is also the final court of appeal for Scotland and Northern Ireland. Either the Court of Appeal or the Appeals Committee of the House of Lords must grant leave for an appeal. Since the Administration of Justice Act 1969, some limited leap-frogging appeals are permitted directly from the High Court to the House of Lords.

§ 12. Judicial Committee of the Privy Council

The Privy Council is also a judicial evolution of the Curia Regis. It was created initially to hear appeals from the Channel Islands and the Isle of Man. Later known as the Privy Council, it assumed the role as the final court of appeals for courts from throughout the Empire. The royal prerogative was its source of power. The Privy Council's minor local jurisdiction diminished when the scope of the royal prerogative was limited following the constitutional conflicts in the Stuart period. The Privy Council later refined its unique role as a judicial body limited to hearing appeals from the Commonwealth, aided by the creation of the Judicial Committee, whose members were limited to professional judges, which assumed responsibility for all judicial matters of the Privy Council. The Judicial Committee survives as part of the English court system. Its judges are those Privy Councillors who have held high judicial office in the United Kingdom or other parts of the Commonwealth. But only a few appointments were made from the Commonwealth prior to 1962, by which time political changes in the Commonwealth had reduced the jurisdiction of the Judicial Committee. Commonwealth nations acquiring independence generally established national appellate courts, terminating or reducing appeals to the Judicial Committee. Canada, India, South Africa and most other former Commonwealth members have abolished appeals to the the Judicial Committee. Australia continues to permit such appeals from state courts, although not from the federal High Court of Australia. New Zealand and a few other former Commonwealth nations continue to use the Judicial Committee as the final court of appeal.

Had Commonwealth representation been increased significantly prior to 1962, the Judicial Committee might have survived as a far more consequential institution. But it never altered its status as a central court sitting in London, requiring Commonwealth Judicial Committee members to travel considerable distances to participate in deliberations. The relative inactivity of the Committee did not demand the full time

presence of its members, and Commonwealth participants usually did not terminate service on their national courts.   Once prestigious, this judicial vestige is
now of minor stature; its future is bound securely to
the fortunes of the Commonwealth.

§ 13. Special Courts

Several special courts with limited jurisdiction supplement the court structure described above. Perhaps
the most visible is the Restrictive Practices Court,
hearing a broad range of issues related to monopolies
and restrictive practices.   It is the most important
court in England to use an aldermanry composition of
judges.   Professional judges from the High Court,
Court of Session in Scotland and Supreme Court of
Northern Ireland, one of whom serves as president,
share the bench with ten lay persons who possess special knowledge of industry, commerce or public affairs.   But these special courts do not share the respect the bar accords the ordinary courts. Of even
less stature are the numerous tribunals which exist in
England with legislative authority to dispense administrative justice. Their procedures are less formal, more
rapid and less expensive than proceedings in the regular courts, but they are criticized for denying individuals their right to appear before the ordinary courts.
Lay participation on tribunals is far more extensive
than in the regular courts. Solicitors may appear as
advocates, but even they are not required in many
tribunals.

The development of special tribunals with lay judges
is viewed by some as a way of preventing social legis-

lation from being excessively strictly construed by the conservative English judiciary. But the judiciary has reacted. The Tribunals and Inquiries Act 1958, increased professional judicial control over the tribunals, foremost through the participation of the Lord Chancellor in appointing members. Further control is exercised by channeling appeals from tribunals to various parts of the Supreme Court, usually to the Queen's Bench Division of the High Court.

Dispute resolution in England by the ordinary courts as a right continues to be eroded. Any encroachment on the role of the ordinary courts by administrative tribunals is generally weighed very carefully. No formal, recognized separate court hierarchy has developed for private and public law issues, as exists in many civil law nations. But there is nearly one for some public matters, such as social security. Administrative justice in England, viewed by many, particularly the organized bar, with less than reverence, nevertheless continues to increase in scope and has a notable effect on the lives of all English citizens.

§ 14. The European Court of Justice

The entry of England into the European Communities by enactment of the European Communities Act 1972, added a judicial institution of then uncertain scope, but of obvious substantial importance, to the administration of justice in England. The 1957 Rome Treaty became part of the law of the United Kingdom, as did those various Community laws which become directly enforceable upon their promulgation.

Because the final authority for the interpretation of Community law is the European Court of Justice in Luxembourg, an important part of English law is being developed by a judicial institution not only with a composition which differs from the ordinary English superior courts, but with a strong balance in favor of judges from civil law systems. One should not identify the court as a civil law court, however, but it does possess a structure likely to create a Community law with predominant influences from civil law jurisprudence.

Of interest is the extent to which decisions of the European Court will bear a resemblance to decisions of civil law courts, disclosing a more abstract nature which may render them less usable as precedent than decisions from common law systems. This nevertheless presupposes that decisions of the Court have some precedential value. Nothing in the organizational structure of the Court suggests such an intention, and the pattern of decisions supports this view. One may well expect, however, that judges of the Court trained in the common law may place greater emphasis on past decisions of the Court, particularly where they contain substantive analysis rather than abstract statements.

The addition of the European Court of Justice to English judicial institutions is one of the most important changes in English common law in several centuries. The lack of an enforcement procedure for the European Court of Justice, however, may mean that its decisions will have less impact in England than decisions of domestic courts. There is evidence of this to-date in some EEC nations, several decisions of the European Court have been ignored by nations against whose interests they have been rendered.

CHAPTER 9

ROLES AND ACTORS

§ 1. Legal Education

Qualification to practice law in England either as a barrister or a solicitor has never required a university legal education, although a law baccalaureate increasingly is the path selected by those intending a legal career. The decision to become a barrister or a solicitor—one may not be both in England—frequently is postponed until graduation. Personal economics may be the deciding factor; becoming a barrister remains more costly. But the large amount of criminal work offers young barristers hope of early remuneration. The non-citizen pays even more dearly, through high fees charged foreign students, although admission as a barrister or solicitor has no direct nationality proscriptions.

The separation of solicitors and barristers evolved during the first two centuries after the Conquest. Persons appearing before the new common law courts were often assisted by one of a number of attorneys or advocates who spent their days milling about the courts. The attorneys or advocates initially were associated with the church, which had a dominant role in many areas of law, but as the church power waned, the advisors primarily were laymen. Sergeants and barristers carved out their niche as courtroom advocates, assisted in preparing the litigation by attorneys or, in the Court of Chancery, solicitors. The distinction between attorneys and solicitors, and the position of sergeant, were later abolished. The separation of the barristers and solicitors, however, has been carefully preserved. It was reinforced by a Royal Commission study in 1979, although there remains tension between the positions.

The education of both barristers and solicitors began as on-the-job training. The division between barristers and solicitors and their governance by different organizations, the Inns of Court (Senate) and the Law Society, respectively, are reflected in the educational process for each role.

University teaching of law was for a long period unrelated to legal practice. Courses in the civil law, principally Roman law, were part of the general, university educational offerings; they were academic and theoretical rather than professional courses. The common law as an academic study was introduced to universities quite late. Blackstone lectured on common law at Oxford in the mid-18th century, as the first Vinerian Professor. A chair also was established at Cambridge, and English law courses were introduced in University College and King's College in London. There was no rush to enroll. The number of students studying law in universities increased slowly. Training for legal practice, contrary to the continental custom, continued to be governed by the profession, not the universities. A modest impetus to the evolution of university law teaching was generated by a study on legal education in 1846 and the subsequent establishment of law degrees at Oxford and Cambridge in the 1850s, followed twenty years later by the creation of law faculties. Law as an academic discipline in England evolved long after it had been firmly established on the continent. Irnerius gave his first lectures on Justinian's Digest at Bologna in the 11th century when legal studies were becoming both systematic and scientific.

Substantive and procedural training is required of those who aspire to be either a barrister or a solicitor. There is some similarity in the training; an aspirant may follow the same path until the final vocational stages. Unique to the English system, however, is the diversity of allowable initial preparation. A strongly coveted premise holds that these professions should admit "mature" individuals from a variety of backgrounds and educational experiences.

Persons interested in a career in law today generally attend one of the approximately fifty universities or polytechnics which offer a first degree in law. Acquiring a law degree with completion of stipulated core subjects fulfills a substantial part of the mandatory barrister or solicitor training.

An expectant barrister next joins one of the four Inns of Court, maintains the required "dining terms" and registers for the vocational training. The vocational or professional stage requires a year in attendance at the Inns of Court School of Law, participating in substantive courses, practical exercises and, ultimately, sitting for Part II examinations. This procedure is not inexpensive; it is undertaken in London and for many constitutes a financial obstacle. Government financial support has helped somewhat.

The professional stage concentrates on practical courses including Procedure and Evidence, both considered elementary courses in United States university legal education. A participant also must select two substantive courses from among Inland Revenue, Family Law, Landlord and Tenant, Sale of Goods, Local Government, Conveyancing, Conflicts of Law, European Community Law, Labor Law, Social Security, and Law of International Trade. Those holding university or polytechnic law degrees often have completed courses in a number of the subjects which are offered in the professional stage.

An historical vestige which remains a mandate for becoming a barrister is "taking dinner" at the chosen Inn of Court. Those reading the law in earlier decades lived in their Inns, but pressures of space ultimately forced them out. Taking meals at the chosen Inn of Court has been substituted for residence and it does offer some collegiality. But the concept of mingling with senior barristers over an evening meal unfortunately has become more of an entry and departure without risking indigestion, or dining if a seat is available, and little more than being witness to the presence of one's seniors.

Completion of the Part II examinations leads next to a call to the Bar and a search for a one year pupillage with a junior barrister, intended to entail additional, supervised, practical instruction. The fortunate pupil may divide his time between two chambers, gaining experience in different areas of concentration. The workload and cramped space of barristers often limits the pupillage to mostly self study in a law library, but the time must be endured before the new barrister may accept his own cases. During the first six months of the pupillage the new barrister may not accept briefs, but even during the last six months he is not likely to have many briefs. He usually will have to plan on supporting himself during the pupillage, and quite possibly for another year as well until his workload increases.

Becoming a solictor is, if not less academic, certainly less expensive. Completing the academic stage, a would-be solicitor registers at the Law Society's College of Law to undertake the vocational or professional stage. There is some parallel to the professional training of a prospective barrister in the Inns of Court School of Law, but the Law Society's teaching is directed to the special function of the solicitor. The candidate then becomes an articled clerk to one or more solicitors or to a governmental unit. He is poorly compensated, but usually is better off than his brethren, the fledgling barristers. When the period of articles is over, the new solicitor's name is added to a list maintained by the Master of the Rolls.

There has not been a total fusion of the education of the barrister and the solicitor, but earning a satisfactory university or polytechnic law degree, or passing the Common Professional Examination by those with a non-law degree, fulfills the academic stage for both prospective barristers and solicitors. Law has become a graduate profession, the school leaver who once could apprentice himself to a barrister or solicitor and on his own study for the exams must now obtain a degree. The unfading distinction in the legal education of barrister and solicitor candidates is at the professional stage. It appears remote that this stage will be merged unless there is an outright fusion of the two functions. That fusion was rejected by the Royal Commission study in 1979, but the changes wrought in the two professions during the past few decades show an inexorable movement towards, rather than away from, fusion.

§ 2. Solicitors

The origin of the solicitor is less elitist than that of the barrister, and the solicitor's work has been less romanticized than the trial advocacy of the wigged and robed barrister. Attorneys who worked directly with clients preparing litigation for disputes before the King's Bench and Common Pleas courts usually did not possess the educational level of barristers. Nor did they present the actual cases in court. The role of advocate was carefully protected by the barristers. The term solicitor initially applied to an attorney appearing in the Chancery Court; that same role was called a proctor before the admiralty and ecclesiastical courts. These attorneys, solicitors and proctors—all later called solicitors—were first jointly housed with barristers in the Inns of Court, but the solicitors were ejected in the late 16th century and organized their own association.

Solicitors outnumber barristers seven to one. The 30,000 practicing and employed solicitors in the United Kingdom are not as concentrated in London as are the barristers. Solicitors practicing in London do not have their offices within monastic chambers like the barristers' Inns of Court. The solicitor has contact with the public and his location reflects this contact, while the barrister, who does not work directly with the public but only with solicitors, may work in a location less accessible to the public.

The life of the solicitor is on the whole more relaxed than the barrister, though the solicitor is less apt to achieve the fame accessible to a successful barrister, which may culminate in appointment to the bench. The solicitor may reach the heights of compensation of the most successful barrister, however, and an average solicitor is more likely to achieve a comfortable financial position than his counterpart at the bar.

Some new solicitors choose to accept a salaried position with a government authority or in industry, but the majority seek employment with a firm of solicitors. Expectation of partnership after some years as a salaried associate parallels the participation in a law firm in the United States, although the solicitor is expected to buy in to the partnership and, unless he has sufficient resources, he may have to remain a salaried employee. A solicitor who is a partner in a large and well known firm may expect sizable financial rewards, and also will benefit from the work of his articled clerks, assistant solicitors and junior partners. Large firms nevertheless are the exception; most solicitors practice alone or in a small group.

Entry to a solicitor's firm begins as an articled clerk to a solicitor, one's "principal," consisting of a two year apprenticeship, ostensibly to provide the clerk experience by way of sitting in with the solicitor on sessions with clients and in court. The more conscientious firms provide their articled clerks with a variety of experiences, including moving them from one department to another where the size of the firm allows specialization. The less fortunate articled clerks, perhaps as many as one-third of them, receive no instruction at all, but pass their days much on their own doing minor, routine tasks (even their own typing), and biding their time until the "training" is over and they qualify as solicitors.

The solicitor traditionally has been a law office practitioner, advising clients on legal, and often personal and business, matters. He does accompany his associated barrister to court to assist in a trial, but the role of courtroom adversary is preserved and protected by the barristers. More recently, solicitors have gained authority to act as advocates in the lower courts. They appear in magistrates' courts, in county courts, and, in limited circumstances approved by the Lord Chancellor, in criminal matters before the Crown Courts. They are chipping away at the foundations of the barristers' preserve, and there is a tension between the two professions of which the public largely is unaware.

The work of the solicitor is concentrated in the areas of conveyancing and estate law, in advising on business matters, and for some, litigation preparation and, in the lower courts, some advocacy. In the major cities large firms of solicitors often concentrate on advice to industry. They are quite similar to large firms in the United States, with the exception of refraining from the advocacy jurisdiction of the barrister.

The practice of the solicitor has changed in small degrees, and like the barrister, the solicitor has carefully preserved his lucrative monopoly powers. The 1979 Royal Commission study of the profession suggested that solicitors be permitted to advertise their skills and to publish brochures. The report nevertheless did not recommend any change in one area that has been strongly criticized for years, the monopoly which solicitors possess on property conveyancing, which guarantees a continued high cost to the public for the transfer of their property, although in exchange for an assurance of expertise in the transaction. Solicitors have rigidly protected their conveyancing monopoly because it is the largest contributor to most solicitors' incomes, and because fees for many other labors of the solicitor, particularly litigation, have not increased with inflation.

Solicitors are self-governed through their professional organization, the Law Society. Membership is voluntary, but about 80 percent join. The Law Society establishes standards for the education of solicitors and disciplines them when errant. It is as conservative as the Inns of Court in defending the domain of the solicitor, but also has promoted the successful encroachment of the solicitor into some of the territory of the barrister, including advocacy before the county courts and, to a limited degree, the Crown Courts.

§ 3. Barristers

There are few institutions in England more tradition bound than that of the some 3,000 practicing barristers (another 1,000 in government). Isolated in their

Inns of Court, barristers view with disdain any encroachment on their domain by the larger group of solicitors. The 1979 Royal Commission report brought a breath of relief to the barristers; it recommended perpetuation of the division of the profession.

Four Inns of Court survive: Gray's Inn, Lincoln's Inn, Inner Temple and Middle Temple. Sergeants Inn, composed of the more senior barristers, and the Chancery Inn, earlier were merged with other Inns. The Inns originated in the medieval guild form of association of practitioners, fully established by the 14th century. They brought together aspiring advocates to live and work. The members of the bar held practice court sessions or moots, and closely counseled the professional, spiritual and personal development of the fledgling barristers. The result was an unusual personal closeness and professional unity, which, through the process of judicial selection, also characterized the bench. Initially the Inns even functioned as residences for the barristers and their students, but pressures of space ultimately reduced the Inns to barristers offices, or "chambers," for dining, and as residences for benchers, the senior members of the Inns.

Barristers comprise the "Bar." A barrister functions individually, working with a solicitor who has retained him for a court appearance, to give special advice or for the preparation of a document. A barrister is required to accept briefs when asked by a solicitor, and a highly regarded barrister will have a heavy workload. His reputation may lead him to seek the role of a Queen's Counsel. The barrister does not have direct contact with the client. Where there is a need to confer with the client the barrister will meet only in the presence of the solicitor, and usually in the chambers of the barrister. Barristers may not form partnerships, as may solicitors, although they do work together in chambers, sharing a clerk and secretarial assistance. The clerk is more of an office manager; he negotiates his barristers' fees with solicitors and receives a commission as compensation. The fees are not fixed, but are set according to the complexity of the case and the reputation of the barrister. The fees are paid to the barrister by the solicitor, who may require an advance from his client to avoid having to pay the barrister without receiving the expected source of that payment, the fee owing from the client, as well as an admonishment from the Law Society.

Barristers do considerable office work, preparing wills, contracts, and drafts and written opinions. But their protected monopoly and the role which makes them so distinctive is as advocates in the Royal Courts and House of Lords. The successful barrister must be able to assimilate rapidly a great number of facts, possess a sound awareness of procedure and the rules of evidence, and use that knowledge in court where his capacity to think and respond immediately will determine his future.

Particular barristers often are sought by solicitors because of the former's specialization, and a firm of solicitors will generally direct work to a select list of barristers. If the work is of only a nominal level of skill, a junior barrister may be associated. For a complex matter, a Queen's Counsel may be preferred.

Barristers with at least ten years experience may decide to "take silk," substituting silk for stuff robes and assuming the title Queen's Counsel. Those who do not choose to be Queen's Counsels (the Lord Chancellor must give his consent) remain junior barristers throughout their careers. About ten percent of English barristers take silk. Queen's Counsel (or leader) status, once limited to barristers working for the Crown, is now sought by barristers in general practice who hope they possess a sufficiently strong reputation to encourage solicitors to retain them for more complex and, consequently, more highly compensated matters, and to limit their work to advocacy and giving oral and written opinions. Until recently a Queen's Counsel had to appear in court with a junior barrister as an assistant, a requirement abolished in an attempt to reduce legal fees. This may assist some who have taken silk unwisely, who did not have a sufficient reputation to draw the higher fees necessary to pay both the Queen's Counsel and a junior barrister. A Queen's Counsel who does not succeed financially must not return to junior status. A way of alleviating an unwise choise is to seek and accept some minor judicial appointment. Seeking Queen's Counsel status thus is one more risk in a profession already filled with obstacles. But if success is achieved as a leader, the financial rewards are quite substantial.

The Senate of the Inns of Court and Bar governs the affairs of barristers. It is composed of some 90 elected and appointed members of the Inns, bar representatives and non-practicing barristers. A committee of the Senate, the Council of Legal Education, is responsible for the lectures, tutorials and practical exercises given to prospective barristers in the Inns of Court School of Law. The Senate represents a comparatively small group, only some 3,000 practicing barristers, of whom fully two-thirds have chambers in London, the remainder practicing mostly in other large cities, with a very few in rural towns. There are now local bars in nearly two dozen cities and towns in England and Wales, which are often more accessible for a pupillage or permanent chambers. The most decentralization of barristers from London which has occurred has directly followed the establishment of permanent courts in provincial centers, and the abolition of the Assizes and Quarter Sessions.

§ 4. The Lawyer in Public Service

Formalization of legal assistance began with the Legal Aid and Advice Act of 1949. It is now under the Legal Aid Act 1974. Legal assistance previously was rendered by a variety of associations. The Act established a national, public scheme, administered by the Law Society, but not a new profession of full-time legal advisors.

The English scheme of legal advice and aid utilizes the services of the general practicing solicitors and barristers rather than promoting the development of a special class of legal aid practitioners. Plans for full-time, paid legal aid solicitors have not been adopted; preference rather has been given to integrating legal advice into the regular framework of legal services. A few neighborhood law centers have been established with full-time, salaried solicitors, but the practice is nowhere nearly as extensive as in the United States. Other centers have a scheme of duty solicitors, adopted in several areas where solicitors are present at magistrates' courts to provide assistance.

The most critical problem facing legal aid in England is the lack of financial support. Without immense government funding, the numerous individual legal advice and aid schemes which exist throughout the country are in jeopardy. The services which they provide are available effectively only to a small percentage of the population. Increased funding would proliferate neighborhood law offices with many new, young solicitors choosing to work full time for the centers, rather than volunteering their services on a part-time basis in conjunction with their professional practices.

§ 5. The Judiciary

Very young judges are not encountered in England. The route to the scarlet and ermine robes and cumbrous wigs of the judiciary is neither by career choice, as in most civil law nations, nor by political appointment or election, as in the United States. Advancing to the English bench is a long and orderly process with appointment rarely granted before the age of 40. That appointment is invariably made from the ranks of barristers. The judiciary thusly created has an esteem unparalleled in other systems. The English legal system owes its reputation, and its reception by others, as much to its personalities as to its principles.

Even were entry procedures to the barrister profession measurably altered, the change would not affect the judiciary for many years. As a barrister progresses through the stages of the profession, from a junior bar member to Queen's Counsel to the bench, a measure of conservatism tends to evolve. Judges rightly appreciate that they have passed stern tests in achieving judicial appointment, and they are not given to very much self-criticism. A few have criticized this process as discouraging any judicial reform suggested from within the judiciary, and as constituting a body which often acts counter to parliamentary enactments by a severely restrictive approach to statutory interpretation.

The English judiciary certainly is not an aggregation of judicial activists, but that is one of its noteworthy strengths. The nature of legal reform in England rarely has involved drastic alteration, but the evolution and modification of current institutions to accommodate changing social needs. There is no reason why the legal profession cannot adjust where necessary, and avoid the dislocations of any extreme and abrupt fundamental changes. The current structure has matured over centuries and is viewed from many areas of the world as a crucial structure to an orderly society, as an irreplaceable backbone to a system which has provided strength to the nation in numerous times of national crises.

Entry into the judiciary only after long years as a barrister, generally at least ten years for the High Court, illustrates that becoming a judge signifies the culmination of a career rather than the pursuit of a new one. Few judges ever leave the bench to commence a new endeavor. A judge who does step down often elicits a negative response from the bar, partially because the prestige and a life peerage, if granted, do not terminate with the judicial resignation.

Barristers are drawn to the judiciary at the height of their careers, for the most part from the position of Queen's Counsel, because of the prestige, the challenge and a knighthood or peerage if appointed to the High Court or above. The move distinctly is not motivated by monetary gain. Judicial salaries are notably less than the earnings of a successful barrister. Nor will the salary increase to a meaningful degree if a judge later moves to a higher court. Where salary differentials exist between superior court judicial positions they are nominal, and thus promotion is not sought for financial gain. Furthermore, there is no overwhelming expectation of periodic promotion, although the selection of judges for the superior courts frequently involves elevation from a lower judicial level. The view of the English barrister toward his role and future as a judge thus contrasts with that of the civil law judge, where promotion through the full hierarchy is a major expectation and, in fact, a necessity of the system since few judicial appointments are made from outside the ranks of professional judges.

The English judiciary staffing the superior courts is a relatively small group, fewer than 100, but increasing as more persons turn to the courts to resolve disputes. The increased number of judges in England has only modestly diminished judicial prestige. The enhanced role of legislation in contrast to judge made law has had a more severe impact. The judges of England with a lasting place in history—Mansfield, Coke, Bacon—thrived in an era where there were few judges and little challenge to the preeminance of precedent as the source of the common law. The judiciary in the United States may be associated with judicial activism, but the English judiciary tends not to issue rulings which grant to individuals rights that demand substantial national expenditure, believing that area to be the responsibility of Parliament.

The appointment of English judges to the superior court from among the barristers is a convention dating to the 13th century. The absence of elected judges lends a consistency to the English judiciary which does not exist in the United States, where the selection practice varies from one state to another, and even within a particular state with respect to different levels of the judiciary. A benefit of a judiciary homogeneous in experience and reputation, both within a given level of the court system and from one level to another, is the lack of a sense of need for an appeal to reach a more experienced or competent judge. The English system tends to assure one of meeting competency at even the lowest level, thereby reducing the indispensability of an appeal for a fair hearing.

Judges hold office for life, they may be removed by the sovereign only if in breach of good behavior and only at the request of both the House of Lords and House of Commons. Removal has never occurred. Lifetime service is permitted of judicial appointees to age 70 or 75, virtually a decade longer than allowed other government officials. Before the age limit of 75 was placed on superior court judges, many served to a very advanced age; Lord Halsbury sat nearly until his death at 93, exceeding Oliver Wendell Holmes' service until 90. Permitting lengthy service does reduce the possibility of a judge retiring and returning to other full time work, although it may result in ineffective service by judges who become incapacitated in later years.

Life peerages are invariably granted to the Lord Chancellor, the Lords of Appeal, the Master of the Rolls, the Lord Chief Justice, the President of the Family Division of the High Court, and occasionally to other judges of the Royal Courts. Every judge of the High Court or Court of Appeal is knighted, if they are not peers. As peers, they may sit as legislators in the House of Lords, but convention dictates that they avoid political issues and not stray far afield from law reform.

Additional to the appointment to ordinary and special courts staffed by professional judges, lesser judicial appointments are available as a master, or registrar, or as a stipendiary magistrate. Masters and registrars undertake the duties of processing cases before trial, a task left to ordinary judges in many nations. The English master has developed a reputation for a remarkable expertise in passing judgment on pre-trial motions, and especially in reducing the issues to be heard by the judge by overseeing the collection of facts and seeking the agreement of the litigants on minor issues. Not infrequently is the work of the master so effective that the dispute is resolved without the need of a trial. If trial is nevertheless required, the master may assign it to a County Court or determine that it should be heard in the High Court in London or on circuit.

A second minor judicial position is an appointment to a magistrates' court, to sit individually in a large city, in contrast to the lay magistrates who convene in collegiate form in the rural areas. The professional magistrate, called a stipendiary magistrate, assumes repetitious and intense work, handling a vast number of minor criminal cases. He generally sits daily, which may produce a boredom that is not a burden to the lay magistrate in the rural areas, who serves only weekly or every second week.

CHAPTER 10

PROCEDURE

§ 1. Civil Procedure

English civil procedure developed internally, that is, within the court system itself, to meet immediate needs. Rules which resolved questions of how the course of an action would proceed were established on-the-spot by the King's Courts. The development of English civil procedure, particularly since the 16th century, has constituted a process of refinement, of periodic alterations to correct immediate deficiencies which distracted the court from reaching a just result. This development contrasts significantly with the more methodical, external development of civil procedure in most civil law nations, where it is guided by legislative enactments and by the writings of law faculty, detached from any particular, current dispute. The civil law lawyer consequently views his system of procedure as more logical and rational in development.

An extraordinary transformation has occurred in English civil procedure from its dominant role in the early stages of the formation of English law. That dominance was demonstrated by the inflexible forms of action in the writ process, reflected in the statement "where there is no writ there is no right." Comparatively little substantive law existed in the initial decades of the development of English law, it evolved over a long period of time through judicial pronouncements, each issued within the strict procedural framework. The legal relationships of ordinary persons, such as in contracts and torts, grew slowly from the aggregation of specific decisions. As substantive legal rules accumulated in the reported decisions, the dominant role of the strict procedural elements declined. English civil procedure is considerably more flexible than during the early centuries of its development. There is no longer any general attitude that procedure overshadows the substantive law. Once governed by an almost mystical unwritten scheme, for a century now English civil procedure substantially has been codified. Rules of the Supreme Court, originally authorized by the Judicature Acts 1873, now regulate most civil proceedings in the Supreme Court, and there are corresponding rules for the county courts and for criminal proceedings in the magistrates' courts.

The complexity of the pretrial stage of an action initially depends on the rules regulating service of process. In a federal system, such as the United States, the serving of process to obtain jurisdiction over a person located in a different governmental unit meets with numerous conflicts. Such complexity does not exist within England, although similar issues will demand an adaptation of English procedural law to the jurisdictional conflicts arising from England's participation in the European Economic Community and its expected ratification of the Accession Convention to the EEC Convention on Jurisdiction and the Enforcement of Judgments 1968.

Civil proceedings begin by the appropriate court office issuing a writ of summons to commence the action. Service of the writ is carried out by the parties or by the court. Effecting service outside of England is subject to court discretion and whether the foreign nation is a member of The Hague Convention 1965 on service abroad or has a bilateral treaty with the United Kingdom. Order 11 of the Rules of the Supreme Court regulate this practice, altering the common law view that a court may not entertain an in personam action against a person who is not served in England.

The writ includes only enough information to apprise the defendant of the nature of the action. It is unlike the earlier, strict forms of action, which required a plaintiff to choose his form correctly or face dismissal. The writ is a command in the name of the sovereign to enter an appearance before the court. The "appearance" is accomplished by sending an acknowledgment of service to the court office which issued the writ.

The pleadings follow the appearance, and are quite similar to the process in other common law systems. But they tend to be briefer and more specific than American pleadings. The function of the pleading stage is to establish the issues for trial. But neither party wishes to disclose more than what is required. Beyond the broadly stated allegations and denials, the parties will be made to produce certain documents or, quite rarely, answer specific written interrogatories, but the English discovery system does not allow a pretrial oral deposition. The pretrial stage thus appears to be almost exclusively a written, documentary process. But this is not so, the applications, such as those for injunctions or discovery or to strike certain pleadings, are argued orally. And, as is true of most appeals, the oral arguments are made without briefs. Some of the pretrial work is accomplished by solicitors, but the barristers who will argue at the trial consult and draft required documents.

The English legal system contributes to the pretrial stage the expertise of a "master" (District "registrar" in the provinces). They are former barristers or solicitors who accept this position of less prestige, but less pressure, than a judge, and who are as skillful in procedure as the judges who will try the final issues are in interpreting substantive law. Masters perform numerous functions intended to refine the case for trial, or bring it to an early conclusion by way of settlement or withdrawal. They rule on interlocutory requests for interrogatories or the discovery of documents, proposed amendments to the pleadings and requirements for security. If the master has performed his task well, the issues will have been narrowed to those truly in conflict. Documenting evidence will have been collected, and the judge at trial will have been relieved of confronting many procedural conflicts which may burden the proceeding and confuse the participants. Acting in the quiet of his office or a hearing room, away from the publicity, openness and formality of the courtroom, the master plays an important role in preparing cases so that the oral, trial stage may proceed without delay, and in contributing to litigation a degree of uniformity which allows the trial stage to focus on the substantive issues. His is not an unhurried role, however, and he often pressures parties to resolve the case themselves.

The English trial is an oral process. This was necessarily so in earlier times when jury members were usually illiterate; presenting written evidence would have been futile. But the oral process also is mandated by the nature of the trial today. Continuation of the deliberate and often time consuming written procedures which dominate the pretrial stage is no longer appropriate when all the parties have gathered for the trial. The parties expect its conduct to proceed without undue postponement. The English trial, as in most common law nations, is "an event." It begins with all parties present and proceeds to its conclusion while they remain. This oral proceeding exhibits the skills of the English barrister. The solicitor, having participated in preparing the matter for trial, quietly sits in court during the trial, frequently engaging in whispered conversation with the barrister, offering advice and searching the files for needed documents. Solicitors do appear as advocates in the county courts, but the High Court remains almost exclusively the domain of the barrister. The English view their trial stage as necessitating rapid comprehension and response, skills which are often not possessed by trial lawyers in nations which do not limit trial advocacy to specialists, including the United States. It is impossible for a judge to be able to be highly knowledgeable in very technical and scientific matters. The nature of the English trial, a predominantly oral hearing proceeding without interruption (in theory often more than practice) until its conclusion, does not afford time for judicial study of complex issues. The reaction has been to create numerous tribunals, each designed to deal competently with special matters. However fragmented and unsystematic the tribunals may be, they offer a composition and procedure usually both less expensive and less restricted by rules and conventions than the ordinary courts.

The oral process of an English civil trial is familiar to any common law system observer. Counsel for the plaintiff makes a statement of his client's case, and next calls his witnesses, each of whom may be cross-examined by defense counsel and reexamined by the plaintiff's counsel, if thought appropriate. When the plaintiff's case has been presented, the defense initiates a similar presentation of witnesses, with cross-examination by the plaintiff. Both counsel give final summaries, and a decision then is rendered by the judge. But the English civil trial judge often plays an active role in directly questioning the parties, to clarify for his own sake conflicting or unclear matters, or even to commence a new line of questioning which he may perceive as important, but which had been ignored by counsel. Judicial participation is important in a civil trial where either party may decide not to introduce evidence. The judge may be able to extract what one counsel prefers not to mention, and the other ignores.

Although England's civil procedure once followed extremely strict procedures, an English trial today appears less disrupted by the application of strict rules of evidence. Evidence precluded in the United States often is admitted unchallenged in an English proceeding, and a barrister certainly is more hesitant in objecting to a line of inquiry presented by the judge than by opposing counsel.

English common law almost never affords the parties a trial with judge and jury in civil cases. The use of a civil trial jury varies throughout common law systems. The United States extends the right to trial by jury well beyond practice in England. Trial by judge alone has not always been the English practice. At early common law, a jury was the norm, except in the Chancery Court. The Judicature Acts, fusing law and equity initially were responsible for the reduction of jury trials in civil cases. Later laws specifically limited their use. Most civil disputes in England are tried by a judge sitting alone. The concept that the essence of the common law system is trial by jury, appears to the English lawyer to be carried to an unnecessary extreme in the United States. The importance of the jury in the development of English common law is associated with the *criminal* legal process. The civil process in England developed with relatively little access for disputants to a trial by jury.

§ 2. Criminal Procedure

Changes which have transpired in the procedure of a criminal process in England since the Conquest, are no less striking than the demise of the forms of action and the merger of law and equity in civil procedure. Until the late 16th century, an accused was detained until trial with no opportunity to prepare a defense. He was not informed of the evidence to be used against him, or of those who would testify for the prosecution. Nor could he call any witnesses on his own behalf. He could not even have counsel were he accused of treason or a felony. He stood isolated against the state. The changes in criminal procedure in the last few centuries, and most importantly since the mid to late 19th century, are almost without exception changes of benefit to the accused. But there is less public criticism in England than in the United States that the balance has swung too far in favor of protecting the interests of the accused, to the detriment of society.

The English criminal process is accusatorial rather than inquisitorial. Pollock has noted that, "Courts of justice are public; they judge between the parties, and do not undertake an official inquiry not even in criminal cases or in affairs of State." The case against the accused is investigated, prepared and directed through the courts by a party, usually a public official representing the Crown, not by the judges or magistrates as in an inquisitorial system. But the English judge or magistrate may actively participate in the trial, asking questions directly of the accused and witnesses, calling witnesses (rarely) and thus bringing an inquisitorial element to the trial to a greater degree than in the United States.

The decision to prosecute is not reserved by the state. With exceptions which are increasing in scope, *anyone*, not only public prosecutors or other officials, or even those with an interest in the matter, may act as a prosecutor. The system of prosecution is thus much more widely diffused than in the United States. But a privately initiated prosecution occurs only in exceptional cases, most often where the citizen (or more often a group opposed to something) believes public authorities have improperly refused to prosecute an action. Private prosecution is discouraged, the costs must be borne by the citizen. Although private prosecution is used rarely, it illustrates the conceptual aspect of the common law criminal process, that a *citizen*, either public or private, must commence and pursue the action, and that the role played by the person or group which determines guilt or innocence is only a minor part in the preparation and presentation of the suit.

Civil procedure tends to be not greatly dissimilar between different courts, the amount in controversy usually determines the level of court with jurisdiction. There is a greater variation of procedural characteristics in criminal proceedings in different courts, directly related to the seriousness of the offense. Seriousness is usually the basis in any legal tradition for determining which criminal procedure will apply. While the goal in civil litigation is to determine liability and damages, a criminal proceeding may involve, in addition to determination of guilt, an educational element, loss of freedom or physical retribution, or a mandated work requirement. Offenses are classified, the least serious (summary offenses in England, misdemeanors in the United States) may require nothing more than the payment of a fine by mail, with a notation in the court records of the financial satisfaction of the wrong. As the summary offense becomes more serious in England, persons must appear in person before the magistrates' court, to be tried by lay peers (or in the large cities a single professional stipendiary magistrate) without a jury. The procedure is less formal than more serious crimes demand (indictable offenses, not unlike the felony in the United States), where a jury will be convened and rules of evidence become stricter and more carefully followed. The complexity of the procedure in a criminal prosecution is directly related to the gravity of what society may demand for one's guilt. No such indictable-summary classification existed during the early years of the development of common law. Other than trial by ordeal, all trials were by judge and jury. To use the current labels, all were indictable.

It is the police who most often prosecute in the magistrates' courts. This function is the most distinguishing characteristic in contrast to the role of police in the United States. But many towns have appointed local solicitors as prosecutors. This has alleviated some of the criticism of "police advocacy." A police prosecutor usually lacks the indifferent attitude as to the outcome of the case, which is quite necessary if the prosecutor, as an advocate, is to assist the court in reaching a just conclusion. The state is not in a win or lose position, it wins as much if an innocent person is acquitted as when a guilty person is convicted. A prosecuting solicitor does represent the chief constable, but he has a greater detachment than a member of the police force. The movement is towards a more independent and unified prosecuting procedure, except for very minor and routine matters.

Where the crime is more serious, the actual prosecution, though not the investigation, is undertaken by the Director of Public Prosecutions, an official who, with a large staff, also handles government actions and cases the Director believes merit his intervention. His role illustrates the more complex mechanisms of criminal procedure as the offense is either more serious, or of more interest to the government.

The English defense process is more common to that in the United States than the prosecution. As Karlen has pointed out, the early American system "was more generous" in allowing legal representation to the defendant, but in terms of both allowance and funding of defense counsel, the two systems are not now greatly divergent. English legal aid does tend to exist more within the traditional professional structure than in the United States, where separate public defender offices have prevailed. That English professional structure, where barristers and judges have common roots and comprise a homogeneous fraternity, tends to give an American observer the impression that there is a closer bond between counsel and the judge than counsel and his client, a bond that, as Karlen notes, may "inhibit the presentation of a strong defense."

The accused somehow must be brought before the authorities. How that is done varies; it may or may not involve a warrant, it may be by an arrest or a summons without arrest, and it may be accomplished by a public official, the police or by a private citizen. Of importance to criminal procedure is both the lawfulness of the act itself, such as the arrest, and the consequences of an unlawful act at this stage of the trial, particularly as to the exclusion of evidence obtained incident to an unlawful action.

The English law of arrest may seem vague to an American observer, it has evolved from suits for false imprisonment and resisting arrest. Warrants are used less frequently in England, both because of the pattern of success in issuing summons (mostly limited in the United States to traffic violations) even for some serious crimes, and because the issuance of a warrant may require a concurrent decision as to bail, which is not part of the warrant process in the United States.

The English policeman is more limited in arresting for offenses committed in his presence; if a misdemeanor either it must constitute a breach of the peace, which is not clearly defined in English law, or the officer must rely on an increasing number of specific statutes. The limitations on the English policeman's powers reflects the relatively homogeneous nature of the population, and the absence of fear on the part of a citizen stopped by a policeman. But that is changing rapidly in the larger cities, the negative caution an American feels if stopped by police increasingly is shared by many persons in England. It affects the relationship at the time a policeman has little more than a suspicion, and it brings to the relationship the adversary element of the later stages of the criminal process.

There is no greater disparity between the work of the police in England and the United States than in the use of evidence obtained in an unlawful search. A common law criminal adjudication must be based on facts admitted into evidence, not a hypothetical problem. The facts admitted thus are the foundation of the process. Evidence discovered during an illegal search may be relevant to the case, but some systems exclude that evidence because of the method of its acquisition. That is the position of the United States procedure.

Although he does not prepare the case, it is the judge who determines the relevancy of evidence, his decision guided by limiting statutes and a considerable bulk of precedent. The English judge must not only rule on what evidence counsel may admit, but, unlike an American judge, he may himself participate in molding the finished product, the final aggregate of facts upon which either he or the jury will decide guilt or innocence. The judge may recall witnesses or introduce new witnesses (rarely), and he may question witnesses either to remove doubt based on earlier testimony, or to inquire more deeply into matters which he believes were only superficially treated.

The discretionary power of the judge in other common law nations, including the United States, is limited severely. American criminal verdicts are appealed far more often than in England. There is a sense that the process requires both trial and appeal, a view that has not existed in England, but one that is changing. The English criminal trial stage thus is the controlling location in the criminal process, but that control center shifts to the appellate stage in the United States.

The right to a jury trial exists in most common law nations. But the procedural elements vary markedly. The English jury tends to remain, as Lord Devlin has noted, "predominantly male, middle-aged, middle-minded and middle-class." Pressures for a more representative jury have been less visible than in the United States. But the most notable distinction in the selection process is the absence of a voir dire examination, allowing counsel to challenge the fitness of prospective jurors. In theory, the English advocate may challenge for cause, but it is not done often. Nor are available preemptory challenges frequently used; the rule is to accept those persons called to serve by the administrative machinery, however haphazard that process may be.

The second striking difference in the jury procedure involves the verdict. But it is a difference which is diminishing. The verdict in English criminal law long mandated unanimity. The Criminal Justice Act 1967, introduced a major change, the majority verdict. A jury is informed initially that it should reach a unanimous verdict. If it does not, it is then told that although it should continue to try to reach a unanimous verdict, a majority verdict will be accepted. The English majority verdict does not mean a bare majority, as is accepted in Scotland, however, but rather permits only two dissents where there are at least 11 jurors.

The majority verdict in criminal cases is a practice whose time has come. It is being adopted in various states in the United States, and the pattern has been to allow a smaller majority than the English view. The accused is believed to have enough in his favor under modern procedural rules, and the impact of a single (or small minority) obstinate juror is thought to justify this important change from the early common law adherence to the unanimous verdict. Thus the difference is not between or among common law nation systems, but between contemporary practice and the historical mandate of a unanimous verdict.

The criminal procedure of different common law nations may reflect very contrasting treatment, but there is a more common element to the sentencing process, namely judicial discretion. Although there is some limited movement toward mandatory, fixed sentences, the generally wide judicial discretion contrasts with the more strict trial procedures. There is one feature in English sentencing which is unknown in the United States. Where a defendant, having been found guilty by a magistrates' court, is believed by the magistrates to have committed a crime for which the magistrates lack authority to grant sufficient sentencing, the magistrates may refer the matter to the Crown Court for the imposition of sentence. A defendant appearing before a magistrates' court must thus be aware that the sentencing limitations of the magistrates' courts are supplemented by those of the Crown Court. If a defendant before a magistrates' court believes there is a likelihood of a reference to the Crown Court for sentencing, he may well prefer to have the entire matter referred to the Crown Court for trial. The reason accused persons tend to avoid requesting a trial in the Crown Court, however, is an expectation of a modest sentence by magistrates in return for an almost certain conviction.

Criminal trials are much in the mind of American observers, willing or otherwise. They are given a heavy dosage of newspaper reporting of the accused and what he has done, and how the trial is proceeding. Now the television media are beginning to enter the courtroom. The public's right to know in the United States has little parallel in England. Reporting of the proceeding is restricted. Only formal, record matters, such as the names of those charged, the nature of the charge and the result is allowed at the committal proceeding. The evidence may not be discussed, unless permitted by the defendant, or unless the accused is not committed for trial. The same rule holds true during the trial, the media must await the verdict. Except in a few circumstances, the trial is open to the public. The limitation is not on the public nature of the trial, long an important part of English law, but on what use is made of information about the proceedings, whether or not that information is gathered at the trial or elsewhere.

§ 3. Appellate Review

In the early development of the common law, an appeal lay only to challenge an error on the record. One sought a writ of error, and then pursued a process which to us seems unwieldy. A review of the judgment, alleging that the court reached the wrong conclusion, later was recognized in the Chancery Court. Thus appeals developed as part of the common law, recognized not by statute, but in the same manner as other rights, as the "way things ought to be" by the judiciary. When the rural courts were abolished, the right of appeal was incorporated into the statutory framework, the primary source being the Judicature Acts.

An appellant now seeks to reverse the judgment as incorrect in law, which in a narrow sense constitutes a rehearing since the judgment may be reversed or some other judgment substituted. But it is not a rehearing in the manner of the rehearing of a civil law appellate court, where new evidence will be heard and there is a de novo proceeding. New evidence may be presented in the English appeal, but it very rarely is, and is accepted only where it could not have been obtained for use at the trial, suggests an important influence on the result and seems reasonably creditable. The most frequent acceptance of new evidence is in an interlocutory appeal, not an appeal from the trial judgment.

Although the appellate court does rehear the case, English judges are far more hesitant to interfere with the discretionary power of judges than in the United States. But they do often overrule procedural determinations.

The statutory scheme designates the Court of Appeal as the appellate body of the supreme court to which appeals are directed from divisions of the High Court, from the county courts or from interlocutory orders of judges in chambers or masters on pretrial issue.

The Court of Appeal uniquely is an appellate court, a characteristic also of the judicial role of the House of Lords. Both have very limited, special original jurisdiction. The trial courts, contrastingly, possess an extremely qualified role in the appellate process.

The Court of Appeal has become the appellate court into which are channelled appeals from both lower civil and criminal courts. Prior to the Criminal Appeal Act 1966, there was a special Court of Criminal Appeal.

But the appeal of criminal cases has a brief history. Before 1848 there was no appeal in criminal matters for indictable offenses, the only recourse was to seek a pardon where there was an apparent mistake. Appeals on issues of law were established first in the Court for Crown Cases Act 1848, but restricted to technical errors. The centralized role of the Court of Appeal as the exclusive civil and criminal appellate court is further supported by its jurisdiction over appeals from courts of special jurisdiction and tribunals. These special courts do not have a full procedural hierarchy, including special appellate courts, such as exists in many civil law systems.

A new appellate level was added to English law by entrance into the European Economic Community. The European Court of Justice in Luxembourg interprets the Treaty of Rome, and English courts confronted with such an issue may refer the matter to this European Court, and must do so if there is no judicial remedy from the English court before which the case is pending.

The Treaty is unlike English legislation. The latter are more exact and judges tend to limit their application only to those circumstances which precisely fit the wording of the statute. But the Treaty often states general principles, and where English courts interpret its provisions, the judges must consider the intent and spirit of the Treaty. They must not act as "traditional" English judges.

As in the United States, some appeals are a matter of right, others require judicial permission. In England, immediately after a decision is rendered by the Court of Appeal, a party may ask the court for leave to appeal. The judges usually respond immediately, rather than reserving judgment. If the request is denied, then the party may ask the House of Lords to permit the appeal, thus giving two chances for the review. The Appeal Committee of the House of Lords hears oral arguments on the petition, and, much like the judges of the Court of Appeal, responds immediately without reserving judgment.

For the most part the English appeal follows an orderly process through each step in the judicial hierarchy. Direct appeals which omit one level, the "leap frogging" process, are presented to the House of Lords from the High Court, but only in very limited cases where there is agreement of the parties and a question of law of some public importance.

The emphasis on an oral process and the infrequency of reserving judgment distinguish English appellate procedure from the process in the United States. The oral focus is most evident during the actual appellate argument before the court. It is not preceded by lengthy and sometime printed briefs, the cumbrous work product of the American attorney. A paper, the "case," is presented by each side in the House of Lords. It is supposed to be merely an outline and not discuss supporting legal propositions or authorities, but they often are too long. The record of appeal, which is furnished to the judges from the lower court, provides much of the information that in the United States is included in counsel's briefs. The lower court judgment in England usually includes an outline of the evidence, the authorities which the judge relied upon in reaching the decision and his reasoned decision.

The inordinately long time of the English oral proceeding is attributable to the reading of the record of appeal and the authorities relied upon by counsel. Some experimentation in reducing this time has been attempted, where the judges at the beginning of the oral arguments were expected to have read the pleadings, the order under appeal, the notice of appeal and the judgment below. This practice tends to be used in long cases and has functioned reasonably well in the Restrictive Practices Court.

The oral arguments are not limited in time, and may go on for days or even weeks. It is rarely predictable how long the oral arguments will last. The court may interrupt counsel, accept his proposition and dispense with the reading of authorities. It may further, after the appellant's argument, immediately state that it has not been persuaded by the appellant and render judgment.

After the conclusion of the oral arguments, the view of each judge usually is given orally, although in the House of Lords decisions are generally reserved and written. How very different from the United States, where judges invariably reserve judgment and counsel must wait weeks or even months to know the outcome of their efforts.

The nature of the English appeal requires the judge to spend most of his time on the bench, very little time is spent in chambers. He generally hears oral presentations morning and afternoon of every day throughout the term. The American judge in contrast works many hours in chambers and receives substantial aid from one or more clerks and personal secretaries.

The need for law clerks largely is absent in England. Since extensive briefs are not used and judges render their opinions extemporaneously upon completion of oral argument, clerks serve little purpose prior to the appeal. Nor are they later needed, it is the law reporters who check the facts and citations and make the cases more readable, not law clerks. But the law reporter has a far more important role in the English system, he determines which decisions will be published in Law Reports, and thus join the accessible fabric of the common law of England.

There are few appellate judges in England, some two dozen on the Court of Appeal and House of Lords. They all sit in London, the appellate process is highly centralized. But the process does not require the presence of the clients, it is a written and oral documentary process. The centralization and limited number of judges does offer a consistency in decision making generally absent in the United States, further enhanced by the process of appointing appellate judges, discussed earlier, which creates a judiciary more consistently competent than in common law systems where judicial selection more closely approximates that in the United States.

The relatively small number of judges in England is possible by the limited frequency of appeal. Although the incident of appeal has been increasing troublesomely in the last decade, nevertheless it is correct to note that there remains a greater public belief in England than in the United States that issues are dealt with competently at lower levels and that there is little likelihood of a reversal on appeal. The recent increase in appeals has placed a substantial burden on the appellate court structure, and it has altered the nature of lower court proceedings. The preservation of the right to appeal and its documentation has assumed an important role in course of the trial stage.

CHAPTER 11

RULES

§ 1. Sources of Law

Sources of law pertain not to how an ordinary citizen believes his conduct is governed, but to where courts look in determining what legal rules are applicable to resolve a specific dispute. Tradition often separates sources into written and unwritten. It is a confusing distinction, intended to contrast laws which have been formally enacted from those which have not been enacted, the latter including judicial decisions and customs, and, important in English law, conventions and the royal prerogative. The variety of sources of English law attest to its nature as a *method* of administering justice.

Classification of sources is less important than their assigned values, particularly when the sources represent conflicting rules. How judges perceive the value of different sources additionally affects the manner in which they will apply a governing source of law. Value allocation to sources within a system is a slow, evolutionary process. English judges traditionally have been less inclined to defer unquestionably to legislation, particularly social reform legislation, than United States judges. Disdain for social legislation has diminished slowly. The legal profession in England has bred an independent and pervasive sense of what is right. Paramount is a sensitivity for preserving an individual right to contract freely and to alienate property. Social change is thought to be introduced appropriately through the adaptation of precedent to new circumstances, not by means of legislation. The judiciary believes that due accord to social change is illustrated by the development of common law decisions. Although there is no dispute that legislation is the source of law which has authority over all other sources, the fabric of the common law is its precedent, and the vast number of volumes of "unwritten" law is the foremost distinguishing feature of the common law tradition.

§ 2. Precedent

In any legal system, what judges have said in addressing issues in earlier disputes is likely to be of interest in subsequent cases with similar facts. If a judge assumes that earlier decisions in his court and in higher courts were dealt with competently, there is no reason to suppose, in the absence of changed circumstances, that a similar result would be inappropriate. Continuity and predictability of the law are positive attributes. The theoretical *usefulness* of prior case law should not be any less in a legal system where judges do not have to follow earlier decisions, than where they are compelled to follow them, presupposing access to the substantive law in the earlier cases through an effective reporting system. When the rules denominating sources of law in a system exclude precedent as the primary source of law, precedent nonetheless retains value. Precedent is often noted in a civil law case as *teaching* something, a use which refers to the form of assistance cases may provide in determining how statutory law is interpreted most wisely. Where that precedent becomes a primary source of law, as in common law systems, the case does more than teach judges something, it exists separately as law to be followed, or distinguished. For centuries English precedent not only existed as law, as it continues to do today, but it existed as the primary source of law, giving way partially only to legislative enactments of Parliament after the civil war, and later being overshadowed by legislation as a source of social reform in the mid-19th century.

Case law binding upon courts may have assumed a diminished role in the English legal system, but legislation faces a gauntlet of interpretation by the courts. Decisions which interpret legislation become a source of law as much as the laws which they interpret. The existence of interpretive decisions of a parliamentary act tends to arouse a sense of comfort with English lawyers and judges. Until judicially interpreted, laws are frequently believed to lack the authority which arises with judicial sanctification. While this should in no way diminish the fact of the supremacy of Parliament, it does illustrate that where the interpretations of statutes possess independent status and authority, the statute alone may be viewed as incomplete until it has been interpreted.

Certainty, precision and flexibility are thought to be characteristics of precedent as a binding source of law. Once a decision has been rendered involving particular facts, there is some assurance that in a subsequent identical fact situation a similar conclusion will be reached. Common law system lawyers nevertheless have become exceptionally skillful at distinguishing fact situations, at making it difficult to accept that identical situations ever recur. The aggregate of judicial decisions in England constitutes an extensive framework, illustrating how varying disputed facts have been resolved. To the English lawyer it is inconceivable that these variations could be foreseen, or included, in statutes. The most exhaustive code cannot offer solutions to all possible situations. It must of necessity have some measure of abstractness. A civil law system judge has the task of resolving a case from broad statutory principles and underlying theories of the "essence."

English common law has attributes both of flexibility and rigidity. Decisions are less binding than might at first be assumed. They are also distinguishable, to a degree that sometimes suggests inappropriateness rather than difference. The English judge, nevertheless, often is more reluctant than American judges to ignore a decision which appears to dictate what may seem at the time to be an inappropriate or unjust resolution. The resulting opinion may state that however regrettable a particular decision might appear, the law on the subject is settled by earlier precedent, and any change must be mandated by an act of Parliament. The degree of rigidity of a common law system thus depends on judicial attitude. The greater homogeneity of judges in England, in contrast to the diversity that exists in the United States with an extensive state court system, tends to identify the English system as one of stronger judicial compulsion to follow precedent, and of fewer variances in attitudes throughout the judicial system.

No system possesses a written law governing all conceivable disputes. Judges must therefore create new law. It may not be very obvious to an observer of a common law system that a judge has "made" law. What effectively is new law may appear to have at least some identity with elements of one or more previous decisions, in contrast to a similar situation in a civil law system, where the judge made law may have at best a tenuous identification with abstract statutes.

It is not always possible to distinguish a legal principle in a case, or *ratio decidendi*, from additional rule-like statements which in fact are ancillary to the decision, and not binding, but considered only *obiter dicta*. If it is difficult for a civil law observer to separate law from dictum in reading a common law decision, some comfort should be found in the fact that often persons trained in the common law cannot agree on the distinction in a given case.

Judges must know which decisions are to be followed, and which at most have value as soundly reasoned judgments to be read for guidance or "teaching" in the civil law sense. Within the domestic court structure in England, House of Lords' decisions are binding upon all other lower courts, even though there may be no line of appeal to the House of Lords. The Lords decided in 1966 to overrule a decision more than half a century old, which had held the Lords strictly bound by its own previous rulings. The House of Lords decided it would henceforth only be compelled to follow earlier decisions when it believed the decision appropriate. The source of this new rule was not a case, but a policy statement of the Lords. Whatever flexibility the House of Lords thus may have granted itself, it expectedly has continued in practice to adhere to its earlier decisions in all but a very few instances.

As one moves down through the system the rule tends to remain consistent. Higher court decisions are followed by lower courts, both in the civil and criminal courts. And courts tend to accept their own earlier rulings. There are of course variations, for example the decisions of High Court judges sitting alone at first instance are not binding on other High Court judges, although they are of persuasive authority. And the decisions of the inferior courts are not binding within the inferior court system, not so much for the reason that they lack the value of decisions of the superior courts, but because they are generally not reported.

Participation in the European Community, and the consequent delegation of the interpretation of any Community instrument to the European Court has added to the English system of legal rules the question of the binding nature of decisions of the European Court on English courts. Also of importance is how the English judge on the European Court will view and use earlier judgments of that Court. Decisions worded in the abstract, in the manner of civil law cases, may prove of relatively minor use in decisions in the national units.

Precedents are only as functional as their reporting. English law reports developed very slowly, without government participation. They continue to be the product of a private enterprise system which chooses which cases shall be reported, often on the basis of the economics of including a particular judgment. Yearbooks developed in the late 13th century, consisting essentially of notes compiled by advocates, but under no pretext that they were to be used by judges as precedent. But they were used for that purpose occasionally, increasingly so by the 15th century. When publication of the yearbooks ceased, private reports were produced, initially under the name of the particular law reporter. They proliferated for three centuries until, in the mid-19th century, a semiofficial council was formed for the purpose of reporting cases in England and Wales. Their Law Reports, which have now replaced most of the private series, are not the exclusive publication of cases, but convention suggests that they are the reports which should be referred to when citing decisions.

The system remains quite informal. Not all cases are reported, and citations often are made to unreported decisions, or to a series other than the Law Reports. Substantial duplication exists, a case may be reported in three or four different series, and additionally included in periodicals. Recommendations have been offered to make reporting official, and also to produce an authenticated transcript filed with the court of record for a decision, a practice prevalent in other common law systems. English reports are produced by barrister-reporters who are present in court to hear judgments. The authenticity of the report thus occurs not from the fact that it is included in the Law Reports, but rather because a barrister was present at the delivery of the judgment, and has vouched for the accuracy of his work.

The format of reporting largely determines its usefulness as precedent. Effective employment as precedent is possible only where a decision is reported in a form which makes it usable by judges in future cases. The form of reporting has thus tended to develop in a style which assures the utility of these private ventures. Reported cases in England, as in the United States, briefly outline the facts and the legal issue which has been presented, and give reasons, often quite lengthy, for reaching a particular decision. But in English cases, facts are perceived differently than in the United States. Factual differentiation often is carried to an extreme in the United States, certainly more than in England. English precedent consequently is more likely to serve as a forceful value in future cases.

§ 3. Custom

Custom as a source of law is present in every legal tradition. The English common law has drawn extensively upon local custom; the Normans did not import a legal system from the continent. Local custom in England assumed an important function in aiding English judges in resolving specific disputes. Custom was a basis for much of the early criminal law, as well as for such family prescriptions as the rights of parents.

In this sense custom was an integral part of the common law.

Some local custom also existed separate from the common law, usually involving rules which were applicable to a very small group of people within a local community. These rules constituted exceptions to the common law. Local custom separate from the common law included rules regulating local fishermen, such as where they could dry their nets, or stipulating the characteristics of a right of way. Custom in this form differs from custom which is part of the common law only in its narrow and limited application, and its variance to the common law. With the passage of time, local customs often come to be modified to evolve into general customs which are integrated as part of the common law.

The initial establishment of custom requires proof that it existed uninterrupted for a long period of time, and that it existed by common consent rather than by the use of force. Also, it must be consistent with other customs, contain certainty and be accepted as obligatory and of significant importance. And it must be reasonable.

§ 4. Conventions

Conventions are an influential source of English law, and, along with custom, constitute the unwritten legal sources. Convention dictates expected conduct in the functioning of the judicial system as well as other institutions. No act of Parliament specifies that there must be a Prime Minister, nor outlines the method by which the Prime Minister is chosen. It is according to convention that a Prime Minister is selected from the parliamentary or majority party, and that if the Prime Minister fails on a vote of confidence or a major government proposal, a resignation should follow. Convention additionally limits the conduct of the sovereign. It is convention which caused King Edward to abdicate; a monarch should not marry a divorced person. It is also by convention that the sovereign carefully limits any exercise of the royal prerogative, and follows the advice of the Prime Minister in making cabinet and ministerial appointments and in granting royal assent to acts of Parliament.

Within the judicial structure, convention has long played a role in determining the respect to be given to the decisions of other courts, the right to issue dissents and the commencement of certain disputes before a specific court, even though other courts possess concurrent jurisdiction. The several courts acts have codified and altered convention, but it remains an integral element of the structure of these institutions.

Convention exists in every society; it is a part of every legal system. It prevails more successfully in a system where there is little emphasis on the codification of rules. Convention thus is less important in civil law systems. A homogeneous society probably is more conducive to admitting convention where tradition plays an important role, where the expectations of one individual with regard to the conduct of others tend to be common throughout the population. Convention is a flexible source of law, but nevertheless a source of exceptional importance in the machinery of justice in England.

§ 5. Royal Prerogative

Powers of the English monarch are severely limited. Sovereignty of the crown, as contrasted with sovereignty of Parliament, is essentially a sovereignty symbolizing loyalty to the monarch. The power of the monarch, called the royal prerogative, includes various rights exercised directly by the sovereign, with a subordinate sense of the prerogative constituting powers exercised by the government on behalf of the sovereign.

The judicial system was highly centralized in the beginning years of Norman rule in England. The king was the supreme source of justice. Various devices such as the writ system allowed the royal courts to increase their jurisdiction at the expense of local, rural courts. The power of the king went unchallenged until the Magna Carta 1215, the first formal check on royal power acceded to by the king. The will of the king was no longer the law, though several centuries later civil strife occurred over the issue of the scope of royal power. The use of the royal prerogative surged in the 16th century with the establishment of the Star Chamber. Stuart kings extensively enlarged the royal prerogative, based on their conceptions of the king's divine right. This challenge was met by common law advocates, and by the end of the 17th century the prerogative was returned to a state of diminished exercise. The royal prerogative was never again the source of authority for the creation of new courts, such as the Star Chamber.

The royal prerogative diminished even further with the Petition of Right Act 1860, which increased a citizen's ability to seek recourse against the sovereign for alleged wrongs. The sovereign's immunity from civil proceedings again was altered by the Crown Proceedings Act 1947, all but eliminating ancient rules restricting procedures against the sovereign.

Comparatively little remains of the royal prerogative, although the monarch plays an important role in the functioning of the government. A few formal powers remain, essentially summoning and dissolving Parliament, rendering royal assent to bills, presiding over the Privy Council, conferring honors, granting pardons, appointing some state officers, approving cabinet and minister appointments, appointing leading clerics, and concluding treaties. Many of these are illusory powers, nevertheless, the monarch does not personally select the Prime Minister, but acts according to the will of the leaders of the parliamentary party. It is unlikely that the royal prerogative will increase in scope in the future. The monarchy is more a symbol than a source of authority, the royal prerogative is at the command of Parliament.

§ 6. Legislation

The authority of legislation in England or the United States, or in any other common law nation, may appear quite fundamental to observers in each nation. Enactments of the principal legislative bodies become law which must be followed. In the United States, complex questions about the effectiveness of the legislation may arise because of the existence of both federal and state legislatures. Is the matter enumerated in the Constitution for the federal congress? Is the matter one of specific residual delegation to the states, and thus not for federal action? These questions do not arise in England; parliamentary enactments are not questioned by challenging legislative competence. With few exceptions, Parliament is sovereign in legislating domestic law. It may enact unwise laws which the courts nevertheless in theory are bound to apply. The English constitution does not contain fundamental rights which may lead to parliamentary decrees being invalidated by the courts as unconstitutional. This should not suggest, however, that there exists an unchallenged acceptance of all acts of Parliament. The vast amount of statutory law is thought by many to be inconsistent with a threat to the stability of the common law. Legislation gains authority when judicially interpreted and methods of judicial interpretation by the English courts are more highly refined than in the United States. Absent the ability to rule legislation unconstitutional, the English courts have finely tuned a system by which legislation is interpreted. Courts thus have significant influence on the post-enactment development of statutory law, since enacted law is only effective when the courts permit it to be applied.

Any statute is subject to being viewed from different perspectives. In attempting to determine the intention of the legislature, one might consult its members to attempt to learn their intent, a method which would be both impossible in application, because of the number of legislators, and which would give legislators an undesirable role in judicial interpretation. More appropriate is to consider the enactment in view of the circumstances of its passage. But it is a third method, illustrative of the reservations which the English judiciary have for legislation, which has prevailed. It is strictly construing legislation according to its literal meaning.

Courts initially will attempt to interpret laws according to their literal or grammatical sense, even allowing the possibility of an undesirable result. They will not permit the result to be absurd or repugnant, however, or to be inconsistent with the balance of the enactment, but will vary the interpretation only to the degree necessary to avoid such a conclusion. In the event that a proposed interpretation continues to appear absurd, the provision may be considered in the context of the entire enactment, not just in the light of the purportedly applicable portion. Thus, the judiciary may look to an act's preamble, if present, but they tend not to consider marginal notes. Notes may more accurately reflect the intent of the draftsmen than of Parliament. Little attention is paid to punctuation, which is considered an item of personal preference. A court may consider the social, political and economic circumstances which led to the enactment, as well as debates which transpired as the proposal passed through various stages in Parliament. Inquiries may be made as to the state of the law before the act, what the act was intended to correct as an apparent defect in the common law, and the reason for the interest in such a change. Other methods of judicial interpretation of legislation may apply in particular circumstances, such as the presumption that an interpretation should avoid repetition or redundancy, and that where specifics are expressed, other alternatives should be excluded.

Judicial interpretation of legislation enacted by the European Community is of too recent occurrence to classify. Under the European Communities Act 1972, questions involving the meaning of Community enactments are treated as questions of law in accordance with principles embodied in judicial decisions of the European Court. These principles will develop over time, presumably incorporating a mixture of judicial interpretation concepts of all of the Community members. An English court interpreting Community enactments in the future thus will be required to apply rules established by the Community, rather than traditional concepts of judicial interpretation of domestic English legislation.

§ 7. The Constitution

No single constitutional document exists in England as in many other civil and common law nations. English constitutional law is thus frequently noted as being based on an "unwritten constitution." That contains more myth than truth. It is true only in the sense that constitutional law is not contained in a single document; the complex and abstract nature of the English Constitution results from it being an aggregation of numerous sources, mostly written but all identifiable. Changes in any of the sources which comprise the English Constitution will alter its total structure, making it more flexible than many constitutions.

The Constitution is affected by most traditional sources of English law, including the royal prerogative, conventions, common law, a few of the more important acts of Parliament, and, more recently, the addition of acts of the European Communities. Clarity of identifying the English Constitution is dependent upon recognizing its sources. The existence of custom, conventions and the royal prerogative do not render this an easy task.

The most important elements of the English Constitution are several statutory laws enacted by Parliament. The Act of Union with Scotland 1707, while classified as a parliamentary act, has a special status over most other acts, a status given also to the Bill of Rights 1689. The Act of Settlement 1700, and the Habeas Corpus Act 1679, are additionally constituent elements of English constitutionalism. Uniquely important is the European Communities Act 1972, which joined England to the European Communities. This added a new source of law, the law-making bodies of the Communities. Community law takes precedence over domestic English law. If not applied by the English courts, it will be by the European Court of Justice.

Added to these acts is the impact on constitutionalism by power delegated by Parliament, affecting such important areas as immigration. A final element identifiable with Parliament is parliamentary privilege, involving such rights as freedom of speech and house debate, its source both in statutory and common law.

External to the direct and indirect effects of acts of Parliament on the English Constitution are custom and the English common law. The most significant constitutional aspect of the common law is the role of judicial decisions in protecting civil liberties. The 16th century Bill of Rights does not guarantee individual liberties. Where such rights are protected, the sources of law are various conventions, judicial decisions and statutes. A contemporary, written bill of rights in England has been sought by many for years.

A final element of the British Constitution is that part of custom referred to as conventions, an important part of the framework of both the Constitution and ordinary English law. The source of conventions and their enforcement is less identifiable than other constitutional elements. Convention evolves principally from a non-judicial precedent established over decades, if not centuries, of consistent conduct. Pressures for continuance are the expectations of the public and the convenience of the existence of the conventions.

In addition to the absence of a single written constitutional document, there is no court with authority to rule on the issue of constitutionality of acts of Parliament. A parliamentary act is supreme. If it conflicts with an earlier act of Parliament, or with precedent, the earlier law is modified, not violated. This might suggest that it is absolutely clear that no act of Parliament can be challenged. For Parliament to pass an act inconsistent with the Act of Union with Scotland, or with the European Communities Act, but which was not intentionally directed to altering those important acts, a court would face the difficult problem of construing them as abolishing or amending those earlier acts, or being unintentionally in violation of those acts and thus invalid. What measure of parliamentary activity is necessary to amend or abrogate an important earlier parliamentary act is unclear, particularly where that earlier act is part of the aggregate which collectively is known as the English Constitution. But it does appear that legislation in England is assigned different values, not by Parliament, but by those through whose test it must survive, the English judiciary. Though they may not declare an act unconstitutional, they are most adept at nullifying the impact of parliamentary acts viewed as particularly objectionable to the administration of justice.

§ 8. The Law of the European Economic Community

Ratification of the Treaty of Accession and the European Communities Act 1972, initiated England's entry into the European Communities (European Economic Community, European Coal and Steel Community, and European Atomic Energy Community). England follows the dualist theory of international law; a treaty does not by accession become the law of the United Kingdom. The Treaty of Accession was thus not self-executing; Parliament had to act to give England's participation legal standing. Parliament not only accepted Community law existing at the time of the

Act, but it agreed to adopt directly applicable Community legislation of the Council or Commission enacted subsequent to entry. Parliament thus delegated law making power to Community institutions, although limited to rights and obligations created by the text of the treaties.

Community legislation which is not directly applicable requires parliamentary action to become effective in the United Kingdom. Such legislation may be implemented by statute or, the more likely course under the 1972 Act, by subordinate legislation adopted by the English executive under delegated authority.

Community law includes sources beyond the treaties and secondary legislation. Decisions of the European Court of Justice may become an important source of law, both as precedent in that Court and in courts in the United Kingdom. A decision of the Court of Justice does not nullify a member state law, but the decision must be followed in member state courts if it pertains to the meaning or effect of the treaties, or the meaning or validity of a Community instrument. United Kingdom courts are bound by European Court of Justice decisions. Were Community law to become unacceptable in the United Kingdom, the only method to renounce that law would be political, not judicial, mandating a withdrawal from the Community by repealing the European Communities Act. The effect of any action less than withdrawal, such as an act of Parliament in conflict with the European Communities Act, remains a matter of some debate. The traditional view that one Parliament cannot bind another tends to prevail. Parliament has been sensitive in avoiding passing laws in conflict with the acts of union and of emancipation of the colonies and dominions; it would seem similarly aware of problems associated with passing laws in conflict with participation in the Communities.

United Kingdom Courts do attempt to apply Community law as required, but there are some obstacles of interpretation. Community legislation, drafted by persons trained in the civil law, tends to be general, without either the precision identified with English legislation or useful interpretation clauses. English judges thus are obliged to speculate as to what was intended by the drafters. The noteworthy English decisions to date, guided considerably by rulings of Master of the Rolls Lord Denning, illustrate a distinct inclination to reach conclusions without a request for European Court interpretative rulings, but which do comply with the spirit of the treaties and are consistent with other Community law. If the English courts consistently avoid requesting interpretive rulings, a body of United Kingdom domestic precedent interpreting Community law will develop which may be quite different from Community law as a whole.

The entry of the United Kingdom into the European Communities has required a most important submission of domestic law to an external law-making body. Other treaty obligations have raised similar issues touching upon the sensitive question of English parliamentary sovereignty, including England's participation in GATT, the United Nations and the European Convention on Human Rights.

§ 9. Reception of Roman Law

Roman law is not a direct source of law of the English legal system. There has been an indirect effect on the development of the English legal system from the Roman law, however, principally from the area of canon law. Early English ecclesiastical courts were attended by advocates and presided over by Chancellors whose educational experience at Oxford and Cambridge included the study of civil law. English family and succession law, including the formalities of wills, thus demonstrate some rules not dissimilar to those of Roman law.

Where early English courts were not aided by precedent and turned to opinions of such writers as Bracton, there was a further indirect application of Roman law principles. Bracton's treatise reflects his knowledge of and respect for Roman law, influenced by the writings commissioned by the Roman ruler Justinian. Bracton's classification of bailments follows directly the Roman categorization. It subsequently was adopted in an early English decision. In other instances, judges have considered Roman doctrines when difficult questions were presented, and there was no direct, traditional source of English law as a guide.

All legal systems tend to benefit from others, particularly as comparative legal study becomes more prevalent. Where there has been no attempt to codify vast areas of the law, there are bound to be gaps which require judges to seek guidance from other sources. Other legal systems in civilized nations, whether they are common or civil law systems, may provide that guidance. If the Roman law has been considered appropriate guidance in a particular case, that should not suggest that there has been a reception of the Roman law. Reception means a direct acceptance of the Roman law as a principal source of law. That has not been a characteristic of the development of English common law.

§ 10.   Divisions of Law—Law and Equity

Where alternative systems of justice exist, conflict is bound to occur. Equity supplemented the common law by offering compatible remedies in some cases, but in others it produced a direct conflict with the common law. The Court of Chancery often issued an equitable injunction ordering an individual to cease an action which had been commanded by a common law court. The success of the equitable remedies depended on the ability of the sovereign to exercise prerogative powers. Objections to the injunctive power of Chancery ultimately waned in the early 18th century, when the rules of equity had become nearly as rigid as those of the common law. The Judicature Acts 1873, finally abolished the conflict by transferring the powers of the common law courts and courts of equity to the newly established Supreme Court of Judicature. No division of the High Court may issue an injunction to restrain a proceeding in another division, ending the most controversial conflict between the two systems. The fusion nevertheless was not absolute. Traditionally legal remedies remained a matter of right, those of equity continued to be discretionary. But the administrative conflicts were abolished, the systems no longer possess any substantial measure of conflict.

§ 11. Divisions of Law—Public and Private Law

Division of common law systems into private and public law is referred to infrequently. A division is more often noted in terms of the law of torts or the law of property, all part of what is known as substantive, as opposed to procedural law. Were the system to be classified as public and private law, private law would include laws of contracts, torts and property. Additionally so categorized would be family law, succession and trusts. Criminal law would constitute a major part of the public law, which would further embody constitutional and administrative law, and procedure. Civil law nations often employ entirely separate hierarchies of courts for public and private law. While there are specific common law courts in England for criminal law, the principal criminal law courts, the Crown Courts, are part of the Supreme Court of Judicature. Appeals may lie to different divisions, but both civil and criminal matters are heard in the same appellate court. The other major section of public law, the law of the constitution, is allocated in the main to administrative tribunals, but the common law appellate court system retains jurisdiction over most administrative appeals.

§ 12. Divisions of Law—The Law Merchant

Commercial law is often separately administered in civil law nations. It evolved within the fairs and markets of the Middle Ages, creating what became known as the law merchant. Commercial law might have developed within England as a largely separate system existing parallel to the common law. But it substantially had assimilated into the common law by the 17th century, although it retained a separate significance, because judges recognized that commercial rules chiefly were based on the practices of merchants and traders. Commercial usage constituted custom. The common law rule requiring proof of the existence of a custom from a very early time was not required in commercial litigation. Current custom was acceptable as long as it did not conflict with common law decisions. In the late 19th century, most of the law merchant was incorporated into statutes, including the Bills of Exchange Act of 1882, the Partnership Act 1890, and the Sale of Goods Act 1893. While the law merchant had its own separate and important origin, little of that isolation remains today in English law.

SELECTED BIBLIOGRAPHY

A. Babington, *The Rule of Law in Britain from the Roman Occupation to the Present Day* (Barry Rose Publishers, London 1978).

Lord Denning, *The Discipline of Law* (Butterworths 1979).

A. Dicey, *Introduction to the Study of the Law of the Constitution* (London 1924).

W.S. Holdsworth, *A History of English Law* (London 1913–1966).

R.M. Jackson, *The Machinery of Justice in England* (7th ed.) (Cambridge 1977).

P.S. James, *Introduction to the English System* (9th ed.) (Butterworths 1976).

H.F. Jolowicz, *Historical Introduction to the Study of Roman Law* (Cambridge 1952).

D. Karlen, *Anglo-American Criminal Justice* (Oxford 1967).

F. Pollock & F.W. Maitland, *History of English Law* (Cambridge 1898).

Royal Commission on Legal Services Report (H.M.S.O., London 1979).

K. Smith & D.J. Keenan, *English Law* (5th ed.) (Pitman 1976).

R.J. Walker & M.G. Walker, *The English Legal System* (3d ed.) (Butterworths 1972).

G. Williams, *Learning the Law* (10th ed.) (Stevens 1978).

PART THREE

THE SOCIALIST LAW TRADITION

CHAPTER 12

HISTORY, CULTURE AND DISTRIBUTION

§ 1. The Historical Foundations of Socialist Law

For purely ideological reasons, Marxian socialist commentators treat with benign neglect the fact that the architects of socialist law derived inspiration not only from foreign non-Marxian legal systems but also from the prerevolutionary laws of the respective countries. They present socialist law as if it were a monument to the ingenuity and originality of the socialist legal mind. Socialist law was founded, if one were to rely exclusively on Marxian socialist writings on the origins of that law, upon a clean slate by men who were equipped with nothing other than the teachings of Karl Marx, Frederick Engels, and Vladimir Lenin and a burning determination to sever the umbilical cord linking the new socialist systems with the inequitable past. In other words, one is led to believe that historically socialist law is a system with a future but without a past.

The founding fathers of the individual socialist legal systems may very well have regarded other non-Marxian systems' notions of law as "almost ridiculous", just as the ancient Romans attributed no importance to outside influences in designing Roman law. But to any knowledgeable student of comparative legal systems, the path to socialist law is paved with stones which were consciously or subconsciously borrowed from other legal systems. Socialist law as we know it today represents a workable harmonization of the principles of natural justice, the concepts of natural law, Roman law, the civil law tradition, the prerevolutionary tradition of the individual country and the general tenets of Marxism-Leninism. This is not to suggest, however, that there is nothing that is original within socialist law. All it means is that, as the discussion which follows indicates, not all of the institutions and ideas that went into the making of socialist law are indigenous to it.

In modern practice the term "natural justice" usually denotes the general principles and minimum standards of fairness in adjudicating a dispute, embodying the specific requirements that no man be judge in his own case, that each side be heard, and no man be condemned unheard. These principles of natural justice permeate socialist criminal and civil procedural rules.

A close analysis of the substantive provisions of socialist law also indicates that many natural law precepts form part of socialist positive law. Without recognizing natural law as higher law by which the validity of positive law could be and is measured, socialist positive law has consciously or subconsciously internalized some of the general principles of natural law. In receiving some of the transplantable elements of natural law, the socialist lawmaker takes the clear position that the unreceived portion of natural law thinking does not constitute part of socialist law, and that if and when a principle of natural law cannot be reconciled with socialist positive law, the latter must prevail.

Among some of the principles of natural law that have found their way into socialist positive law is the social contract theory, *i. e.*, the principle of self-preservation in pursuance of which man sought to find security by transferring all his natural rights to the sovereign (the state) and promising to obey that sovereign. Under this theory, as developed by Hobbes, the delegation of power by the citizens to the state is unconditional, and the exercise of the delegated authority by the sovereign is absolute. This theory of social compact permeates socialist constitutional law. The other notable principles of natural law that have found their way into socialist law are: the principle of sanctity of contracts which Grotius crystallized into the doctrine of *pacta sunt servanda* [obligations voluntarily undertaken must be fulfilled] in his study of the nature of international law; the obligation to repair damage done by one's fault to others—which permeates socialist law of torts; the concept of *aequum et bonum* [equity] which is readily visible in socialist law of restitution.

Roman law influence on socialist law was received through prerevolutionary law which in turn was heavily influenced by medieval German scholarship. By contrast, the civil law tradition filtered into socialist law, not only through the respective prerevolutionary laws which had adhered closely to that tradition, but also through the overt willingness of the drafters of the early socialist codes to look to the experiences of civilian codifications, especially of the Napoleonic and German codifications.

But, whereas the external forms and the internal divisions of socialist law, as well as its attitude towards the sources of law, the role of the judiciary and judicial procedure are essentially in the civilian mold, the substantive rules of socialist law are heavily laden with the principles of Marxism-Leninism and inspired by the indigenous culture of the individual countries. Thus, the similarity between the civil law and the socialist law traditions is one of form more than of substance. Remarkably, the common law tradition has had virtually no impact on the development of socialist law.

Because Soviet law is the oldest, the most exported and most copied of the socialist legal systems, we would like at this point to take a closer look at the historical relationship between prerevolutionary Russian law, Soviet legal tradition and the civil law tradition.

Vis-à-vis prerevolutionary Russian law, Soviet law represents one step forward and two steps backward. Except for the brief period between 1917 and 1920, Soviet law seems to have retained the essential characteristics of prerevolutionary law. Russia prior to 1917 was essentially *pays de droit écrit*, [a region of written laws] even though the Asiatic region of the vast

Russian Empire was more or less *pays de droit coutumier* [a region of customary laws].

The tradition of codification in Russia goes quite far back as is evidenced by the following litany of codes that had existed in Russia prior to 1971: the Russkaia Pravda [Russian Law] was adopted in the eleventh century. This was followed by the Sudebniki (Court Manuals) of 1497 and 1550; the Stoglav (One Hundred Articles) of 1551; and the much more comprehensive Sobornoe Ulozhenie (Code) of 1649. Between 1700 and 1829 there were many unsuccessful attempts at further codification of Russian law. Finally, in 1830, Mikhael Speranskii published a Complete Collection (Polnoe Sobranie) of the Laws of the Russian Empire, consisting of a 42 volume reproduction, arranged in chronological order, of the more than 30,000 legislative enactments which had been promulgated since 1649. This was followed in 1832 by the 16 volume Svod Zakonov (Code of Laws) which was a systematic codification of the whole Russian law, branch by branch. The 1832 Svod Zakonov contained altogether 60,000 articles. With few exceptions it embraced virtually all branches of Russian law and came into force in 1835. New editions of the Svod Zakonov appeared in 1842 and 1857 and it was in force until 1918. A new Criminal Code was enacted in 1845. Following the great law reforms of the early 1860s other codes were promulgated. The last of the tsarist codes were the Criminal Code of 1903 and the Draft Civil Code of 1913.

When the Bolsheviks seized political power in Russia in 1917, they adopted a nihilistic and apocalyptic attitude towards law in general. They set out to destroy tsarist law and dismantle all prerevolutionary legal institutions. Like the French revolutionaries, the Russian Bolsheviks sought to break with the past. In reality, however, they did not and, in fact, they could not do so. In order to create a new legal order, they had to fall back on the old prerevolutionary Russian legal tradition. Russian tradition became Soviet tradition in lawmaking. The tradition was one of codification and not of judge made law.

But the Russian revolutionaries did not embark upon codification right away after the 1917 revolution. In fact, codification of Russian law was put off for almost five years. Serious codification of Russian law began with the beginning of the era of the New Economic Policy in 1921. During the bridge years (1917–1920) Russia effectively operated a system of judge made laws and judges were called upon to administer revolutionary justice based upon their revolutionary consciousness.

The most prominent and influential legal thinker of the precodification era was V.I. Lenin, the founder of the Soviet state. There is a general presumption that Lenin acted under the impact of traditional Romanist thinking in devising his new lawmaking system. Lenin was not only a positivist with a touch of class, but also a lawyer of the Romanist tradition. All of the influential legal thinkers of the precodification era were trained in the Romanist tradition. In devising a new legal system for Russia, they subconsciously drew upon their Romanist background.

During the bridge years the Russian lawmakers, as a matter of policy, adopted the position that all tsarist laws were to be abrogated to the extent that they were incompatible with the new order and that, pending the promulgation of new laws to replace the old tsarist laws, the judges of the revolutionary tribunals were to make laws. In doing so the judges were to be guided by their revolutionary consciousness and socialist customs. But this experimentation with judge made law was to be seen a a temporary deviation from the inherent tradition of Bolshevism, *i. e.*, the tradition of codification, the tradition of legislative positivism.

It was further decided by the Bolsheviks that immediately after the transition period all laws should be codified. The code that they evisaged was one that would be so comprehensive in its coverage as to render lawmaking by judges unnecessary. The code was to serve as a direction to the judges from above. At the outset it was decided that Soviet codification was not to resemble the codification of the first French Empire. The Napoleonic emphasis upon codification for long periods of time, if not for eternity, was to be avoided. The new Soviet code must be flexible and amenable to periodic changes. Once the laws were codified, the judges were to apply the norms of the code and other statutory laws, no matter how inequitable or wicked the results of such application might seem to the judges. The Soviet codifier further had in mind a system in which the judges would lack the authority to interpret legislative law. All requests for statutory interpretation shall be referred to the legislature. The reasoning behind such a rule was that, to the Russian lawmakers, to interpret a statute was tantamount to a legislative activity; and once the new codes were put in place the courts must not be permitted to legislate under any circumstance.

The era of codification of Soviet law began in 1922. If the years 1919–1920 are seen as the years primarily of the accumulation of experience, then 1922–1923 will go down in the history of Soviet law as the years of the reworking and promulgation of the codes. The era of codification needs to be explained not as a retraction from the revolutionary policies of the bridge years, but rather as a natural extension of these formative years of Soviet law. In other words, Russian codification was not a retreat from the revolutionary legislative policies of the bridge years. Rather, it was crystallization of the experience of the judges and of the desire of the lawgivers during the bridge years. The Russian codifiers perceived a code as a legal expression of a political ideology and not merely as an ideologically colorless collection of rules. To them a code was an embodiment of a new political ideology, a perfection of reason, and a self-evident, internally logical restatement of the operational rules in a given area of the law.

Through codification the Russian legislature sought to unify and systematize the laws throughout the country, to consolidate the revolutionary ideology of the new regime, to introduce a more precise formulation into the legal norms, and to update and reform the isolated revolutionary legislation of the bridge years. For the most part, the codes were a legislative reenactment of the jurisprudence of the revolutionary

tribunals during the formative years. The most prominent legal philosopher of the era of codification was
E.B. Pashukanis.

Whereas the prerevolutionary Russian law was dominated by the German school within the civil law tradition—an influence which was passed on to the
post–1917 architects of Soviet law, the drafters of the
new Soviet codes consciously looked to the experience
of the French codifiers for inspiration. What the Sovi-
ets ended up with was a civil code whose provisions
were quite obviously influenced largely by the German
Civil Code, the Swiss Civil Code, and the Russian
Draft Civil Code of 1913, but whose style and language were much closer to those of the French Civil
Code. In many respects the Russian Civil Code of
1922 sought to blend the best elements of German codification with the lofty ideals of the French codes. In
this respect the post–1917 Russian codifiers were un-
willing beneficiaries of the mistakes of their German
and French predecessors.

But whereas the Russian code writers admired the
codification system that was undertaken in revolutionary France, they condemned the phenomenon which
they called the deification of the Napoleonic Code.
Goikhbarg likened the Napoleonic Code to an eccele-
siastical liturgy. By contrast, the drafters of the first
Russian codes perceived an ideal socialist code not as a
legal dogma, but rather as a legal platform for political action. A true socialist code is not intended to last
for all ages. Unlike the Napoleonic Code, the Russian
Civil Code was not designed to serve all sorts of political regimes. A socialist code must continually reflect

alterations in the everchanging political, social, and economic programs of the socialist state which is embarked upon the construction of a communist society. In the view of Goikhbarg, "legislative lawmaking was to be the primary instrument of social restructuring, but it was to be a different kind of legislating from that of bourgeois France. The proletarian codes are not to be eternal, but subject to amendment or replacement when necessary to meet the everchanging needs of a working class in power."

The impact of legal scholars on the development of Soviet law during the bridge years (1917–1920) and during the first wave of codifications (1921–1926) was remarkable. Men like Lenin, Stuchka, Lunacharskii, Goikhbarg, Kozlovskii, and Pashukanis left lasting prints on the life of Soviet law. The reign of legal scholarship in Soviet law ended with the conclusion of the first generation of codification. Thereafter, the influence of jurists on the fate of Soviet law dwindled. In the succeeding years the only jurist that had any influence on the development of Soviet law comparable to that of the early jurists was Andrei Vyshinskii. All the other countries within the socialist legal family, by some accident of history, share a somewhat similar historical linkage with the civil law tradition.

§ 2. The Socialist Legal System as an Autonomous Legal Family

a. *The Nature of the Problem*

For many years students of comparative law have openly debated the issue whether the socialist legal system deserves to be placed in a separate chamber in the house of the law alongside the other two major legal systems of the modern world, *i. e.*, the common law and the civil law. The issue, more specifically, was whether socialist law was sufficiently different from the civil law system as to be segregated from the latter. On this fundamental question there are two major schools of thought among Western scholars— the first school takes the position that socialist law is different enough in its peculiarities as to be granted an independent status vis-à-vis the other two major legal systems. The second school, on the other hand, argues that nothing in socialist law makes it radically different from the civil law. Accordingly, this latter school concludes that socialist law rather represents only a shade of the civil law family just in the same way that one may speak of the French, German or the Latin American variations of the civil law.

We subscribe to the position that socialist law is an autonomous legal system to be essentially distinguished from the other contemporary families of law. We quite agree that when judged by the habit of thinking of lawyers who operate within the system, socialist law is very similar to civil law. But it is equally true that socialist law has since attained some degree of quantitative growth in terms of its substantive provisions. Such internal growth has been such as to make it qualitatively different from the civil law. The qualitative transformation of socialist law into an autonomous system of law took place first in the Soviet Union in the mid-1930s. Thus, in terms of its conceptual framework and the habit of thinking by its principal actors socialist law is of the civil law mold. But, if judged by its substantive provisions it has an entirely different quality from any modern civil law. The conclusion that we reach from this is that socialist law is different from any other principal legal system in its general essence and substantive content, but continues to retain its similarity to the civil law in terms of its external form, internal division, conceptual framework, and habit of thinking adopted by lawyers who operate within it.

b. *Criteria for Categorizing Laws Into Legal Families*

There is no unanimity among Western comparativists as to the criteria to be used in categorizing legal systems into legal families. If one takes just the substantive rules as the criteria for the categorization of legal systems, one may speak of two major groups of law—"bourgeois" or "capitalist" law and socialist law. In this context the bourgeois or capitalist laws would include the civil law and the common law systems. Among the characteristic features of the bourgeois-capitalist group of legal systems, if one were to adopt this dualist approach, are the following fundamental principles of law: the sanctity of private property rights (subject, of course, to a few limitations and regulation); the placement of heavy emphasis on individual freedom and the superimposition of individual interests over those of the society; and the imposition in greater or lesser degrees of constitutional checks and balances on the exercise of governmental power. The essence of all of these devices would be the preservation and perpetuation of the capitalist economic status quo. Judged by these criteria, socialist law stands in direct contrast to bourgeois law. One can fully appreciate the qualities of socialist law only if they are contrasted with the basic features of the other two major legal systems. For a discussion of the comparative characteristic features of the civil law and the common law systems, the reader should turn to Parts Two and Three respectively of this Nutshell.

c.   The Common Core of the Socialist Legal System

The question to be asked in this analysis is: what makes socialist law socialist? In other words, what elements constitute the common core of the socialist legal system? On this latter question there is presently no unanimity among Western commentators. There are three dominant Western schools of thought on the question. The first school lists those elements which are typical only of the socialist legal systems. The second school not only disagrees with some of the elements identified by the first school as endemic to socialist law, but also repudiates the first school's entire approach to the question. Instead, the second school puts forward its own model for comparing socialist law. The major difference between the first two schools is that whereas the first school emphasizes the social, economic and political features of socialist law, the second school tends to accentuate the pseudo-religious aspects of socialist law. The latter proposes that, based on these criteria, one really should be comparing the socialist legal system not with the common law and the civil law systems, but with other religious systems such as Muslim law, canon law, and Talmudic law.

The major fault with these two approaches to the comparison of the socialist legal tradition is that each treats socialist law only and exclusively in terms of either-or, *i. e.*, either as a social-economic-political category or as a pseudo-religious system. Neither of these schools of thought, in our opinion, has come up with a model sufficiently comprehensive to properly identify this multi-dimensional phenomenon known as socialist law.

We take the position that the uniqueness of socialist law lies not only in its social, economic, and political features, but also, and equally so, in its pseudo-religious character. Socialist law concerns itself not only with the political organization of society and the social and economic welfare of the citizens, but also with the spiritual welfare of the individual. To disregard the educational element of socialist law is as incomplete an analysis of socialist law as it is to dismiss the social, economic and political concerns of that system.

Consequently, we propose to treat socialist law in its three dimensions: as a conceptual-formalistic category; as an historical, political, economic, and social category; and as a pseudo-religious category. In each of these categories socialist law has different opposites. When viewed from the standpoint of the first two dimensions, socialist law may be compared with the common and civil law traditions. But when looked at from the third perspective, it is comparable only to such other religious legal systems as Muslim law, canon law, Talmudic law and Hindu law.

d. *Socialist Law as a Conceptual-Formalistic Category*

Socialist law as a conceptual-formalistic category deals with the conceptual framework of the law, with the attitude of socialist courts, and with socialist judicial procedure. From this vantage point, no major differences can be identified between socialist law and the civil law. In this regard socialist law still preserves its civil law roots and, therefore, can be properly contrasted with common law as the valid opposite.

As a conceptual-formalistic category the socialist legal system is characterized by the following features, some of which are borrowed from the civil law: the tradition of codification; legislation is recognized as the preeminent source of law; deductive reasoning; and an inquisitorial procedure. But unlike the situation that prevails under the civil law system, socialist law, for ideological reasons, does not recognize the division of law into public and private law. Rather all law is perceived as public law. Within this arrangement the state professes a legitimate interest in all disputes arising within the society no matter how "private" they may be.

Legal scholarship has never played the same dominant role under the socialist legal system that it played under the civil law system. In direct contrast to the situation which prevailed under the civil law system, socialist legal scholarship was only designed as a rationalizing process by which legal scholars attempt to scientifically justify a particular rule of law or policy adopted by the socialist state. Thus, legal scholarship, instead of being a forerunner of legislation, often acts as its appendage. Much more than their civil law counterparts, socialist courts are conceived, at least in theory, as judicial slot machines whose primary function is to identify and mechanically apply the laws of the state.

With the notable exception of Yugoslavia, judicial review of acts of the legislature is unknown under the socialist legal system. Instead of the doctrine of separation of powers which one finds more or less in all the bourgeois legal systems, socialist legal systems adopt the doctrine of unity of powers.

e. *Socialist Law as an Historical, Political, Economic and Social Category*

The historical mission of socialist law is to advance society toward socialism and ultimately toward communism—the latter being the more advanced stage of socialism. To achieve this goal, socialist law seeks to liquidate all capitalist and feudal forms of property ownership, to consolidate socialist economic relations and to lift domestic relations from the level of capitalist decadence. More than anything else, socialist legal rules are seen as an instrument of social engineering —a weapon in the hands of the political governors aimed at achieving the set political goal through the coercion of general compliance.

Viewed from this perspective, the socialist legal system is characterized by elements such as an uncompromising recognition of the supreme leadership of the omnipotent Communist Party, state ownership of land, and the collectivization of the use of land. One must point out, however, that there are notable variations in the agrarian policies of the individual socialist states. For example, in some of them land is not nationalized and in others agriculture is not collectivized. Other characteristics of socialist law include features such as national economic planning as the central core of economic development, total mobilization of the population for social involvement, less than enthusiastic accommodation of private ownership (here also one notices national variations in each of the socialist systems), and the doctrinal rejection of the Romanist division of law into public and private law.

f. Socialist Law as a Pseudo-Religious Category

Socialist law as a pseudo-religious category stands in contrast to Hindu law, canon law, Talmudic law, and Islamic law. Seen from this vantage point, socialist law is a philosophy of life whose basic task is the fundamental remaking of the conscience of the people. the purpose of this law is, through an intricate network of legal rules, to inculcate in the people such ideals as high moral soundness, unwavering belief in the idealness of life under communism, and self-sacrifice for the common good.

As a pseudo-religious legal system, socialist law operates on the assumption that man has been corrupted by his socio-economic environment and as such has become evil; that the present imperfect man needs to be cleansed of his evil ways and that the task of transforming society from capitalism to communism must be carried out at the same time as the reformation of man himself. Since the present man by virtue of his imperfection cannot live under communism, socialist law implicitly operates on the assumption that only the "new man" may enter the promised land—the lawless state of monolithic tranquility and dynamic equilibrium known as communism. Accordingly, this aspect of socialist law is characterized by its emphasis on the educational role of law. The social goal of this law is to create the new communist man who will not only willingly embrace atheism and look upon religion as an opiate, but also would be purged of all the evil propensities of the present imperfect man.

To accomplish this socialist law mobilizes all available legal, quasi-legal and social institutions for this purpose. These include the courts, the procuracy, the legal professions, the comrades' courts, the people's militia, the auxiliary police force, the trade union organizations, and numerous other social organizations. This system calls upon everyone to be his brother's keeper, to come to the rescue of a fellow citizen in the times of need, and to love one another. Among some of the moral virtues which socialist law seeks to inculcate in the "new man" are love for the fatherland (patriotism), international solidarity among the toiling masses of the world, hatred for the class enemy, unmitigated support for communist party policies, selfless sacrifice for the benefit of society, socialist humanism (*i. e.* humanism that furthers the cause

of socialism and is founded upon socialist moral principles), respect for socialist property, honorable attitude
toward state and social duty, respect for the honor and
dignity of one's fellow citizens and for the rules of socialist communal life, love of one's neighbor, and love
for work and the dignity of labor. Viewed from this
perspective, socialist law does not merely seek to regulate legal relations as of today, but more importantly,
it seeks to prepare society for the ultimate demise of
law.

As a pseudo-religious category socialist law is not a
science. Some of its intrinsic tenets are neither scientific nor internally logical. A juxtaposition of some of
its legislative principles indicates that it is replete with
inconsistencies. Perhaps that is purposefully so. The
discipline it most closely parallels is probably theology.
As an instrument of social engineering as well as a
doctrine of redemption it operates on the premise that
if you can affect the belief of the people and make
them think a new magic has been found, even if your
reasoning is all wrong, you can probably change the
system. In a sense it is a challenge of faith. It is
dogmatic, yet pragmatic at times.

In conclusion, we do concede the fact that the roots
of the socialist legal system are traceable to the civil
law system. This in itself may have been one of the
greatest accidents of history. As it happened, Marxian socialist revolutions spread only to those countries
which, before the revolution, were members of the civil law family. But, what is perhaps more noteworthy
here is that while embarking upon a comprehensive re-
construction of their social, economic, and political sys-

tems, these countries saw fit to retain the civil law infrastructure of their prerevolutionary legal systems. The result of this unique and unprecedented experiment in legal transplantation is the creation of a legal tradition that is qualitatively different from the one from which it so heavily borrowed.

One of the elements of radical departure of contemporary socialist law from the civil law is the fact that under the socialist legal system private law has lost its Romanist preeminence and all law is now considered to be public law. Also, the professional bench in the civil law tradition has been democratized and socialized in the socialist legal tradition. Under the socialist legal system, law is totally subordinated to the prevailing socio-economic and political conditions. Law is only a conduit between politics and economics and to that effect law is immediately preempted whenever it conflicts with overriding economic or political considerations. In short, the socialist legal tradition is civil law à la Marxism-Leninism. Nevertheless, it is an autonomous legal tradition in its own right.

§ 3. Marxism-Leninism on the Nature and Functions of Law

Among the major contributions of socialist law to comparative jurisprudence is its general theory on the nature and functions of law. Socialist legal thinking on these questions was essentially shaped by the writings of Karl Marx, Frederick Engels and Vladimir Lenin. Subsequent Soviet and other socialist legal thinkers have made contributions to this general theory. In this section of the analysis we propose to search the Marxian theory of law for answers to the following critical questions: What is law? What is the nature of the relationship between law, politics, economics and morality? What is the relationship between natural law and positive law? Must law incorporate public morality for it to be legitimate? Is an immoral law law at all? Under what circumstances, if any, do citizens have the right to disobey the law? Is there a zone of individual privacy that ought to be precluded from legal regulation? Will there be law under communism?

Generally speaking, Marxist-Leninist theory on the origin, nature, and functions of law may be reduced to the following fundamental tenets: The present man is imperfect and evil by nature; his imperfection, however, is historical and arose directly as a result of his socio-economic and political environment; law is a coercive order or a sovereign command, not a set of rules imposed by the people from below or a set of rules which spring from within the group; law, as an historical phenomenon, emerged as an instrument for regulating the external conduct of the evil man; man's evil nature resulted from and was sustained by the exploitative nature of the environment created by the slave-owning society, feudalism, and capitalism; even though a causal connection no longer exists between the environment under socialism and man's evil nature, the socialist man is nevertheless still imperfect primarily as a result of the cumulative effect of the past environments on his inner being; the historical mission of socialist law is to cleanse man of his evil nature and to prepare him for the ultimate demise of law under communism. In other words, since the present man was corrupted by his environment, the task of socialist law is to remold man in his original image. To return to his original, pre-law state of being is to prepare him for life in a post-law society.

A second set of fundamental tenets of Marxian jurisprudence includes the following: Because law is an order emanating from the sovereign lawgiver, an individual citizen has no right to disobey the law whether on the ground of conscientious objection or as a form of civil disobedience; law selectively incorporates certain rules of morality, but the legitimacy of law does not derive from its moral base; even though the laws of a bourgeois society are immoral in absolute terms and even though the laws of a socialist society, on the other hand, come closest to reflecting the morality of the majority, an immoral law is law nevertheless; and the province of the law is all-embracing and all-encompassing. Accordingly, there is no zone of individual privacy that is precluded from legal regulation. A lawmaker, however, may impose certain limitations on his power to legislate on certain matters of individual privacy. Subject to such self-imposed restraints, the power of the sovereign to legislate is absolute. No area of human conduct lies outside the reach of the long arms of the law. As to the relationship between natural law and positive law, the Marxist-Leninist does not share the view that natural law is superior to the laws of man. To him no law stands above positive law. To him the power of the sovereign to enact laws is neither governed by any divine destiny nor is it subject to any limitation imposed by a non-existent divine law. In Lenin's characterization "law is, in the final analysis, a political pressure. It is concentrated politics." In the words of Frederick Engels, "In the final analysis, everything that is legal is rooted in politics."

In other words, to the Marxist-Leninist *lex est ancilla politicae* [law is the ancillary of politics]. In socialist literature law is defined as "a system of universally binding norms, guaranteed by the state and reflecting the will of the governing class in a given state but which, upon the triumph of socialism, reflects the will of all the people". A more pedantic definition of law, provided by a socialist commentator, suggests that "Law is an internally interconnected totality of rules of human conduct in a given society, which are either established or enforced by the state, are predetermined by the dominant economic relationships in the given society, reflect the will of the governing classes (or of the whole people in the case of a socialist society), are designed to regulate social relationships in the given society, and are guaranteed enforcement through the invocation of the coercive powers of the state." These definitions fully embody the dominant Marxist-Leninist teachings on the nature and functions of law. To the Marxist-Leninist, law is an historical phenomenon, a class category, an element of the superstructure, an active conduit between the economic basis and the rest of the superstructure, and an instrument of social engineering. The contents of law are determined by economics and law itself is ancillary to politics. Accordingly, law is not and cannot be apolitical or neutral to class consciousness.

To the Marxist-Leninist the emergence and continued existence of law is inseparably linked with the emergence and continued existence of the state. To him the state is an organization of the political power of the ruling class, a specific form of political organization through which the governing class asserts its authority over the entire society. But under advanced socialism the state is perceived as the organization of the political power of the whole people. Like law, the state is an historical phenomenon. It is not eternal. In the primitive society when there were no economic classes and no notions of private property there was no state. Historically speaking, the state arose only after the emergence of private property and the resultant division of society into antagonistic economic classes. The state was devised as a machine for the preservation of the dictatorship of one class over another. Thanks to the device known as the state, the economically dominant class also acquired political dominance over the economically powerless class. The state, like law, is an element of the superstructure. Its nature and form are predetermined and preconditioned by the economic basis over which it is superimposed. But because the relationship which exists between the state and the economic basis is of a dialectical nature, the state also exerts reciprocal influence on the development of its own economic basis.

Socialist law operates as its own grave-digger. By consciously engineering the advent of communism it lays the groundwork for its own demise. The fact that there would be no laws under communism should not be taken to mean that anarchy would reign in that society. All it means is that law will be replaced by a system of rules of communist morality to be enforced through a system of orchestrated social pressure. In order to prepare society for the ultimate replacement of law with rules of communist morality, it is anticipated that during socialism the rigid demarcation between legal norms and moral rules would be gradually eliminated. It follows, therefore, that one of the characteristic tendencies of the development of socialist law is the gradual but programmed convergence of the rules of law and morality. Thus, whereas socialist law started out by incorporating the rules of morality prevailing among the governing majority classes, it is expected to end its development by being fully assimilated into the rules of communist morality.

The envisaged state of affairs under communism is deceptively similar to the conditions that prevailed during the primitive society. In both societies, economic classes, private property, the state, and law were or would be nonexistent. In both systems governance was or would be by non-legal rules of morality. Because of the consensual nature of these rules, they would or would not be enforced through any form of external coercion. These similarities have prompted some commentators to refer to the early society as a form of early communism. To the Marxist-Leninist, however, the early society represented not communism, but communalism. It is at best a form of primitive communism.

§ 4. The Distribution of Socialist Law

The Soviet system is the oldest national legal system within the socialist legal family. The system itself dates back to 1917, but it did not fully mature into a distinct socialist law until the mid-1930s. The Soviet model has since been adopted in different parts of the world, ranging from Eastern Europe to central and southeast Asia to the Caribbean region and to some parts of Africa. Whereas the English language is virtually the *lingua franca* of the common law system, the socialist legal system, like the civil law system, has not evolved a *lingua franca*. The Russian language, however, is the most influential as well as the most internationally used language within the family of socialist law.

The groups of countries that have received socialist law may be divided into two major categories, *i. e.*, the older socialist countries and the new or emerging socialist states. The following countries fall within the first category: Poland, Bulgaria, Hungary, Czechoslovakia, Romania, Yugoslavia, the German Democratic Republic, Albania, the People's Republic of China, the People's Republic of Vietnam, the People's Democratic Republic of Korea, Mongolia, and Cuba. The Mongolian system is the oldest national legal system within this sub-group, and the youngest is Cuba. Of every ten persons in the world today six live under socialist law.

Among the new or emerging socialist legal systems of the modern world are: Democratic Republic of Kampuchea (Cambodia), Laos, Mozambique, Angola,

Somalia, Libya, Ethiopia, Guinea, and Guyana. It is perhaps worth noting that of all the countries in both groups of socialist legal systems, only Guyana had a non-civil law prerevolutionary legal system. As a former British colony Guyana had a common law system prior to independence. Some people may wish to include Tanzania within this second group of new socialist states. Tanzania has infused a number of socialist notions into its legal system, but nevertheless the post-independence Tanzanian legal system has not undergone sufficient qualitative transformation to qualify it for inclusion within the family of new socialist legal systems. At this point Tanzania's flirtations with the traditions of socialist law do not affect the core of that country's legal system.

CHAPTER 13

LEGAL STRUCTURES

The administration of law in a socialist system is an extremely complex process. Unlike the administration of law in a traditional Western system, it is not a monopoly of the governmental agencies. It is not uncommon for an entire branch of socialist law to be administered totally by a nongovernmental organization by virtue of blanket delegation from the socialist state. This is the situation with labor law which, along with other related social legislations, is wholly administered by the trade union organizations. The administration of the other branches of socialist law, *e. g.*, criminal law and administrative law, is shared among governmental agencies and nongovernmental organizations. Because of this idiosyncratic element of the socialist legal system, any discussion of the administration of socialist law cannot be confined to an analysis of traditional legal institutions.

The institutions discussed here exist in all of the socialist legal systems even though they may go by different names. The forms of intervention by the respective communist parties in the administration of the relevant national laws may vary in degree as one moves from one system to another. The essence of such intervention, however, is the same in all of the socialist legal systems.

[*285*]

§ 1. The Communist Party

In each socialist country there is typically only one political party, *i. e.*, the Communist Party. In the few socialist systems where there is a multiparty system, all the other political parties, as a condition of their permission to operate, must acknowledge the leading role of the Communist Party. The Communist Party's influence over the administration of law in a socialist state is as dominant and pervasive as it is over law-making. That role may be reduced to the three basic functions of the party as political guardian, moral tutor, and keeper of the socialist legal conscience. Within the socialist legal system the Party is as omnipotent as its is omnipresent. Nevertheless, the Party maintains a parallel existence with the socialist state. Technically speaking, the Party machine is not an integral part of the legal superstructure, and the Party ideological decisions and directives that have not been formally received into the law are not an organic part of the state's legal norms.

The relationship between Party policy decisions and the state's legal norms is quite similar in many respects to the relationship between equity and the common law under the English legal system. Just in the same way that equity is a gloss over common law, so are the Communist Party decisions a gloss over the state's legal rules. Just in the same way that a rule of common law must yield if it conflicts with a principle of equity, any legal rule that is inconsistent with an ideological principle of the Party must yield to the latter. Until there is a total disappearance of laws in the socialist state, Party norms must of necessity lean on the state's legal norms just in the same way that equity cannot exist today without the prerequisite backup from the common law. However, unlike the situation in English law where the administration of equity has since been transferred to the common law courts, Party policies that have not been incorporated into the state's legal norms are enforced not by the regular courts, but by a parallel system of Party machinery.

From yet another perspective the Communist Party is to the socialist legal system what the brain is to the human body. Like the human brain the Party neither seeks to displace nor to compete with all the other instrumentalities of the state body politic. Vis-à-vis all the other institutions within the socialist legal system, *i. e.*, the legislative, executive and judicial agencies, the Party operates very much as did the *deus ex machina* in Greek mythology. It is the only thinking organ within the socialist system. Once it has thought out what is best for the society, it sends out impulses through its numerous tentacles to the various appendages of the socialist legal body. Once those "messages" are received they are carried out by the respective addressee through a process which is tantamount to a reflex action. The Party stands behind every legislative activity in the socialist state. It directly oversees the execution and implementation of legislative policies throughout the country. It hovers over the adjudicative processes at all levels of the judicial system.

In discussing the role of the Party within the socialist legal system, a third analogy that readily comes to mind is that of papal infallibility in Catholic theology. Because the Party is the preeminent interpreter of the material sources of socialist law, it is generally regarded as being infallible in these matters. In promulgating its ideological policies, the Party derives inspiration and guidance from a higher law, *i. e.*, the laws of dialectical and historical materialism. The principle of the infallibility of the Party is functionally equivalent to the doctrine of papal infallibility.

The constitutional status of the Party has no parallel in any Western legal system. The Party is for all practical purposes not only extra-constitutional, but also supra-constitutional in the sense that it neither derives its authority from the state constitution nor is the exercise of its inherent powers meaningfully limited by constitutional constraints. The leadership role of the Communist Party is too complex to be reduced to any constitutional formulas. Perhaps the best way to describe the role of the Party within the socialist political system is to regard it as the mind, the honor and the conscience of the socialist society. Socialist legal norms merely capture this political reality.

The life of the Party is governed by two basic documents, notably, the Program of the Party and the Rules (Constitution) of the Party. The former maps out the path for the future development of the Party, whereas the latter regulates the detailed aspects of life within the Party. The Party Constitution is a more elastic and dynamic document. As an operational document it changes more frequently than does the Party program. From its inception the Party is designed to be an elitist rather than a mass organization.

At any given time the membership of the Party ranges from 15–25 percent of the total adult population of the given socialist state.

In order to maintain its operational distance from the state apparatus without losing touch with the latter, the Party has devised numerous methods of asserting its leadership role with respect to the state agencies. These include promulgation of policy directives and instructions that are binding on the state agencies, the exercise of control over personnel matters in all state agencies, the exercise of general supervision (oversight) over the day-to-day activities of the state agencies, and the establishment of Party groups within every state agency and social organization.

The most important problems of state, society, and economics must be solved in the light of Party directives and instructions. The Party, on the other hand, exercises its monopoly over personnel policy in the various state agencies by reserving to itself the right to appoint to key positions the most qualified individuals who are devoted to the communist cause. Within every state agency there is a nomenclature list indicating the positions which can only be filled on the basis of a Party recommendation. The Party must be consulted both before appointments are made, and before any dismissal. There is thus some assurance that these state agencies will only appoint individuals prescribed by the Party, mostly on the basis of the nomenclature list. Party secrecy rules prohibit any member from disclosing even the existence of a Party nomenclature list. Personnel policy orders issued by the Party must be obeyed, including positions which are filled by elections.

In exercise of its general supervision over the activities of the individual state agencies, the party points out the defects in the activity of corresponding organs of state and instructs the latter on ways to eliminate them. In all state agencies a Party group is established if there are at least three members of the Party. The task of these Party groups is to intensify the influence of the Party within the agency in question and to implement party policies among nonparty members inside such agencies. In all of their activities Party groups within such bodies are guided by the Rules (Constitution) and Program of the Party.

§ 2. The Trade Union Organizations

In all of the socialist states typically there is one national organization of all the individual trade unions. This nongovernmental (though not necessarily independent of government control) trade union organization monopolizes the right to represent the interest of all the workers. It operates in close alliance with the Communist Party and the state. Recent developments in Poland (*i. e.*, the establishment of trade union organizations that are independent of government control) make that country an exception rather than the norm in matters of trade union-state relationships. For the purpose of this analysis we shall treat the Polish situation as an aberration.

The official socialist national organization of trade unions (NOTU) performs functions that are essentially governmental in nature. Key positions within the organization are concentrated in the hands of Communist Party members. The socialist countries reject the "principle of professionalism" as the basis for organizing workers and instead adopt the so-called "production principle".

Broadly speaking, the NOTU functions as a school of administration and economic management, a platform for the exercise of the workers' right of legislative initiative, a mechanism for protecting the legal rights and interests of workers, administrator of the state social insurance and pensions benefits, administrator of holiday and health resorts, co-administrator of housing for workers, a mechanism for cultural education of workers, promoter and organizer of sporting events, and promoter of the foreign policy of the country concerned.

As the school for administration and economic management, the NOTU provides the workers with an unprecedented opportunity to participate actively in the administration of certain governmental social services as well as in the management of the national economy. As a platform for the exercise of the workers' right of legislative initiative, the NOTU affords the workers the opportunity to participate in the preparation and drafting of major social legislation which directly affects labor and labor relations. This right empowers the NOTU to propose legislation before the national parliaments. What all of this means is that the NOTUs are granted an official standing within the legislative processes: they may propose new legislation and comment on draft legislation which is initiated by government agencies.

As a mechanism for protecting the legal rights and interests of workers, the NOTU constantly seeks to improve the living and working conditions of trade union members. NOTU performs its protective functions through a combination of methods including participation in the formulation of all governmental policies directed at improving workers' wages as well as at material and moral incentives to workers, and oversight over the implementation and observance of labor legislation relating to work safety and labor standards. Also, as part of its protective functions, NOTU monitors the actions of the management to make sure that the latter observes state norms relating to working hours and vacations. Another method by which the NOTU protects the interests of workers is through the negotiation and conclusion of collective bargaining agreements.

The NOTU serves as the sole administrator of state social insurance and pension benefits. As a mechanism for cultural education of workers, the NOTU works in close collaboration with the Communist Party in the creation of the "new man". As the promoter and organizer of sporting events, the NOTU organizes various sporting activities for its members. In collaboration with the State Committee on Physical Education and Sports and with the Central Committee of the Communist Youth Organizations, the NOTU directs all sporting activities throughout the country.

Lastly, the NOTU serves as an instrument of the given country's foreign policy. According to its charter, NOTU considers itself to be an integral part of the international trade union movement. The NOTU maintains special contacts with the NOTUs in the other socialist countries. Card-carrying members of NOTUs are routinely included on the staffs of the embassies, foreign trade missions, consulates, and diplomatic missions of the respective socialist countries.

The role of the NOTUs in the administration of socialist law can best be illustrated by noting the fact that the typical NOTU performs tasks which, under the present United States law, are allotted to various federal departments and agencies such as the United States Department of Labor, the National Labor Relations Board, the Department of Health and Human Services, the Department of Education, the Department of Housing and Urban Development, the Civil Service Commission, and the Occupational Safety and Health Administration. In addition to performing the functions of the above-named governmental agencies and departments, NOTUs also subsume all of the functions of the American trade union organizations.

The fact that the NOTU is virtually an instrumentality of the socialist state raises the question of whether it can effectively represent the interests of its members in those situations in which workers' demands run counter to those of the government and management. The traditional response to such question by the socialist governments is that because the socialist state is a workers' state the interests of the state are never antagonistic to those of the workers. The history of trade union-state relationships in the socialist countries belies such an assertion.

§ 3. The Legislature

In theory, socialist constitutional law rejects the doctrine of the separation of powers into the three traditional departments of government. The rationale for such rejection is that, it is argued, the socialist state has a special mission to perform and that in doing so, it cannot afford to build artificial walls separating one branch of government from the other. Under this socialist view all the departments of government must work in unity and usually under the guidance of the Communist Party. In practice, however, socialist constitutions adopt systems of government which amount to a functional separation of powers among the three departments of government. The philosophical underpinnings nevertheless are quite different from the rationale which underlies the separation of powers under the American constitutional system.

Very clearly, the legislature is supreme, followed by the executive branch. The judiciary is regarded as the least dangerous branch of government. In short, the socialist states adhere to the doctrine of unity of powers in principle, but in practice devise a system of functional separation of powers among three unequal departments of government all of which operate under the general political guidance of the Party.

Generally speaking, the legislative branch of the socialist government is inferior only to the Communist Party and to the state constitution. This means that acts of the legislature must conform to provisions of the constitution and must not conflict with the Party policy line. This does not mean that the legislature cannot amend the constitution. It certainly can and usually does. But until the constitution is amended the legislature must conform its legislative acts to the prescriptions of the constitution which operates as the supreme law of the land.

The socialist parliament is a "working organ" in the sense that it is not a body of professional politicians, it meets only once or twice each year, its sessions last from three to seven days during each meeting, it may meet in extraordinary sessions if circumstances so demand, the members retain their jobs while they serve in the parliament, but they are compensated for expenses incurred in connection with their performance of their parliamentary duties. To qualify for election to parliament one does not necessarily have to be a member of the Communist Party. In the federal socialist systems (*i. e.*, U.S.S.R., Yugoslavia and Czechoslovakia) it is not unusual for the same person to be elected to the federal and state legislatures at the same time.

In the federal systems where the federal parliaments have two chambers with equal power, no one chamber has more power or a wider jurisdiction than the other on any question. The unitary states, however, as a rule have only one-chamber legislatures.

The typical socialist parliament has many members in comparison with its Western counterparts. For example, the USSR Supreme Soviet has 1500 deputies.

Because of the large size of the socialist parliament, coupled with the fact that the legislature meets only once or twice per year, legislative committees are formed and meet on a regular basis. The committees are responsible for a thorough study of all legislative proposals. By the time the parliament convenes, they prepare the bills to be presented to the full house. Additionally, the socialist legislature typically creates an executive organ within itself. The designation of such executive organs of the legislature (not to be confused with the executive branch of government) varies from state to state, *e. g.*, presidium (in the U.S.S.R., Bulgaria and Albania), standing committee (in the P.R.C. and Viet Nam), council of state (in Poland), etc. The executive organ is a working arm of the legislature. Its members are elected by and from among members of parliament. It sits all year round and acts as caretaker while the full house is in recess. It is quite uncommon for a deputy who is not a member of the Communist Party to be elected to serve on this executive organ.

§ 4. The Executive

The executive department is the second most important functional branch of a socialist government. It assumes different names in different socialist countries, *i. e.*, the council of ministers (U.S.S.R.), the federal executive council (Yugoslavia), the government (Albania), the state council (P.R.C.) and the cabinet (Korea), etc.

The difference in their designations notwithstanding, the executive institutions occupy the same position within the socialist constitutional structure, *i. e.*, they execute the laws and the general program of socio-economic and political development as promulgated by the legislature and by the Communist Party.

All the socialist countries have a cabinet of parliamentarians. This means that all members of the cabinet are required to be members of, appointed by, accountable to, and may be voted out of office by the parliament. The chairman of the cabinet is responsible for coordinating the activities of the various ministries (cabinet departments). He recommends individuals who may serve in his cabinet.

In addition to the ministries, there are state committees which perform almost identical functions with the ministries. Generally, the state committees are created to take charge of highly sensitive or highly specialized areas of state government. Sometimes state committees are organized within the administrative system of a cabinet department. Some of the chairmen of the state committees are ex officio members of the cabinet. On the whole, the state committees are quite similar to the independent administrative agencies in the United States. Examples of notable Soviet state committees are the State Committee on Science and Technology, the State Committee of Cinematography, the State Committee on Press and the Television, the State Committee on Printing and Publication and the Committee on State Security (KGB).

§ 5. Judicial and Quasi-Judicial Institutions

a. Regular Courts (General Civil and Criminal Jurisdiction)

To a considerable extent the quality of justice under any national legal system depends upon the quality of the principal legal actors under that system, *i. e.*, members of the bench and bar. However, in inquisitorial systems such as those of the socialist states, the quality of the members of the bar has relatively less impact on the outcome of a case before a court than does the quality of the members of the bench. In other words, the quality of justice in socialist courts, to an extent that is even far greater than would be the case under an adversary system, depends on the calibre of the judges.

In many respects the socialist judicial system is similar to, but at the same time quite distinguishable from, those of the major continental European systems, noticeably those of France and Germany. The system of courts in the individual socialist countries depends, among other things, on whether the country in question is a federal or unitary state. In some of the federal states [USSR and Czechoslovakia] there are both federal and state courts. Typically, the courts are structured into three hierarchies, *i. e.* courts of original jurisdiction, intermediate courts of appeal and the supreme courts. Only one country within the socialist legal system (Yugoslavia) has a supreme constitutional court which has jurisdiction to review acts of the legislature for conformity with the basic law.

The socialist judiciary is stripped of the trappings of the black-robed infallibility generally associated with the common law judiciary. Neither in theory nor in practice is the socialist court regarded as a co-equal branch of the socialist government. Rather, it is inferior both to the legislature and to the executive branch of government. It is in every respect the least dangerous branch of the socialist government. In light of this lowly position of the courts, judicial activism has no place in the socialist legal system. Accordingly, the socialist court must bow to the legislative command however absurd, however unjust, and however wicked.

In essence, therefore, the primary function of the socialist court is to apply a predetermined law to the facts of a given case. The respective supreme courts have the extra function of superintending and coordinating the general application of law as well as synthesizing the general principles of that law. This is not to say, however, that the socialist judge always operates like a judicial slot machine. He may be, in a few instances, a creative adjudicator. This is especially so in the area of tort law where statutory law has been known to follow case law. Also, it must always be borne in mind that the socialist court is both a court of law and of justice. However, it dispenses not neutral or classless or apolitical justice, but socialist justice which is "justice with a touch of class." What this means is that the socialist judge is required in each case to consider whether or not a judgment would further the cause of communism.

It seems that there is a contradiction between the assertion that judicial activism has no place in the socialist system and the view that the socialist court does not always behave like a judicial slot machine. The contradiction is only apparent. Depending on the ascertainable intention of the omnipotent legislator, the socialist judge may behave either as a judicial slot machine or as a creative adjudicator.

In the exercise of its enlightened discretion the socialist legislature delegates some discretion to the judge, but in doing so it defines the outer perimeters of such discretion. The judge is thereby authorized to tailor the judgment in the case to meet the particular circumstances of the case. This is particularly so in criminal law where the statute establishes the minimum and maximum punishments, but delegates to the judge the power to determine the exact punishment for individual cases. In the area of private law the legislature endows the judge with the power to construe and enforce contracts in such a way as to educate the parties and to further the cause of communism. In all of these instances the discretion of the judge is defined, structured, and confined by the legislature.

Where the lawmaker wishes to strip the judge of all discretionary authority, it simply adopts a peremptory norm. This is the case when the norm of constitutional or criminal or family law imposes certain specific duties on citizens. In the latter set of cases the socialist judge has no choice but to enforce such duties even if he thinks that they are inherently unjust or irreconcilable with his conscience.

In short, the difference between a socialist judge and a common law judge is that, unlike the latter, the socialist judge cannot invoke the principle of equity or of natural justice, to set aside an applicable (and readily ascertainable) statutory law. Unlike the American judge, the socialist judge cannot create new constitutional rights by simply asserting that these fall within the penumbras of or are ancillary to or derivative from enumerated constitutional rights. Unlike the common law judge, the socialist judge does not have any inherent equity jurisdiction. He resorts to *aequum et bonum* only if specifically authorized to do so by statute, and this generally happens only if and when there is no law to apply in the case.

Under the general heading of "regular courts", all courts which exercise general civil and criminal jurisdiction have been included here. At the lowest level within the regular court system (people's district courts) the same judges, with minor variations in certain localities, generally handle both civil and criminal cases. This tends to require the people's district court judges to become generalists in the law since they handle civil and criminal cases on alternate days. Further up the judicial ladder, one begins to notice some sort of specialization among the judges. As a rule the superior courts are organized into chambers with different judges sitting in the respective chambers. The jurisdiction of the regular courts is carefully delineated by statute from those of the numerous quasi-judicial agencies that are also charged with the settlement of disputes.

Among the miscellaneous general principles of socialist court organization are the fact that all the judges of the regular courts are elected, are accountable to their electors, are independent and subservient only to the law, as well as the requirement that all trial courts must sit in panels which must include lay judges. Even though all the judges are civil servants in the sense that they are administratively part of the civil service and are integrated into the system of the Ministry of Justice, all the judges of all levels of the court system are elected. Because of the "principle of accountability" all judges are required to give periodic reports of their activities to the bodies that elected them. Any individual judge who is found to be incapable of carrying out his judicial commission may be recalled by his electors prior to the completion of his term of office. The "principle of independence" means, among other things, that criminal action may not be initiated against a judge or a lay assessor, nor may he be arrested or removed from office without the prior consent of an official of the corresponding legislative council. Under "the principle of collegiality" whenever a court acts as a court of first instance the law requires that the proceedings must include participation by lay assessors, generally in the ratio of one judge and two lay assessors.

In the trial courts the judges as well as the lay assessors decide both questions of law and fact. The lay assessors have the same procedural standing as does .the law judge, *i.e.*, they have equal access to all the facts in the case, access to all the evidence and the right to vote on questions of law and fact. Decisions by the trial court are taken by a simple majority vote. Before the members of the court vote on the issues of law, the law judge generally instructs the lay assessors on the law of the case. But generally the law judge votes last so that his authority would not influence the opinion of the lay assessors. Because of the majority rule it follows that, in principle, the two lay assessors can combine to outvote the law judge. But in practice this rarely happens. The law judge is generally the dominant figure on the bench; and he, by virtue of his "power of persuasion", tends to lead the court to go his way. The law judge also presides at the trial, but the privilege of presiding may be assigned to any one of the lay judges. In the true sense of the term the law (presiding) judge is the governor of the trial proceedings and it will be very rare indeed for the law judge to find himself in the minority on any question of law or fact voted upon by the court.

Like the law judge, the lay assessors are all elected. Periodically, a pool of lay assessors is elected throughout the country. A lay assessor may not be required to serve for more than two weeks per year unless, in the interest of preserving the continuity of the bench during a particular trial, a lay assessor is required to do so in order to complete a trial in progress. Like the law judge, the lay assessors are accountable to and removable by those who elected them. Membership of the Communist Party is not a prerequisite for election as a judge or lay assessor. In practice, however, a disproportionate number of Communist Party members are elected to these positions.

b. Economic Courts

In the socialist system the economic courts operate as a separate quasi-judicial pyramid apart from that of the regular courts. They culminate in one supreme court, the supreme economic court. Like the regular court the economic court is a collegial body, and the procedure they employ is quite similar to that of the regular courts. However, there are more dissimilarities than there are similarities between these two sets of courts. The economic courts operate more as courts of arbitration than as regular courts. Whereas the regular courts tend to apply "law" in the narrow sense of the term, the economic courts resort to extra-legal rules such as economic plans as their main body of applicable law. Unlike the regular courts which operate as a separate department of the socialist government alongside the legislative and executive department, the economic courts are administratively integrated into the executive department of government. In other words, the economic courts are instrumentalities of the executive branch of the Soviet government.

There are other noteworthy differences between the economic courts and the regular courts. All levels of the regular courts are stripped of all lawmaking powers, but the supreme economic court is typically entrusted with some lawmaking powers, notably the authority to promulgate rules of procedure for the inferior economic courts. In a regular court the presiding judge is usually a trained lawyer who at trial is joined by two lay assessors, while in the economic court the permanent arbitrator is not a lawyer. He is

most likely to be a chemist, an engineer or an econo-
mist. At trial he is joined not by two impartial lay assessors, but by two partisan representatives of the
parties in the dispute. Further, in a regular court the
presiding judge as well as the lay assessors are elected, but the arbitrators who sit in the economic courts
are appointed.

In order to fully appreciate the value of the economic courts within the socialist legal system, one has to
understand the role of economic planning. Socialist
economic development is guided by economic planning.
Periodically, the state adopts an economic plan for the
development of the national economy over a period of
time, often five years. Based on this general plan
each affected enterprise is required to enter into a
"plan contract" with another related enterprise for the
supply of the raw materials needed to meet its production plan. All disputes arising from such planning
contracts are resolved by the economic courts set up
specifically for this purpose. The regular courts play
no role in resolving these "economic" disputes.

There are many policy reasons for removing planning contract disputes from the jurisdiction of the regular courts. A thorough understanding of the nature
of these economic disputes calls for a special expertise
which the regular courts do not have. Additionally
the resolution of the disputes calls for speed which the
regular courts cannot provide because of the multiple
appellate reviews that exist within the regular court
system. The rules governing the construction of planning contracts are somewhat different from those
used in the interpretation of private contracts. Gener-

ally, in interpreting a planning contract, an economic court attempts to balance the economic interests of the state agencies concerned against the overall interests of the state as a whole.

c. Labor Courts

Alongside the regular courts most socialist countries also operate a system of labor courts to handle all contentious labor disputes between the management and an individual employee. These labor courts go by different names in the different socialist systems. For example, in the Soviet Union they are referred to as commissions on labor disputes. Typically, these courts are administratively integrated into the local trade union organizations. They handle only disputes arising from an individual worker's employment contract. Prominent among disputes that are not assigned to the jurisdiction of the labor courts are disputes arising out of collective bargaining agreements. Decisions of labor courts are generally appealable by either party to the regular courts. Specific statutes may grant original jurisdiction over certain labor disputes to the regular courts. The trade union organization and the administration of the enterprise nominate equal number of arbitrators to sit on these labor courts. Typically, lawyers neither sit as judges (arbitrators) on these courts nor serve as counsel before these courts.

d. Administrative Courts

In an effort to reduce the caseload of the regular courts the socialist countries have devised a parallel system of administrative courts, which in the different countries assume different names, such as administrative commissions.   These administrative courts, however, do not constitute a separate pyramid from the regular court system, in the sense that there is no separate supreme administrative court comparable to the French Council of State.   In special instances, appeals from the decision of an administrative court may be taken to the regular courts.   Like the economic courts these administrative courts are operationally an integral part of the executive department of government.

The jurisdiction of the administrative courts is intentionally limited to minor administrative offenses committed by individual citizens or officials.   The administrative courts, for example, are neither authorized to entertain suits by private citizens against the government resulting from injury suffered as a result of the actions of a governmental agency nor empowered to hear employee grievances against the government. Typically, there is no single statute that lists the types of cases that may go before the administrative courts. Rather, individual courts are generally organized at the levels of the regional, city and village councils. Structurally, they function as organs of and are supervised by the executive committees of the corresponding legislative councils.   The court consists of members of the corresponding legislative councils who are assigned to serve on them along with representatives of the various social organizations.   A court generally consists of a president, one vice president, a secretary and not fewer than four regular members of the court. The chairman or vice chairman of the executive committee of the corresponding legislative council serves as the *ex officio* chairman of the court. The term of office of the members of the administrative court corresponds to the term of office of the respective legislative council. The administrative courts are responsible to and accountable before their supervising executive committees of the legislative councils.

The defendant before an administrative court enjoys a certain measure of due process rights. He has, among other rights, the right to familiarize himself with the materials of the case, to offer explanations to the charges, to call witnesses, and to confront adverse witnesses at the hearing. Glaringly absent from the due process rights which the offender enjoys before an administrative court is the right to counsel. In an effort not to totally "judicialize" proceedings before these courts, the law does not grant a defendant a right to the assistance of counsel, whether retained or appointed. The defendant must act as his own counsel in all proceedings before the commission.

Depending on the nature of the administrative violation, an administrative court may either issue a written or oral warning to the defendant or assess a fine against him. If the violation is job-related the warning is entered in his employment file. The court may impose any other sanction established by the statute under which the defendant was tried and convicted, and in appropriate instances, may transfer the case to a comrade's court for the application of a less stringent "measure of social pressure".

e. Comrades' Courts

The comrades' courts are a permanent fixture in all of the socialist systems. The functions of these courts roughly correspond to those of a small claims court in an American jurisdiction. But the functions of the comrades' courts go far beyond those of an American small claims court. In addition to handling minor disputes among citizens the comrades' court serves as a universal enforcer of the rules of communist morality. They are courts of the future in the sense that they now operate as an understudy for the regular courts and are intended to replace the regular courts once the society attains full communism. The procedure before these courts is extremely informal, substantially inquisitorial, speedy and specifically designed to reform the defendant as well as educate the public at large.

Officially, the comrades' courts are designated as social organizations. In reality, however, these courts enjoy a semi-official status in the sense that the general structure, organization and functions of the comrades' courts are regulated by statute, their activities are subject to general procuratorial oversight, and some of their activities overlap those of state agencies with corresponding functions. The operational direction and coordination of the activities of the comrades' courts are carried out both by the executive committee of the corresponding legislative council as well as by the local trade union organization.

The comrades' courts have many notable features. Prominent among them is the fact that they are non-professional, quasi-judicial tribunals staffed by neighbors and fellow workers. Branches of the comrades' courts are set up in factories, enterprises, apartment buildings, neighborhoods, colleges and universities, collective (cooperative) farms, villages, as well as among any other identifiable group of citizens with at least 50 persons. However, in individual instances, with the consent of the superior trade union organ or of the executive committee of a corresponding local council, comrades' courts may be set up in collectives where there are fewer than 50 persons.

Because the comrades' courts proceedings are deemed to be of a noncriminal nature, they cannot hand down a criminal punishment. They may demand a public apology, give a comradely warning, social censure or a social reprimand with or without publication in the press, extract a small fine, recommend to the appropriate administration to fire, demote, or transfer the offender, recommend eviction of an offender from a public housing project, or recommend that an official should be required to make compensatory payment in case of damage caused to property.

Collaboration between the comrades' courts and the regular courts proceeds along two levels. A comrades' court may transfer any case to a regular criminal court if the comrades' court feels that there are enough grounds for criminal rather than social sanction. The regular criminal court must also transfer to the comrades' court any case before it if it feels that the crime committed does not pose any serious danger or the personality of the defendant is such that he could be re-educated through means of social pressure.

Members of the comrades' courts are elected to a fixed term of office, usually two years, at a general meeting of the collective to be served by the court in question. Members are accountable to and removable by those who elected them. Accordingly, all comrades' courts present reports of their activities to their electors at least once a year. In an effort to avoid an undesirable judicialization of the court's proceedings, the rules do not permit the participation of professional counsel or prosecutors in hearings before the courts.

The comrades' courts have three types of jurisdiction—exclusive, alternative, and transfer (referral). Among some of the cases that go before the comrades' courts are violations of work discipline; petty stealing of state, social or personal property; public drunkenness; acts of petty hooliganism; general disturbance of public peace either in one's place of residence or in any public place; public manifestation of an unworthy attitude towards women; failure to respect one's parents; failure to show respect for one's seniors; use of obscene words in public places; walking on public lawns, where a sign specifically says "Don't Walk on the Grass"; property disputes involving small amounts if both parties agree to go before a comrades' court; and any other anti-social behavior which does not constitute a crime or for which the criminal code has waived criminal sanction.

Under the general principle of *res judicata* the comrades' court is precluded from taking up any case (whether civil or criminal) in which a court of law has entered a definitive ruling on the merits. A comrades' court is also forbidden to entertain any case which is currently pending before a regular court. The regular courts are similarly precluded, under the same concept of law, from entertaining any case that had been definitively dealt with on the merits or is being heard by the comrades' court.

Parties before the comrades' court enjoy a measure of due process of law but the process is remarkably less rigid than in proceedings before the regular courts. One due process right which is clearly enjoyed by parties before the comrades' courts is the protection against double jeopardy. Under this doctrine a comrades' court shall not subject anyone to further sanction for conduct flowing from the same set of facts for which a defendant has already been placed in jeopardy by a regular court of law. However, the fact that some other administrative organ has already imposed a fine on an offender for a particular conduct does not preclude the comrades' court from taking up the case and imposing a separate sanction on the offender if he is found guilty of the conduct as charged.

Other due process protections enjoyed by parties before the comrades' court involve the right of a defendant to be informed of the charges against him, the right to be present at one's trial and to present evidence, the right to confront adverse witnesses, and the right to trial by an impartial tribunal. The decision of a comrade's court is not appealable to a regular court.

§ 6. Procuratorial and Criminal Investigative Agencies

a. The Procuracy

For the sake of convenience, detailed discussion of the nature and functions of the office of the procuracy has been integrated into Section C (2) below.

b. Criminal Investigative Agencies

One of the characteristic features of the inquisitorial criminal procedural system is the thoroughness with which a case is packaged before the commencement of the trial. At the pre-trial stages of the proceedings a criminal case goes through several checkpoints, one of which occurs upon the completion of the preliminary investigation into the case. Some socialist systems, notably that of the U.S.S.R., draw an artificial distinction between preliminary inquiry and preliminary investigation. Generally speaking, preliminary inquiry is a preparatory procedural step which, in those cases where the law mandates the conduct of a preliminary investigation, is antecedent to a full preliminary investigation. Under this system the agencies that conduct preliminary inquiry are different in most cases from those that carry out preliminary investigation. Most other socialist countries do not follow the Soviet arrangement in this regard. Typically, these other countries maintain only one unified system of criminal investigative agencies.

§ 7. Agencies for the Registration and Safekeeping of Public Records

a. *Notarial Offices*

For a detailed discussion of the profession of the notary and of the organization of the notarial offices see Section C (2)v below.

b. *Bureaus of the Office for the Registry of Civil Acts*

The Office for the Registry of Civil Acts (ORCA) is charged with the registration of legal facts as well as with the safekeeping of public documents relating to civil status. Typically, the ORCA is charged with the registration of acts of civil status such as births, adoptions, establishment of paternity, marriage, divorce, change of name, and all deaths (including civil deaths). All such acts are registered with the ORCA pursuant to the provisions of the relevant family code. The ORCA is established in every city or village and administratively is attached to and operates under the guidance of the executive committee of the corresponding level of the legislative council.

In registering the acts of civil status, the bureau of ORCA is required to make the appropriate entry in the register and issue a certificate to the registrant stating the fact so registered. The ORCA, unlike the notarial office, does not engage in any extensive investigation into the veracity of the facts which it is called upon to record. It is only a recording bureau and as such it simply records facts as they are presented to it by the registering parties. If there is any dispute as to the facts in question, *e. g.*, if the paternity of a child born out of wedlock is being contested, the registration clerk of the ORCA bureau must refer the case to a regular court for resolution. The ORCA, however, is required to verify the identity of persons who call upon it to perform any act of registration.

Along with the notarial offices, the ORCA is the major keeper of public records in the socialist countries. But unlike in the case of the notarial office, officials of the ORCA are not lawyers and do not need to have legal education in order to hold their office. They do not even need to have knowledge of the law beyond that of the enabling statute of the ORCA and of the relevant family code of the jurisdiction where they function. But like notaries, officials of the ORCA are civil servants who are paid a fixed salary. The ORCA operates in close collaboration with other government agencies, notably the police department and the selective service system. For example, in the enforcement of domestic passport rules the police department relies on information supplied by the ORCA. Similarly, in the administration of the military draft law the selective service system relies on the ORCA in drawing up a list of eligible enlistees.

CHAPTER 14

ROLES AND ACTORS

§ 1. Legal Education

Legal education in the socialist countries follows the tradition of legal education in continental European countries. It is offered at the undergraduate level, it is free, it is "non-professional" in the American sense, it is under the exclusive control of the universities and not of the professions, and it blends the teaching of purely legal subjects with the teaching of other humanitarian subjects. In the socialist countries, as in continental Western Europe, law is regarded as a humanizing discipline.

Unlike the situation in the United States where, typically, applicants for admission to the law school are required to hold the bachelor's degree, in the socialist systems the first degree in law is treated as an undergraduate degree. For admission an applicant must hold a general secondary school certificate, not be older than 35 years, have had two years of post-secondary school practical experience, and pass an entrance examination.

Like most other programs in the socialist countries, the law school curriculum is highly centralized. The syllabus is worked out and approved by the central Ministry of Higher and Secondary Education and is obligatory for all institutions teaching law throughout the country. The curriculum is divided into two parts. Part 1 stresses the social and economic sciences, and

[*316*]

Part 2 deals with the legal sciences. All of the subjects in both parts are mandatory. The function of the socialist undergraduate legal education is not to produce narrow specialists, but rather to produce generalists in the law.

The Part 1 (social and economic sciences) courses generally include History of the Communist Party, Marxist-Leninist Philosophy (which is subdivided into Historical Materialism and Dialectical Materialism), Fundamentals of Scientific Communism, Foreign Language, Jurisprudence, History of Political Thought, Legal History, Accounting for Lawyers, Latin, Law and Computers, Roman Law, Judicial Psychology, and Forensic Medicine and Psychiatry. The Part 2 (legal sciences) courses cover the traditional law courses.

Each course lasts for one semester and is generally followed by a final examination at the end of each semester. All examinations are oral and administered by a panel of two or three examiners, usually the same instructors who taught the course in which the student is being examined.

In addition to the examinations, each student must write a thesis during his last semester and take a comprehensive state examination which tests his knowledge, depending on his choice, in either public law or private law subjects. One major defect of this system is that it does not adequately teach the students any writing skills. The only time a student is required to write anything is at the very end of his studies, *i. e.*, when he writes his thesis. Because the examinations are oral and are conducted by the same instructors who had conducted the semester-long lectures or seminars, and as such tend to know the students individually, subjective judgments cannot be totally ruled out in the examination processes. The second criticism of this system is that there are too many obligatory subjects which the students must take during their stay at the law school. The system tends to produce narrow generalists. The students spend so much time accumulating informational knowledge that they hardly have any time left to reflect over the issues raised in the individual courses.

Until recently, the duration of law school studies was generally five years, but in the mid-1960s this was reduced to four. Under the four-year program the students are required to undergo a clinical apprenticeship during their seventh semester. Such apprenticeship must be spent in one of several institutions such as the courts, the procuracy, or any of the administrative agencies. The students are usually not given any choice as to the institution where they wish to undergo their clinical apprenticeship. There is generally no correlation between the institution where a student underwent his clinical apprenticeship and his ultimate job assignment upon graduation from law school.

The method of teaching law in these countries consists of a combination of lectures and tutorials. The lectures are delivered to a large audience, ordinarily to an entire class of first or second year students. The lectures traditionally are read only by full or, in limited cases, by associate professors. Thereafter, the classes are broken up into tutorial groups of between five to ten students. The tutorials are typically conducted by an associate or assistant professor or by a teaching assistant. The tutorial groups meet about three times per week to discuss and analyze the issues raised in the general lectures. Attendance at the general lectures is generally not obligatory, but as a rule almost all students attend these lectures. Attendance at the tutorial sessions is mandatory.

Legal education in the socialist countries is offered in university law faculties as well as in research law institutes. Because legal education in the socialist countries is of a non-professional character, the university law faculties tend to stress theoretical knowledge rather than practical skills. On the other hand, the law institutes (which typically are not affiliated with a university) are designed primarily for the part-time students and for those who are studying law through correspondence. These law institutes tend to stress the so-called practical subjects. Except for these differences in emphasis the curriculum of studies is the same in both the university law faculties and in the law institutes. Because of its part-time nature, the duration of studies in the law institutes is normally longer by at least one year.

The students at the university law faculties, who must be full-time students, pay no tuition fees. They are supplied with free books by the law library and receive a monthly subsistence allowance (stipend) from the state depending on the income bracket of the student's parents. The amount of the stipend is increased by about 25 percent for the excellent student.

The academic staff of a university law faculty includes a dean who is elected by the faculty council from the senior teaching staff [the senior teaching staff consists of only the full professors], full professors, associate professors, assistant professors, and teaching assistants. At the law institutes the academic staff additionally includes senior research fellows, junior research fellows, and senior instructors. Each law faculty is divided into departments, and each department is chaired by a full professor. The highest honor that can be bestowed on a legal scholar in these countries is election as a full or corresponding member of the national Academy of Sciences.

The following law degrees are conferred on persons who successfully complete the prescribed course of studies and fulfill other requirements: Bachelor of Laws; Master of Laws; Candidate of Juridicial Sciences (which roughly corresponds to an English Ph.D. degree in Law or an American J.S.D. degree); and Doctor of Juridicial Sciences (which has no counterpart under the American system). Socialist universities seldom grant honorary degrees.

§ 2. The Legal Profession

As a professional group socialist lawyers lack political power or social prestige. If official predictions are to come true, *i. e.*, that law in the socialist society will ultimately wither away under full communism, each new day brings the socialist legal profession closer to its demise. There is nothing to suggest, however, that any action at this time by the socialist legal profession is an act in contemplation of death. It is too early to begin to plan a funeral service for the legal profession in any socialist country. All indications point to the fact that the legal profession in the socialist countries is here to stay. Except for the advocates, all other members of the legal profession are state employees whose status is similar to that of any other civil servant. Like the situation in the United States, but unlike that of Germany, France or England, the legal profession is integrated, with admission to a considerable extent controlled by the university law faculties.

The organization of the legal profession in the socialist countries is similar to that of the United States and quite unlike that of France, Germany or England. Typically, in a socialist country there is only one legal profession. There are no institutional barriers to horizontal mobility from one branch of the profession to another. An advocate may choose to become a jurisconsult or procurator or vice versa without having to undergo any retraining process. Similarly, a procurator may move onto the bench without having to face any requalification problems. The training and professional requirements for admission to any branch of the profession are virtually the same. Except for the prospective advocate who has to undergo some post-law school apprenticeship in a law office before becoming a full-fledged advocate and the prospective legal scholar who needs further post-graduate training, the other branches of the socialist legal profession do not have any specific professional training, beyond receiving the first law degree, for their prospective members.

a.   Judges

In contrast to his American counterpart, the socialist judge is a faceless and humble civil servant whose judicial opinions are often rendered anonymously, whose dissenting opinions are entered in the records of the case [these court records are closed to members of the general public] but never reported, and whose decisions are only randomly and selectively reported. He is stripped of all elements of the cult of the black-robed infallibility which has evolved around his American colleague.   Elevation to the socialist bench is an overtly political process.

b.   Procurators

The procuracy is a formidable institution within a socialist legal system.   It comes very close to, but nevertheless falls short of, being the fourth branch of the socialist state.   Its functions are executive in nature yet it exercises supervisory oversight over the executive branch of government.   Organizationally, it is an extension of the legislative branch.   Judging by the scope of his political power, the Procurator General wields more authority than the chief justice of the nation's Supreme Court.   In terms of social prestige within the legal profession, the inferior procurators yield only to the legal scholars and justices of the respective supreme courts.   Measured by the extent of its functions, the procuracy has no counterpart in any modern Western legal system.   Because of his proximity to the centers of political authority, the Procurator General is the most powerful jurist in the entire country.

Structurally, the procuracy is a hierarchical, central-ized and independent organization, free of all interfer-ence from the local legislative councils. It is organ-ized according to the threefold principles of independence, uniformity, and centralization. Procurators are ranked hierarchically into military-type classifications. They wear military-type uniforms which designate their ranks and they operate in a strict hierarchy of vertical command. Each procurator is responsible to his superior, as well as for the actions of his subordinate procurators.

There are two parallel systems of the procuracy— the civilian procuracy and the military procuracy, both of which culminate in a single Procurator General. Administrative subdivisions of the procuracy roughly correspond to the administrative divisions of the coun-try in question. The Procurator General is generally appointed by and responsible to the national legisla-ture. The subordinate procurators are in turn ap-pointed by the Procurator General.

Unlike all the other members of the legal profession whose functions are essentially one-dimensional, the functions of the procurators are multi-faceted and span virtually all aspects of life in a socialist society. In its capacity as the penultimate guardian of socialist legality and guarantor of socialist rule of law, the procuracy's presence looms over virtually all legal pro-ceedings as well as over quasi-legal proceedings in such social organizations as the comrades' courts, the trade union organizations and the collective (coopera-tive) farms. The procuracy performs numerous clear-ly distinguishable but sometimes overlapping functions, acting as criminal investigator, grand jury, criminal prosecutor, judicial ombudsman, governmental (executive) ombudsman, general ombudsman, prison ombudsman, military ombudsman, and propagandist of socialist law.

As the criminal investigator, the procurator has responsibility for conducting the pretrial investigation in every criminal case. He conducts such investigation either personally or through criminal investigators over whom he maintains close supervision. As the grand jury he makes the determination whether or not to indict an accused. As the criminal prosecutor he handles all criminal prosecutions on behalf of the state. As a judicial ombudsman his function is to oversee all judicial proceedings, even those in which he is also serving as the public prosecutor. The procurator's prosecutorial and ombudsman functions within the context of the same judicial proceedings are not necessarily performed by the same procurator. As the executive ombudsman he oversees all activities by agencies of the executive department of government. His general ombudsman activities include oversight over the activities of all social organizations as well as private individuals. Similarly, as both the prison and military ombudsman he oversees the operations of the prison insitutions and the military establishments. In his capacity as propagandist of the law he organizes public lectures and seminars on different aspects of the law. He is perhaps the most respected member of the legal profession.

c. Advocates (Private Practitioners)

The profession of the advocate is the last "free profession" in most of the socialist countries, and he is the legal actor closest to a private practitioner in a Western legal system. The advocate is not a civil servant. His professional fees are the sole source of his income. He may not concurrently hold any other salaried position. This rule is intended to preserve the professional independence of an advocate as well as to shield him from any extraneous influence in his activities. Exemptions from this rule are made for those advocates who wish to pursue part-time teaching or academic research.

Advocates belong to professional associations called the college of advocates. The aggregate of all existing colleges of advocates is the "bar". In the Soviet Union, for example, an advocate operates out of a law office known as a jurisconsultatsiia. To equate the socialist concept of "bar" with an American, or the English, bar would be incorrect, however. Unlike the situation in the United States where one has to be admitted to the bar in order to practice law in any of its forms, one does not have to belong to the socialist bar in order to engage in the practice of law. Members of the other branches of the socialist legal profession practice law in various forms. One, however, has to belong to the bar in order to engage in the activities of an advocate. In a general sense an advocate is one who pleads cases before trial or appellate courts and the "bar" roughly corresponds to an association of such advocates. In the latter sense the socialist bar is integrated.

Unlike the English bar whose barrister members engage principally in advocacy while leaving the legal paperwork to the solicitors, there are no functional equivalents of the solicitors under the respective socialist systems. Accordingly, members of the bar do not confine themselves principally to the practice of advocacy. In contrast to the English barristers who have a near monopoly over advocacy in the superior courts, socialist advocates do not have a monopoly over advocacy in any level of the regular courts. As a social organization the bar retains control over much of its internal affairs, *i. e.*, admission of new members, disciplinary action against members, assignment of members to law offices, appointment and removal of managers of law offices, determination of the scale for the distribution of income within a law office, the determination of the size of a new law office, and the adoption of its own internal rules of procedure and code of discipline.

But unlike some of the other social organizations existing in the socialist countries, the bar is subject to some forms of state control. The basic statute governing its structure and functions is adopted by the legislature, governmental oversight over the activities of the bar is assigned to the ministry of justice, the fee schedule for the compensation of the services of an advocate is established by the state, the professional qualifications for admission to the bar are established by statute, and the categories of services that may be rendered free of charge to members of the public are statutorily defined. Even though the advocate is not a state employee he receives state-administered social security benefits on the same basis as state employees.

The modern socialist advocate, however, cannot be called a "private practitioner" in the true sense of that term. The advocate's law office is only superficially similar to an American law firm. The socialist advocates' law office is neither a partnership nor a professional corporation. Rather, it is just an operational unit of the college of advocates. Whereas an American law firm independently decides who may be associated with it either as a partner or as an associate, members of an advocates' law office are assigned to a particular law office by the presidium (executive committee) of the college of advocates to which the law office belongs. The size of an advocates' law office is determined by the presidium of the college of advocates.

Income within an advocates' law office is a set percentage of the fees generated by the individual advocate. Generally, the law office retains no more than 30 percent of such fees [to cover its overhead expenses] and credits the remainder to the personal account of the member. This means that a member's income is graduated depending on his experience and expertise. In short, a socialist advocate is a "private practitioner" only in the sense that he is not a civil servant and is not paid a fixed salary by the state. His status lies somewhere between that of a private practitioner and a salaried civil servant, but perhaps closer to that of a private lawyer in a Western system.

The university law faculties virtually hold the key to admission to the profession of an advocate. A prospective member of the profession must initially receive the first law degree. For admission to the bar there is no special professional bar examination to be passed. Upon receiving a law degree the prospective advocate must undergo an apprenticeship in a law office for six months. Completion of the apprenticeship allows him to petition the presidium of the college of advocates whose membership he seeks. As an exception to the general rule, any citizen of the state in question who holds a first law degree and has a work experience of at least two years in any other branch of the legal profession may petition the presidium of the college of advocates [whose jurisdiction covers the locality in which he wishes to practice] for admission as an advocate. Persons without the first law degree but who have worked in a law office for at least five years may also be admitted as advocates at the discretion of the presidium of the college. In addition to these general requirements, a prospective advocate must also be of a good moral character and lack a criminal record.

The functions of the advocate subsume those of the barristers and solicitors in England as well as combine the functions of the French avocat, notaire, conseil juridique and avoué. [For a detailed discussion of the role of these respective actors within the French system see Part One and for the English system, see Part Two of this Nutshell]. The advocate performs numerous functions including representation in criminal, civil and administrative proceedings, representation before the economic courts, legal consultation to economic enterprises, organizations and institutions, drafting of various legal documents, free legal counseling to members of the public, special counseling work with persons who are given suspended sentences or released on probation, and promotion of Soviet law.

An advocate is expected in all his undertakings, whether personal or professional, to be law-abiding, morally proper, and to avoid any semblance of impropriety. He is supposed to serve as a model for the "new man" that the state expects everyone to become under full communism. He must in all his acts exude moral purity and show strict respect for law. An advocate may not enter into any contingent fee arrangement with any client. Socialist law views contingent fee arrangements as absolutely immoral, ethically condemnable, and professionally undignified.

Within the bar organization there is a specialized sub-group called the foreign bar whose members specialize in cases with foreign elements, such as representation of foreign citizens in the courts of the socialist country, and the representation of citizens of that nation in foreign courts. Members of the foreign bar who are also members of the regular bar generally are knowledgeable about foreign laws and can function in at least one foreign language.

In addition to the foreign bar, there is yet another sub-group of advocates within the regular bar association whose members act as the exclusive counsels in special instances of political dissidents. Membership in this special group is based not on merit or brilliance as an advocate, but on political trustworthiness and the ideological stability of the individual advocate. Generally, admission to this closed body is open only to persons who are trusted by the system not to put up too zealous a defense of the defendant. An ordinary advocate who does not belong to this group may not be allowed to represent any party in a political case. Unlike the foreign bar, the political bar does not exist officially. In fact, the respective state authorities persistently deny the fact that such a sub-group exists within the bar.

d.   Jurisconsults

The jurisconsult in a typical socialist system roughly corresponds to the American in-house corporate counsel. He is a full-time legal adviser to enterprises, government agencies and institutions, and various economic and social organizations. The jurisconsult gives legal advice in commercial matters, drafts various legal documents, and represents the enterprise in all judicial and quasi-judicial proceedings as well as in arbitration proceedings.

The bulk of the jurisconsult's function consists of what may be described as preventive lawyering. He scrutinizes all decisions, orders, instructions and decrees about to be issued by his enterprise to make sure that they conform with the law; he goes over all draft contracts of the enterprise to make sure that they do not violate the law; he renders legal opinions to his employer on legal questions that might arise in the course of the day-to-day operations of the enterprise; and he routinely informs his employer of new legislation that might affect the operations of the en-

terprise. Typically, the jurisconsult will resort to litigation or arbitration as a step to be taken only spar-
ingly. In fact, he regards resort to litigation as
evidence of failure to contemplate and prevent the dispute in question. He is indeed obligated to refuse to
represent his employer in any litigation or arbitration
if he reaches an inner conviction that his employer has
no case. Like the advocate, he may not prosecute a
frivolous lawsuit on behalf of or defend a justified
claim against his employer.

A jurisconsult may not concurrently hold any other
salaried position. He may not be required to perform
any other duties within the enterprise by his employer.
Administratively the jurisconsults are integrated into
the structure of the Ministry of Justice.

e. Notaries

The socialist notary is cast in the general mold of his
continental European counterpart. But because of the
extraordinary growth of notarial functions in the complex post-industrial capitalist systems of the West, the
socialist notary today resembles the pre-industrial
Western notary. He nevertheless still bears remarkable similarities to his civilian counterparts. Like his
French or German colleague, he is a family counselor,
a commissioned agent in certain commercial transactions, a custodian of public records, and a certifier of
certain facts of legal significance. In the true West
European tradition he operates within a territorially
defined jurisdiction and is not permitted to hold any
other position in addition to being a notary. Thus, unlike the American figure with the same name, he can-

not be both a notary and an attorney at the same time. As in Germany and France, a degree in law is a prerequisite to admission into the profession of a notary in the socialist countries. But in contrast to his contemporary West European counterpart, he is not a private practitioner. He is just an ordinary civil servant.

Unlike his French counterpart he does not have a proprietary interest in his notarial commission. Thus he cannot, unlike the French notaire, pass on his commission by succession to his heir or sell it to a commercial buyer. In direct contrast to his European counterpart, who is a most respected, highly visible and comparatively well paid member of his community, the socialist notary is a humble and often faceless guardian of routines. As a professional group the socialist notaries lack any political clout.

Since one of the major functions of the socialist notary is to notarize documents, it is necessary to point out that under the socialist legal systems there are essentially two types of legal documents, those that require notarization in order to be valid and those that do not need to be notarized to be valid. Among the first category of documents are any contract of sale, exchange or gratuitous transfer of a house or part thereof if at least one of the parties is an individual citizen, any donation of money in excess of a fixed amount, power of attorney relating to certain transactions, wills, etc.

The functions of the socialist notary may be classified under four headings: certification of facts of legal significance, certification of noncontentious legal rights, performance of acts of execution in relation to certain documents, and the protection of property or evidence as well as the safekeeping of public documents.

The socialist notary is not expected to notarize mechanically any transaction or fact or document that is presented to him. As a prelude to giving his stamp of approval to any act, the law requires him, *inter alia*, to verify the substantive capacity of the parties as well as the conformance of the proposed transaction with all procedural requirements. The notary must also certify the authenticity of any document that is presented to him for certification as well as the identity of the persons seeking to notarize a particular document. If the petitioner is an agent of a state or social organization, the notary must verify the instrument which confers the power of attorney on him as well as the scope of his authority. The authenticity of the signatures tendered to be notarized must be verified. Additionally, the notary must insist that any transaction, application or other document must be signed in the presence of the notary. Before notarizing a contract the law also requires the notary to explain to the parties the meaning of the provisions of the contract as well as the legal implications of their contemplated act.

In other words, the law requires the notary not only to look out for possible violations of the law of the particular transaction but also to act as the legal counselor of the parties to the proposed transaction. He usually goes over the draft of a proposed contract with the parties and advises them of their rights and of the best way to protect their interests. If he detects any irregularities or violations in the proposed transaction, the law requires him to withhold his approval until the mandatory requirements have been complied with by the parties or petitioners. Because of his constant dealings with private law matters, it is generally conceded that the notary is perhaps the most knowledgeable about the particular country's private law among all the practicing lawyers. The lives of the average citizens are affected more by the activities of the state notary than by those of any other members of the legal profession.

By law the notary serves also as a private attorney-general in the sense that if in the course of his activities he discovers any violations of the law, he is obligated to report such knowledge to the appropriate authorities so that the requisite actions may be taken. Any refusal by a notary to perform a requested notarial act may be appealed by the aggrieved citizen or institution to a regular court. For each transaction carried out a notary collects from the petitioner a notarial fee in accordance with the set tariffs.

f. *Legal Scholars*

Legal scholars constitute the cream of the legal profession in all of the socialist countries. They play a major role in the training of all the other members of the legal profession and are the most highly compensated of all the lawyers. By virtue of their professional training they are the most knowledgeable about the law. They exert the greatest influence on the development of the law in several ways, through their systematic commentaries on the law, service on legislative drafting committees, service on the consultative committees attached to the respective supreme courts, and teaching law to future members of the profession. Typically, there are two groups of legal scholars in these countries, law teachers and legal research scholars. The latter conduct their research mainly in research institutes.

CHAPTER 15

PROCEDURE

§ 1. Civil Procedure

To say that modern socialist civil procedure blends elements of the Anglo-American adversary system with those of continental European traditions is not to deny the fact that the socialist system of procedure has developed its own unique features. Some of the features of modern socialist civil procedure are completely unknown to the other two systems.

A strikingly unique feature of modern socialist civil procedure is the ubiquitous presence of the procurator throughout the proceedings. The essence of the procurator's participation in these proceedings is to assert and protect the public interest in civil litigation. Even in civil actions where the state is not a party in interest, the procurator may in theory and usually does in practice intervene to protect an assertable interest of the public. The institution of the procuracy is completely unknown to the Anglo-American system. The presence of a functional equivalent of the socialist procuracy, *i. e.*, the public prosecutor, is provided for in continental West European systems of civil procedure. The difference between these two systems, however, is that the presence of the procurator in the socialist system is not only more pervasive, but also more intrusive, than that of the prosecutor in the civil law systems.

Modern socialist rules governing the status and role of parties in a civil action are notably different from those applicable in the United States. Socialist law affords the right to initiate and prosecute a civil suit to a wide range of persons in addition to the parties in interest. The law allows a self-appointed "good Samaritan", notably the procurator to file and prosecute a civil action on behalf of a third party beneficiary. Such good Samaritan action may be filed without the consent or over the objection of the intended third party beneficiary. Even where the third party beneficiary refuses to join the action, the judgment of the court in the case is binding on such third party in whose name the action was prosecuted.

Under modern socialist rules a civil trial may proceed even when the plaintiff elects not to further pursue the case. The reason for this unusual feature is that a socialist court is neither required nor permitted to dismiss a suit for lack of prosecution. While the class action has been found to be a most useful device for the joinder of similarly situated parties under American law, socialist law, like its continental European counterparts, refuses to recognize the class action concept. The closest socialist analogue to the class action is the so-called group action. Even though the group action performs some of the functions generally carried out through the class action device, it is conceptually different from the American class action.

Turning to the rules governing the filing of claims, one further notices several peculiarities of the socialist system in contrast to the American system. There is

a seemingly limitless freedom of the parties in a socialist civil action to amend their claims after the initial
filing; and the system allows a consolidation of a civil
claim with an on-going criminal proceeding where both
actions are founded upon the same factual situation.

On the question of discovery socialist law, like
American law, makes provisions for pre-trial, pre-suit
and pre-pleading discovery of facts. However, the
parties in a socialist civil action do not have anything
near the dazzling array of discovery devices available
to the American party. A socialist civil complainant
has at his disposal only a handful of informal methods
of individual discovery of facts in the case.

American law has a wider range of undiscoverable
information than does socialist law. For example,
under a typical socialist law of pretrial discovery,
much information is discoverable, including defendant's financial ability, expert's information developed
for litigation, investigator's notes and written ideas
and written as well as oral statements of witnesses obtained by an investigator in preparation for trial. In
fact, much of this information under socialist law
would be discovered not by the parties themselves, but
by the pretrial judge as part of the measures undertaken by him in preparation for trial.

Whereas American law recognizes many forms of
adjudication without trial, socialist law generally recognizes only very few such procedures, such as consent judgment, termination with prejudice, and dismissal without prejudice. There is no procedure for
summary judgment. If the formal requirements of a

statement of claims are met by the plaintiff, the case will be tried on the merits unless the plaintiff withdraws it with leave of the court. A claim will not be stricken for failing to disclose a cause of action, no matter how obvious this may be to the pretrial judge. But the defendant may submit a written statement to the court admitting the suit and thereby abort the trial.

There are many noteworthy features of socialist law of evidence. Some of these characteristics are shared by socialist law with its continental European counterparts, but others are unique to the socialist system. Among the characteristics of modern socialist rules of evidence are the following: the general tendency is to admit all relevant and material evidence in a case, including opinion testimony. Typically, however, hearsay testimony is not admissible as evidence even though information derived therefrom may be used collaterally. Hearsay testimony may be admissible as evidence only if the best evidence is unavailable. The free admissibility of evidence is coupled with the principle of free evaluation of evidence by the judge. Unlike the situation under American law where judgment in a criminal trial may not be introduced as evidence in a subsequent trial, under socialist law the trial judgment in a criminal case, once such judgment acquires the force of *res judicata*, is admissible as evidence in a civil action, but is not conclusive as to the fault or liability of the defendant in the civil suit.

Under modern socialist law, unlike under American law, the testimony of a person is not excluded from evidence merely because the testimony is given by a person who has an interest in the outcome of the case. Accordingly, testimony by a party in interest is admissible as evidence under socialist law. Furthermore, under the prevailing socialist law, parties in interest are not regarded as witnesses in their own case. Accordingly, the duty of a witness to tell the truth under pain of possible criminal punishment does not apply to a party in interest who elects to testify in his own behalf. In other words, unlike the witness, a party in interest is not under a legal duty to testify. And when he decides to testify he is not under any legal duty to tell the truth.

When one turns to the issue of pleadings it becomes immediately clear that socialist law, like the laws of the civil law system, adopts what amounts to notice pleadings under the common law. A pleader does not have to allege every essential factual element required by the substantive law to justify relief or to establish a defense. Consistency of the facts alleged is not a prerequisite of proper pleadings under socialist law. There is no requirement of stating a cause of action. Socialist law not only allows a pleader to plead inconsistent claims, but also alternative claims if they are made in good faith. It is generally the duty of the socialist pre-trial judge to straighten out any inconsistencies in the pleadings submitted to him and to reshape any pleadings cast in very general form in order to bring out the issues.

The trial is perhaps the most adversary aspect of socialist civil procedure. Nevertheless, it is dissimilar to the common law trial in many respects. There are noteworthy characteristic features of the socialist trial. The jury is conspicuously absent. Socialist trials are essentially bench trials. The trial is concentrated or continuous. Once a civil trial has started the court trying the case may not interrupt the trial to hear any other case. Because socialist trials are concentrated, there is an extensive pre-trial preparation of the case to shape the issues. Another major feature of the socialist trial hearing is the lack of a verbatim transcript of the trial proceedings. At socialist trials minutes stating the essential points, rather than full transcripts of the proceedings are kept.

Socialist law, like American law, recognizes the universal concept of statute of limitations according to which a specific period is set during which an aggrieved person must institute an action to protect his rights or lawful interests. On this matter, however, socialist law refuses to place procedure over substance. Accordingly, a socialist court or pre-trial judge may not refuse to accept a case simply on the ground that the statute of limitations on the action has run. Rather, the court is required to make a preliminary determination of the reasons why the petitioner failed to comply with the applicable statute of limitations and, if it is satisfied that the reasons are excusable, to proceed to hear the case on the merits.

The next area where socialist civil procedure is markedly different from its American counterpart is on the question of the form and scope of review of judgment. This will be discussed later in the Appellate Review section.

In the area of civil remedies socialist law is characterized by the general provision that a court may
grant more relief than that which is prayed for by the
plaintiff if the interests of justice so demand, and the
general prohibition against the award of pecuniary
compensation for non-pecuniary harm unless the statute specifically provides otherwise. As in all the civil
law systems of Western Europe, socialist law typically
prohibits the award of pecuniary compensation for so-
called emotional harm unless a statute specifically so
provides. But in almost all of the civil law systems of
today there are statutes or judicial decisions which as
a practical matter permit the award of monetary damages for emotional distress. Some of the socialist
states have enacted similar statutes, but there are no
such statutes, nor judicial decisions, in the Soviet system. Consequently, the Soviet system is one of the
few remaining national legal systems where the ban
against the award of pecuniary compensation for non-
pecuniary harm remains unmitigated.

Socialist rules governing the relationship between a
witness and the parties in a civil action are radically
different from those prevailing in American law.
Under socialist law the parties merely nominate witnesses, to be called in a case. The determination
whether or not to call such witnesses, as well as the
determination of the sequence in which the witnesses
are to testify in the trial, is made not by the parties,
but by the pre-trial judge or the court. There are no
pre-trial contacts between the counsel and the prospective witnesses under the prevailing socialist law. This
in turn also means that the parties do not have to

vouch for the veracity of the testimony of the witnesses, including those summoned to the case upon their nomination. The fact that the counsel do not have pre-trial contacts with the witnesses does not mean that the counsel are uninformed of the contents of the testimony of the witnesses prior to the trial. The counsel have full access to the depositions of the witnesses on both sides, which are generally taken by the pre-trial judge either personally or, at his request, by a commissioned judge.

Finally, socialist law, in contrast to American law, is characterized by miscellaneous features such as the general rule that the losing party pays the full costs as well as the full amount or a percentage of the attorney's fees of the prevailing party, unless the statute specifically creates an exemption; the uniquely socialist concept of private (special) rulings of the court which are rendered by the court at the same time that judgments in the case are handed down; and the fact that the socialist court has the power to hold a person in contempt of court and to assess a punitive fine against such a person, but never the power to order the imprisonment of even the most recalcitrant contemnor of the court. By contrast, an American court may, among other measures, order the imprisonment of a contemnor in order to enforce its contempt order.

§ 2. Criminal Procedure

The socialist criminal procedure system is essentially inquisitorial in nature, but it is not totally devoid of elements that are traditionally associated with the adversary system. It is nevertheless, preeminently more inquisitorial than it is adversary. It shares some of its inquisitorial features with the continental civil law systems. At the same time it manifests certain elements peculiar to systems that belong to the socialist legal family.

A striking feature of the socialist inquisitorial system is the continuity of the trial process. From the time the defendant enters his plea to the charge until the conclusion of the trial and judgment, the court may not interrupt the trial in order to undertake any other trial. The principle of continuity of trial is characteristic of all the other inquisitorial systems.

Another major feature of the socialist inquisitorial criminal process is the fact that the trial and the sentencing hearings are integrated into one continuous process. There is no separate pre-sentencing hearing distinct from the trial itself. As a result of this integrated procedure, after the conclusion of the trial the court retires to deliberate not only guilt and innocence, but the appropriate sentence in the case. The practical implication is that the trier of facts is informed of the defendant's prior conviction record before a decision is reached on the question of guilt or innocence.

A socialist trial court has full access to the pre-trial investigative file. Access is afforded not only to the presiding judge, who typically also serves as the pre-trial judge, but also to the other lay members of the court. Hence the socialist court begins to hear a case both with knowledge about the facts of the case and the personal background of the defendant. This contrasts sharply with the adversary system in which the trier of fact is kept in the dark as to the defendant's background and is ill-informed of the details contained in the pre-investigative file.

In contrast to some of the other inquisitorial systems, the socialist counsels play an active role during the conduct of the trial. They are actively involved in the examination of the witnesses as well as in the oral arguments. Typically, the socialist system not only permits direct examination but also cross-examination. By comparison, a socialist cross-examination is perhaps not as rigorous as its American counterpart. The permissibility and use of cross-examination by socialist counsel is one of the adversary elements of the socialist system.

A further principal feature of the socialist system is the oral nature of the criminal trial. The socialist judge is required to reach his decision based solely on evidence presented orally in court. Even though the judge has full access to the pre-trial investigative record of the case, he must close his eyes to whatever is contained in that record that was not brought out in court during trial. It is, however, the responsibility of the presiding judge to make sure that every element of evidence in the record is introduced orally at trial. This principle of orality also requires the judge, in case of any irreconcilable conflict between the recorded pre-trial and oral testimony given during trial, to give priority to the latter.

Unique to the socialist system is the use of social accusers and social defenders during trial. Social accusers and defenders are representatives of the public who are admitted to participate at the trial. They are elected at public meetings of persons who work or live at the same place as the defendant. Without seeking to displace or compete with the state prosecutor, the social accuser lends support to the prosecution. By contrast, the social defender throws his weight behind the cause of the defense counsel. Both the social accuser and the social defender operate independently of the state prosecution and defense counsel, respectively. But unlike the case of the state prosecutor and the defense counsel, the participation of a social accuser or social defender in the criminal process is confined to the trial phase of the proceedings. Even though by law the social accusers and defenders have the same rights that are granted to all the other participants in a criminal trial, their role in practice is essentially that of character witnesses for or against the defendant.

The fact that there may not be any pre-trial contacts or *ex parte* communications between the defense counsel on the one hand and the witnesses, the experts and the victim of the crime on the other, is another characteristic feature of the socialist inquisitorial system. Once a socialist counsel is admitted into the case he usually is granted full access to all depositions, including those of the witnesses, experts and the victim. If he feels that there is need for supplementary questioning of any of these participants he must ask the investigator to carry out the supplementary questioning. Pre-trial contacts or *ex parte* communications between the defense counsel and these other participants in the case are disallowed to prevent any coaching of the witnesses by the defense counsel.

Another notable feature of the socialist inquisitorial system is that the defense counsel is not permitted to engage in any independent pretrial fact gathering. Gathering facts in the case—both incriminating as well as exculpatory—is concentrated in the hands of the criminal investigative agencies. If upon his admission into a case a defense counsel feels that certain evidence has been left out or that there is need for supplementary investigation he must direct his request to the investigator who carries out the needed fact-gathering or taking of testimony.

Closely connected with the foregoing feature of socialist criminal procedure is that even though the court is generally required by law to assess court costs against a convicted criminal defendant, each party in a criminal case (the prosecution and the defense) is expected to bear his own attorneys' fees. This is true even if the defendant is acquitted and regardless of whether or not the attorney was retained or court-appointed. The law mandates the court or procurator to appoint counsel for the defendant in those cases in which the participation of counsel is obligatory if the defendant fails to voluntarily retain counsel. But because the services of a court-appointed counsel are not provided free of charge, the court is required upon the conclusion of the trial to order the defendant to pay the costs of his court-appointed counsel. This general rule is often relaxed to some degree in individual socialist countries.

The socialist criminal procedure system uses a piggyback system which permits the merger of civil claims with a criminal trial. The victim of a crime may elect to institute a civil suit against the defendant to seek compensation for any civil damage suffered as a result of the crime. In some socialist states criminal courts have the discretion whether or not to permit consolidation of a civil suit with a criminal trial. Once admitted into the case the civil plaintiff enjoys the same procedural rights as any of the other participants. The civil plaintiff operates independently of the state prosecution. As such, if the latter decides to retire from the case, the civil plaintiff may continue his action without the participation of the state prosecutor. If the civil plaintiff has already litigated his action in a civil proceeding and was denied recovery, he is barred from relitigating the same issues in the subsequent criminal trial.

During the consolidated trial of the civil and criminal actions different rules of evidence apply to the different actions. Even though the civil action was consolidated with the criminal trial, civil rules of evidence are applied to the civil claims on the theory that a civil suit does not cease to be a civil suit merely because it is being tried within the context of a criminal action.

If the civil plaintiff had already litigated his civil claims in a civil action the criminal court is bound by the findings of fact in the civil proceedings, but such findings of fact do not affect the question of guilt or innocence of the defendant in a criminal trial. Thus, the determination of guilt in a separate civil suit is not only acceptable in the subsequent criminal trial, it is *res judicata* as to those facts, although not as to guilt or innocence. Similarly, the findings of fact in a previous criminal trial are acceptable in a subsequent civil action and are *res judicata* as to those facts, but not as to the determination of fault or liability.

The possibility of conducting a criminal trial without a state prosecutor is perhaps the most "socialist" feature of socialist inquisitorial criminal procedure. A socialist criminal trial is viewed as a tripartite proceeding in which all the three sides, the court, the prosecution and the defense counsel, operate autonomously, yet in collaboration. Under socialist law the responsibility for conducting a state prosecution lies with the state prosecutor, but the actual conduct of the prosecution by a state prosecutor is discretionary, not mandatory. The general theory is that the prosecution's case is self-prosecuting and that the conduct of the prosecution by a prosecutor is dispensable. Upon indictment of the defendant the indicting prosecutor makes a determination whether or not to conduct the prosecution during trial. Even if he decides affirmatively, he may retire from the case at any time during trial, if in the course of the trial proceedings he reaches an inner conviction that the defendant is innocent. The fact, however, that he elected not to prosecute or that the prosecuting procurator elected to drop out of an on-going trial will not abort the trial.

Closely related to the above feature is the absence of prosecutorial discretion. The system strips the indicting procurator of the discretion to indict a defendant if the pretrial investigative file discloses sufficient evidence to enable him to conclude that a crime has been committed. The law, however, requires that before deciding to seek an indictment against the defendant, the indicting procurator must reach an inner conviction that a crime has been committed, that the defendant was the one who committed it, and that the evidence in the pretrial investigation report is sufficient to convict the defendant of the charges. In practice, therefore, if the indicting procurator decides not to prosecute a given case, all he needs to do is to enter a conclusion to the effect that he failed to reach an inner conviction on any of the matters noted above.

Another characteristic feature of the socialist inquisitorial criminal procedure is the absence of a jury as fact finders. As is the case under the West German system, but unlike the situation in the French system, the socialist trial court typically consists of professional and lay judges. The ratio of professional judges to lay judges varies from state to state but typically is one to two. The participation of lay judges is required in all trials regardless of the level of court. The lay assessors, unlike American jurors, have the same procedural rights and obligations as the law judges. They have full access to all pretrial investigative records of the case, they may not be precluded from hearing any available evidence in the case, they vote on questions of law and fact, they participate in decisions relating to guilt or innocence as well as in sentencing, they may put questions to the participants during trial, and they have to give written reasons for their decisions. Since the lay judges are usually not trained in the law, as a rule they are instructed by the law judge on questions of law before being called upon to reach a decision in the case.

One area of the law where socialist criminal procedure systems differ radically among themselves is when the right to counsel attaches. Subject to a few exceptions, a Soviet defendant, for example, is permitted by law to retain counsel only at the conclusion of the preliminary investigation. From the time that he is charged with the commission of a crime, and throughout the conduct of the preliminary investigation, he is not permitted to retain counsel. Such fact-gathering proceedings are thought to be investigative in nature and not yet accusatory, and the presence of counsel in this phase of the proceedings is functionally unnecessary and may even result in mischief. Only in certain instances specifically listed by law is a defendant permitted to retain counsel from the moment he is charged with the commission of a crime. Not all of the socialist countries follow this Soviet practice. In some of them the right of a defendant to the presence of counsel attaches from the moment the suspect is charged with a specific crime.

Thorough pretrial packaging of a case is a feature which the socialist systems share with other non-adversary systems. Before a case goes to trial it is carefully screened, checked and double-checked for errors either in the application of substantive law or in the enforcement of the defendant's procedural guarantees. The practical effect of this system is that cases with low probability of conviction are dropped before trial. Pretrial packaging of the case also accounts in part for the high conviction rate generally associated with all inquisitorial systems. Because of these various pretrial screenings of cases it is estimated: that about 60 percent of all initial complaints are dropped at the pre-indictment phase of the proceedings, *i. e.*, at the conclusion of the preliminary investigation; that about 10 percent of the remaining 40 percent are dropped at the conclusion of the preliminary judicial conference; and that over 99 percent of the cases that actually go to trial end up in conviction.

The socialist inquisitorial procedure is further characterized by the requirement that the prosecution's evidence be open to full pretrial discovery by the defense. This arrangement is intended to remove all elements of surprise from a trial. Pretrial disclosure of the state's evidence to the defense counsel is not selective but total. No evidence that had not been made known to the defense may be introduced during the trial. The defense counsel must be granted full and unimpeded access to the preliminary investigative file upon the conclusion of the investigation. Since the defense counsel is not permitted to engage in any independent pretrial fact-gathering, pretrial discovery of the defense evidence by the prosecution is generally not an issue under the socialist system. Simply put, under the socialist system no strategic advantage is gained by one party withholding evidence from the other party. The socialist trial is not allowed to degenerate into a trial by ambush.

The absence of the guilty plea as a device for aborting a criminal trial is a feature which the socialist system shares with other inquisitorial systems. A typical socialist trial usually commences with the court calling upon the defendant to enter his plea to the charges against him. If he enters a plea of guilty, unlike the situation under American law, the trial does not end at that point. Rather, the court admits his plea of guilty as one piece of evidence in the case and proceeds to trial. Because a socialist trial has a built-in automotive force it may neither be terminated by the failure of the state prosecutor to conduct the prosecution nor by the entry of a plea of guilty by the defendant. A socialist court is obligated to independently corroborate a defendant's guilty plea. To that effect it must reach an inner conviction on the defendant's guilt by looking at the totality of all the evidence in the case.

The socialist systems reject all notions of plea bargaining between the state prosecutor and the defense. The systems adopt the uncompromising position that criminal justice may not be negotiated or bargained away by the state prosecutor. Any plea bargaining agreement reached between the state prosecutor and the defense counsel is frustrated by several built-in devices of the system, including the fact that the court is not obligated to accept the indictment as it is presented by the prosecutor and is able to amend the indictment either in the direction of aggravating or mitigating the situation of the defendant, as long as any such amendment of the indictment by the court does not involve changing the factual elements of the charge. In other words, a defendant may be tried for crimes other than that for which he is indicted by the procurator. Due process requires, however, that the defendant must be afforded adequate opportunity to prepare his defense against the court-amended indictment.

The keeping of stenographic transcripts of the proceedings has become a fixed feature of the American criminal trial, but the socialist systems share a lack of stenographic transcripts of trials with other continental inquisitorial systems. Minutes of the proceedings are kept, however, which must reflect the major points of the trial. To assure that the court reporter records full and comprehensive minutes of the trial proceedings, the presiding judge generally pauses during trial to dictate crucial testimony. Furthermore, the trial participants may, with the permission of the presiding judge, dictate key portions of the testimony for entry into the minutes.

Perhaps the quintessentially socialist feature of criminal procedure is the fact that a socialist criminal court is required to enter private rulings at the same time that it hands down its decision in a given case. A private ruling is an ancillary statement by the court in which it indicates, among other things, what it discovered to be the circumstances that facilitated the commission of the crime, and its recommendation as to how to eliminate such conditions and thereby prevent the recurrence of similar crimes in the future. If the judges feel that criminal or administrative action ought to be instituted against a third party as a result of the facts turned up during the trial, they so recommend to the appropriate authorities. However, in an effort to prevent potential abuse of the institution of private rulings, the law typically requires the court to confine references in its private rulings to only those facts that were raised and established during the trial.

The prosecutor's right to appeal a judgment of acquittal is shared by socialist systems with continental criminal procedural systems. The reason for this rule is that a judgment is not regarded as definitive until a court of appellate review has had an opportunity to look at it. As such the protection against double jeopardy, which socialist law grants to the defendant, attaches only after the court of appellate review has reviewed such judgment. The prosecutor's right to appeal a judgment in a criminal case is not confined to instances in which the prosecutor objects to the acquittal of the defendant. The prosecutor may, for example, petition for appellate review if he feels that the punishment handed down by the court is incommensurably lenient or harsh, that the court failed to take into consideration all the evidence in the case or that the acquittal or conviction is unsupportable by the evidence introduced during the trial.

As is the case during trial the participation of the state prosecutor during appellate review is not mandatory. When a prosecuting procurator decides to appeal the judgment of a trial court, it is left to his discretion whether he wishes to conduct the prosecution of the appeal during the appellate review proceedings. The implication from this arrangement is that the prosecutor's case during such hearings is self-prosecuting.

While maintaining some form of exclusionary rules of evidence the socialist system rejects the doctrine of the fruit of the poisonous tree as the latter is understood in American law. The general rule regarding the admissibility of evidence in the socialist criminal proceedings is that any evidence, whether testimonial or documentary, as long as it is relevant and material and not unduly repetitious, shall be freely admissible. Evidence which is inadmissible is that obtained in violation of the attorney-client privilege or which cannot be verified either because the source is unknown (*e. g.*, anonymous letters) or is unavailable for examination (*e. g.*, hearsay evidence).

Evidence that is obtained in violation of the prescribed procedural rules relating either to the gathering or preservation of such evidence may be inadmissible if the procedural violation is of a criminal nature or is so fundamental to cast doubts on the credibility of the evidence. But if the procedural violation is capable of being cured or neutralized, it may be treated as evidence upon the removal of such procedural infirmity. A particular piece of evidence adjudged to be inadmissible does not render information derived therefrom to be unusable collaterally.

§ 3. Appellate Review

The general question whether a superior court may review the judgment of a court of first instance of necessity involves the issues of finality, timeliness, and mode, as well as scope of review. Under the final judgment rule, review of judgment normally is permitted only of a final judgment. A final judgment is the definitive judgment in the case entered on the merits by the court of first instance. The rationale for the rule is to prevent litigants from appealing every unfavorable judicial decision during the course of litigation and to avoid unnecessary intermediate reviews on the basis of errors that could be rendered moot by the judgment on the merits.

There are instances, however, when a non-final decision may have irremediable consequences. This is the case when an interlocutory (non-final) decision stops further movement of the case. As an exception to the final judgment rule, under socialist law interlocutory decisions are immediately reviewable by a superior court on the theory that such a decision effectively disposes of the case. Certainly, a judicial decision that, even though it is not final, sounds the death knell of a case has the same procedural effects as a final judgment and hence ought to be and is independently reviewable.

The timeliness doctrine requires that a party who wishes to seek a review of the judgment of a court of first instance must do so within the time limit established by law. Normally, the time runs from the time the order or judgment was rendered. A reviewing court may review only those decisions upon which there is a lower court record properly preserved and presented as the basis for the petition for review.

The function of the socialist review of judgment is to determine whether a reversible error has been committed by the lower court. Typically, socialist courts of review do not retry cases. The composition of the court of review is not designed to conduct trials. Because a socialist court of review does not engage in evidentiary hearings, the scope of review is thus less than a *de novo* hearing, but more extensive than review for legal errors only. A socialist court of review verifies not only the correct application of law by the lower court, but also the supportability of the judgment by all the evidence in the case. A socialist court of review thus reviews not only questions of law, but also the weight of evidence in the case for purposes of review of judgment. Evidence in the case may include not only evidence that was introduced and examined at the trial, but also newly discovered evidence which may be introduced for the first time in the course of the review proceedings.

Under socialist law the choice of the form of review of judgment of a court of first instance depends on whether the review is being sought against a judgment that has acquired the effect of *res judicata* or not; who has the right to seek the review in question; whether the review is being sought against a final judgment or against a nonfinal decision having irremediable consequences or against a private (special) ruling; and whether the review of judgment is to be undertaken by the same court that rendered the judgment in question.

Depending on the answers to these questions, socialist law generally recognizes several forms of review of a judgment: cassational appeal, cassational protest, supervisory review, interlocutory appeal, interlocutory protest and redetermination of the case.

Cassational review (not to be confused with the French cassational review) may be sought either through the filing of a cassational appeal or cassational protest. Cassational review is the form used for reviewing the final judgment of a court of original jurisdiction that has not acquired the effect of *res judicata*. If the review is initiated by a procurator it is called a cassational protest. But if it is initiated by any of the participants in the trial other than the procurator, it is called a cassational appeal. A court of cassational review, unlike the trial court, does not contain lay judges. It consists exclusively of law judges. Proceedings in the cassational courts are limited to oral arguments and no evidentiary hearing is conducted. In their oral arguments the participants may raise new points since, by law, they are not required to confine their oral arguments to points already discussed in their written petitions.

In the course of the cassational proceedings the participants may introduce newly discovered evidence in their oral arguments. The admissibility of newly discovered evidence in cassational hearings is subject to the general requirements of relevancy and materiality. Since there is no evidentiary hearing during a cassational review, the person who alleges the existence of newly discovered evidence will be expected to document such evidence in his written petition filed with the court and to introduce orally such evidence during his oral argument.

In reaching its decisions in the case, the court of cassation is required to look to all the evidence in the case, *i. e.*, the records of the case, allegations in the written petitions by the participants and allegations contained in the oral arguments by the participants. Furthermore, the court of cassation must not confine its investigation only to those portions of the judgment or issues in the case that have been appealed by the parties. Rather, it shall check to see whether the judgment of the court of first instance was in accord with the law and well founded, as to both parts of the judgment appealed against and not appealed against. The court of cassation is required to investigate the case with a view to protecting not only the interests of the participants in the cassational review, but also of all possible third parties who may be adversely affected by the decision in the case.

Depending on the findings in the case, the court of cassation is authorized to enter any one of several decisions. It may affirm the judgment of the lower court and deny the cassational appeal or protest (this is done only if the court comes to the inner conviction that the judgment of the court below was in accordance with law and fully substantiated by the evidence in the case), vacate the judgment of the lower court in part or in full and remand the case for a reconsideration by the court of first instance. It may further vacate the judgment of the lower court in part or in full and terminate the proceedings in the case or leave the suit without consideration. Finally, it may amend the judgment in the case without remanding the case to the lower court for further consideration. Whenever there is a need for the collection or further verification of evidence in the case, the court of cassation must remand the case to the court of first instance for an evidentiary hearing. However, if the facts of the case have been established by the court of first instance fully and correctly, but there is an error in the application of substantive law by the lower court, the court of cassation must correct the legal error and render a definitive decision in the case without remanding it to the lower court.

When a court of cassation remands a case for a retrial in a court of first instance the retrial is assigned, at the discretion of the court of cassation, to a court of first instance comprised either of the same members of the court who decided the first case or of different members.

Like the judgment of the court of first instance, the decision of a court of cassation follows an established format. It must contain four component parts: introductory, descriptive, reasoned and operative (resolutive). The information that must be contained in the decision of the court of cassation includes the time and place of the pronouncement of the decision; the title of the court pronouncing the decision and the composition of the court; the name of the procurator who gave conclusions on the question of law in the case as well as the identity of the other participants in the hearing; the name of the person who filed the cassational appeal or protest; a short summary of the substance of the judgment or of the cassational appeal or protest; the materials produced; the explanations of the persons taking part in the hearing of the case in court and the procurator's conclusions on questions of law in the case; the reasons for which the court came to its conclusions and reference to the laws which guided the court; and the ruling of the court in the case. When a court of cassation quashes a judgment and remands for a retrial it thus must state with clarity what circumstances of the case require clarification and what evidence must be obtained, as well as any other step to be taken by the court of first instance.

As to the legal effects of the decisions of the court of cassation vis-à-vis the lower court, the general rule is that "the decisions of a court hearing a case by way of cassation, as set out in the decision, are binding on the court rehearing the case". However, "the court hearing a case by way of cassation is not entitled to establish or treat as established any circumstances which were not established in the judgment or were refuted by it, or to prejudge the question of the credibility or otherwise of any evidence or the superiority of some evidence over others, how the rules of substantive law are to be applied or what judgment ought to be pronounced at the new trial in the case".

As already stated only judgments that have not acquired the effect of *res judicata* are subject to cassational review. Once a judgment or decision becomes *res judicata* it may, nevertheless, be subjected to supervisory review. But unlike an interlocutory review or cassational review which may be initiated by any participant in the case or by a non-participating procurator, the right to initiate a supervisory review is granted only to a limited number of governmental officials. These include the procurator general, the president of the national Supreme Court, the deputy procurator general, and the presidents of the intermediate regional courts and people's district courts.

Generally speaking, the petition for supervisory review is heard by the presidium (mixed chamber) of the court whose judgment is being reviewed. To prevent any interlocking membership of the courts of supervisory review and of the other courts, the general rule is that a member of the presidium of the court who took part in the hearing of a case either in the court of first or cassational instance, may not participate in the hearing of the case by way of supervisory review. If a majority of the members of the court of supervisory review at the intermediate or local court levels are disqualifiable under this rule, the case is sent to the next higher court for supervisory review.

As in the case of cassational review, the scope of review in a supervisory review is less than review *de novo* but more extensive than mere review for legal error. Typically, the law requires the court of supervisory review to check the judgment or decision for conformity with the law and substantiality of evidence. In doing so the court does not confine itself solely to the narrow issues raised by the protest, but rather looks at the entire judgment. Also, the court in reaching its decision in the case looks at all available evidence in the case, including any newly discovered evidence. The court must always bear in mind not just the interests of those persons who are participating in the hearing, but also of third parties who may be adversely affected by the judgment or decision in question.

The right to petition for a redetermination of judgment is granted to all participants in the case as well as to any procurator. The law generally establishes a time limit during which a petition for reconsideration must be filed. Effectively, it is three months from the time that the new evidence was discovered by the petitioner or the date that the sentence of the criminal court acquired legal effect or from the date of entry into legal effect of the sentence or judgment quashing a judgment or decision upon which the judgment or decision to be redetermined was based. Unlike in the case of supervisory review, the right to initiate a redetermination of judgment is not granted to judicial officials, *i. e.*, presidents or vice presidents of the respective courts.

Interlocutory (non-final) decisions may be reviewed by way of interlocutory appeal or protest. Interlocutory decisions either do or do not effectively stop any further movement of a case. If an interlocutory decision stops further motion in a case it is immediately (independently) reviewable by way of interlocutory appeal or protest. But if it does not stop the case, any review must await final judgment, in which case review is considered part of the ordinary cassational appeal or protest.

An interlocutory appeal, in contrast to an interlocutory protest, is an appeal initiated by any participant in the case other than the procurator. When it is initiated by a procurator it is referred to as an interlocutory protest. An interlocutory appeal or protest is also the proper device for reviewing a private (special) ruling in a civil action. All interlocutory appeals or protests are heard by the court that ordinarily has the power of cassational review. The decision of a court of interlocutory review acquires the effect of *res judicata* immediately upon its pronouncement. As such, it is not subject to any further cassational or interlocutory review. It is, however, not immune from review by a court of supervisory review.

The options granted to the court of supervisory review, with one exception, are exactly the same as those which the law grants to the court of cassation. The only difference is that the law authorizes the court of supervisory review to affirm a trial court's judgment or ruling in the case if the latter had been reversed or amended by a court of cassation. For example, if a judgment of a court of first instance was reversed or amended by a court of cassation, but the court of supervisory review agrees with the court of first instance in the case, it shall simply affirm the earlier judgment or decision of the trial court by lifting the infirmity imposed on it by the court of cassation.

When a court of supervisory review orders a new trial in a case, just as with the court of cassation, the law allows the court of supervisory review to send the case to the same or to an entirely different court for retrial. This is the general practice although the court of supervisory review may remand a quashed judgment for a new cassational review, a comparatively rare practice.

One other method of reviewing judgments and decisions that have acquired the effects of *res judicata* is a complete redetermination of the judgment or decision. This is available as a method of review if there is newly discovered evidence in the case. But the newly discovered evidence must be of such a nature that had it been known to the trial court it would have affected the outcome of the case. A redetermination may not be granted on the basis of non-prejudicial newly discovered evidence.

Generally, the redetermination of judgment or decision is handled by the same court that rendered the initial judgment. But if the judgment of a trial court had been amended by a court of cassational or supervisory review or if a superior court had entered a new decision in a case, the petition for redetermination of the judgment or decision is handled by the court that entered the amended or new decision.

§ 4. Methods of Securing Constitutional Supremacy

Students of comparative constitutional law identify two basic methods of securing constitutional supremacy: judicial control and political control over the constitutionality of state actions. The choice of method of achieving this ideal of constitutional justice depends on the legal culture of each country as well as on the history and general ideology of the state in question. Some legal systems resort to a combination of elements drawn from both methods. Others totally repudiate one of these two methods and stick exclusively to the other. Socialist countries, with one notable exception, typically prefer the political control device over the judicial control method.

The judicial control methods include such devices as temporary judicial relief (the writ of *habeas corpus*), implied judicial control (the ability of the French Council of State to review acts of the executive branch for conformity with the general principles of law and to "interpret away" provisions of questionable constitutionality), and judicial review in contentious cases. The latter method may take the form of general judicial review (not limited to fundamental rights but rather to all constitutional and legal rights) and restricted judicial review (limited only to fundamental rights).

The political control over constitutionality takes the forms of exercise of constitutional control by the legislature or the president of the republic, preventive constitutional control in the form of advisory opinions (by the French Council of State) or binding opinions (by the Constitutional Council in France) and separation of powers.

In the socialist countries, with the notable exception of Yugoslavia, there is no form of judicial control over constitutionality of governmental actions. The prevailing method of achieving constitutional justice in these countries is through political control. Usually, the legislature polices its own legislative activities to make sure that they are in conformity with the constitution. But since the socialist legislature typically operates as a continuing constitutional convention, an act of the socialist legislature can rarely be unconstitutional. The socialist constitution is the supreme law of the land only until it is amended by the legislature. The ultimate political control over the legislature is exercised, however, by the Communist Party.

The other method of political control over constitutionality in most of the socialist states is procuratorial supervision over the activities of the executive and judicial departments of government. The general rule in these activities is that all sublegislative acts (acts emanating from the executive departments) must conform with the state constitution in order to be valid. If the procurator determines that an executive act violates the state constitution, he protests the act to the council of ministers (the cabinet), which in turn is empowered to repeal the particular unconstitutional act.

But if the constitutionally offensive act was issued by the council of ministers, the procurator must take his protest directly to the legislature for the appropriate action.

On the other hand, if the procurator determines that the decision of an inferior or intermediate court violates the constitution, he protests the decision to the national supreme court. But if the allegedly unconstitutional decision was handed down by the supreme court itself, virtually all socialist states empower the procurator to take his protest over such a decision directly to the legislature for constitutional review thereof. When this happens the legislature or subdivision constitutes itself into an ad hoc super-supreme court for the purpose of reviewing the decision of the supreme court.

Typically, a socialist court lacks the jurisdiction to entertain constitutional challenges to acts of the legislative or executive branch of government. The only socialist country that has a constitutional court is Yugoslavia. This court is authorized to hear constitutional challenges to actions by the respective branches of the state. If the court finds the challenged acts to be unconstitutional, it has the power to void them.

The general reluctance of the socialist countries to permit any form of judicial review of acts of the legislature or executive branch of government reflects their unwillingness to permit the courts to serve as a check on the exercise of state authority by the other two branches. Protection over the state constitution is a political function performed ultimately by the

Communist Party, penultimately by the legislature and routinely by the council of ministers and the procuracy. The role of the courts in the promotion of constitutional justice is typically limited to appellate review by the superior courts of the judgments of the courts below for conformity with the law, including the constitution.

CHAPTER 16

RULES

§ 1. Divisions of Law

Socialist law rejects both the common law division of law into common law and equity, as well as, at least in theory, the civil law division of public law and private law. There is no system of equity under the socialist legal system, and to the socialist legal mind all law is supposed to be public law. This later position is predicated upon Lenin's assertion that "all law is public law." It must be noted, however, that East European legal scholars interpret Lenin's pronouncement on the possible division of socialist law into private and public law differently from their Soviet counterparts.

Soviet scholars still adhere to what they see as Lenin's categorical and absolute rejection of any possible division of socialist law into public and private law, because such division presupposes the parallel existence of public and private property within the system. Upon restudying Lenin's position on this question, the East European scholars have come to the conclusion that the Soviet theorists have misread Lenin.

Briefly stated, public law is that division of the law which regulates relationships between the citizen and the state or between agencies of the state inter se or between the state and foreign governments. By contrast, private law regulates relationships between private individuals. Accordingly, public law includes several branches: constitutional law, criminal law, enterprise organization (economic) law, foreign relations law, financial law, land law, collective farm law, and correctional labor law. Private law, on the other hand, includes the laws of contract, tort, and property; family law and restitution. Labor law can properly be described as "mixed" or sui generis. It lies somewhere at the border between public law and private law.

A different major division of socialist law is that between substantive law and adjectival law. Substantive law consists of the substantive rules of both public and private law whereas adjectival law consists of the laws of procedure, evidence and remedies. Adjectival law as such includes criminal procedure, civil procedure, administrative procedure, remedies and evidence.

a. Public Law and Private Law

Constitutional law is the queen of the socialist legal system. It is a fulcrum upon which the entire socialist law revolves. As a branch of public law it constitutes the fountainhead of the entire legal order. Its norms constitute the litmus against which all the other norms of socialist law must be tested. Constitutional law defines the structure of the state and apportions powers to the different functional branches of the socialist state. It defines the constitutional status of the Communist Party within the legal system as well as prescribing the fundamental rights and duties of citizens. It articulates the general principles of socialist federalism (where applicable), the electoral system, the political and economic systems, the program for the social and cultural development of the socialist society, and socialist foreign policy and national defense. Within the socialist hierarchy of norms the constitutional norm is supreme. Consequently, any other legal norm that conflicts with this basic norm must yield.

Criminal law articulates the general penal policy of the socialist state. Such questions as what is a crime and what is the purpose of criminal punishment are regulated by the norms of this branch of public law. The law of enterprise organization regulates the economic relationships among the various economic enterprises in the course of their fulfillment of the state economic development plans. Legal relations that fall outside the realm of economic plan contracts, even if they exist between economic enterprises, are generally regulated by other branches of the law. Foreign relations law is the branch of socialist law which regulates, among other things, the authority to conclude an international agreement on behalf of the state, the constitutional procedure for the conclusion of such treaties, the difference between treaties and executive agreements, and the procedure for the reception of international agreements into domestic law.

Financial law, as a branch of socialist law, regulates financial relationships which arise in connection with state activities in the area of accumulation, distribution, redistribution, and expenditure of state budgetary resources. The state carries out these activities through the various financial institutions of the local council, the ministries, and departments, the state banks, the state construction banks, etc. Generally speaking, socialist financial law is determined by financial planning; the state budget is the basic financial plan. From the point of view of subject matter, socialist financial law is subdivided into budgetary, fiscal, state insurance, social insurance, credit, money circulation, and financial control provisions.

Land law regulates legal relations connected with the use of land. Socialist land law is founded on the general principle that nearly all land is nationalized. There are a few socialist countries where small amounts of land may still be held in private hands. This is the exception rather than the rule in socialist law. Typically, the only form of land use in the socialist countries is land tenure or the right of use of land. Land, the subsoil, forests, and all bodies of waters are regarded as *res extra commercium* [a thing that must not be made the object of any commercial transaction]. Any form of commercial or other legal transaction involving land, including buying, selling, mortgaging, leasing, lending, testamentary disposition, and gratuitous transfer, is illegal and deemed to be null and void *ab initio* under most of the national socialist legal systems.

Labor law regulates relations arising from participation of workers and civil servants in the labor process. The labor relations of members of collective (cooperative) farms are regulated not by labor law, but by collective farm law.

Collective farm law as a branch of law is unique to the socialist legal systems. This branch of law regulates the relationships arising from the organization and activities of collective farms, as well as relationships between a collective farm and its members or between two or more collective farms. All relationships arising from participation in a collective farm, *i. e.*, property, labor, administrative, and land use relationships, as well as the implementation of state policy in the collective farms, are regulated by collective farm law. Similar relationships arising within a state farm are regulated not by the norms of collective farm law, but variously by norms of labor law or land law.

Correctional labor law regulates the status as well as articulates the rights and duties of persons who are serving terms in any of the penal institutions. The administration of this branch of law is typically entrusted to the management of the correctional facility and the procuracy.

The laws of contract, tort and restitution constitute the three divisions of the law of obligations in any socialist legal system. Family law, on the other hand, regulates personal and property relationships between spouses *inter se*, as well as between parents and their children and other members of the family. Together with the law of property, these four branches of law constitute the core of socialist private law.

b. *Substantive Law and Adjectival Law*

One of the historical characteristics of the socialist legal system is the preeminence which it gives to substantive over procedural law. It is generally said that in a typical socialist legal system the law of procedure is secreted in the interstices of substantive law. Socialist law has had a blind spot for procedure. Because socialist law of procedure evolved at a much later stage than substantive law, the latter division of the law is more developed and better refined than the former. To the socialist legal mind procedure follows substantive law. The nature and form of the applicable procedure are determined by the nature of the substantive rules in question.

Civil procedure is used for the judicial administration of all the substantive laws embodied in the civil code. In designated instances persons who have exhausted the special procedure contemplated under other branches of the law may, if the issues involved are not of a criminal nature, invoke the powers of the civil courts. Whenever a civil court administers any other substantive law other than civil law, the procedure used is civil.

Criminal procedure regulates the activities of the criminal courts, the procurators, and the criminal investigative agencies in connection with the investigation of a criminal case. It is the procedure used for the administration of the rules of substantive criminal law.

By contrast, administrative procedure is employed by the various administrative agencies in their implementation of the numerous substantive administrative rules and regulations. Administrative procedure in these countries is generally characterized by its informality and speed. Defendants before an administrative tribunal typically enjoy less due process protection than their counterparts before civil and criminal courts. Because the rules of evidence are closely linked with those of procedure, there is no uniform law of evidence that is applicable to all the three procedures described above. Similarly, the nature and form of remedies tend to vary not only from one division of the law to the other, but also from one branch of law to another. The law of remedies is best studied within the context of the individual branches of substantive law.

§ 2. Sources of Law

Generally speaking, the term "sources of law" means the fountainhead from which the stream of law flows. More specifically, the term "source of law" may be used in three different contexts to refer to material, formal or literary sources of law. Material source of law under the socialist system refers to the economic system which predetermines the contents of the law. In discussing the material sources of socialist law, one must bear in mind the same fundamental presumptions of the socialist legal system: the material source of all laws is the socialist economic basis upon which the legal system is mounted; the true nature of this economic basis is reflected in the policies and major ideological decisions of the ruling Communist Party; and because the Communist Party is regarded as infallible by virtue of the fact that it is the final authority in matters of state ideology and general development of the law, any legal norm that conflicts with a Party general directive must yield. The economic basis as interpreted in the policy directives of the Party is the ultimate source of socialist law.

By contrast, the term "formal source of law" refers to the sovereign, the state, or the "will of the people." By this term one means the political power which gives the law its validity and force. The analysis which follows is primarily concerned with the so-called literary sources of socialist law: the sources of binding rules of law or the forms in which legal rules are manifested.

The general attitude of the socialist legal system toward the literary sources of law is close to those of civil law countries, but has lagged behind recent changes in the civil law practices on this question. The role of legislation is stressed in lawmaking; the role of judges in norm creation is almost totally discounted. The attitude of socialist law towards custom as a source of law is somewhat ambivalent. On the one hand it seeks to eradicate all customs from the life of the law. It views custom, particularly bourgeois and prerevolutionary customs, as subversive, evil, and incompatible with the spirit of the new law. On the other hand, it concedes that in some aspects of the law, in the absence of any applicable legislative norm, custom could be resorted to as a source of binding rules of conduct. The role of social organization in lawmaking is granted partial recognition under socialist law.

In discussing the literary sources of law, socialist commentators, like civil law scholars, draw a distinction between the so-called binding (primary) sources and the non-binding (secondary) sources of that law. A non-binding source of law constitutes evidence of what the law is, but lacks a binding character.

The binding sources of law under the socialist system are legislation, sub-legislative acts (sometimes referred to as subordinated legislation or delegated legislation or indirect legislation), acts of social organizations that have received the approval of the state, custom, general principles of socialist law, treaties and conventions, and foreign law. Legislation, as used in this context, refers to all acts adopted by the legislative branch of the socialist state or its subdivisions. The constitution is the supreme form of lawmaking in any socialist state. It is the supreme law of the land in the sense that all other laws within the country must be tested against it for constitutionality. In cases of any conflict between a constitutional rule or any other legal rule in the country, the latter must yield. The adoption of the state constitution is typically reserved exclusively for the legislature.

Next to the constitution within the hierarchy of sources of law are the codes. A code must be distinguished from just any collection of statutes or an assemblage of related legal rules, the code being an internally harmonized, periodically updated, supreme systematization of the legal rules relating to one branch of law. A true code strives not merely to bring together in one place the existing legal rules in one branch of law, but more importantly, to convey in one act, in an internally reconciled and scientifically systematized fashion, all of the accumulated normative materials in the given branch of law. The style of the individual and national codifications within the respective socialist countries follows that of either the French or the German codification.

Organic statutes constitute another form of legislation. A statute may address itself to matters not covered by any code or, in some cases, may be used to fill gaps in the code or to modify a code provision. Periodically, subdivisions of the legislature (the executive organs of the parliament) promulgate rules on different legal relationships. Not all such rules are regarded as binding sources of law, however.

Another major category of sources of socialist law are the sub-legislative acts, emanating from the executive department of the socialist state. In order to be valid these acts must be substantively *intra vires* [within the powers] as determined by the jurisdiction of the issuing authority, be constitutional, and be promulgated in conformity with the established procedure.

Acts of non-governmental organization that have received the approval of the state constitute the next major category of binding sources of socialist law. A unique feature of the socialist legal system is the wholesale delegation of certain traditionally governmental functions to social organizations. In exercise of this delegated responsibility these social organizations promulgate different rules and regulations. Under normal circumstances rules adopted by social (non-governmental) organizations are not regarded as a binding source of law. But once these rules receive the express approval of the state, they become elevated to the level of a legal rule. For example, most rules adopted by the socialist trade union organizations fall within this category of legal rules.

The next major source of law is custom. Custom plays a most significant role as a source of law, but only when so authorized by the legislator. Custom is expressly recognized as a source of law in international trade law, the law regulating merchant shipping, land law, and domestic commercial law. For example, one fundamental principle of socialist commercial law is that in all such transactions individual citizens as well as social organizations are required not only to observe the laws, but also to respect the rules of socialist community life and the moral principles of a society building communism. Business practices and usage among the economic organizations are also treated as sources of socialist enterprise organization law (economic law).

A point that must not be lost is that custom serves as a source of law only if and when legislative law so recognizes it. If the law is silent on the threshold question of whether or not custom should be relied upon in a given situation or if the law specifically rejects custom as a source of law, the courts must not look to custom for a rule of law.

General principles of socialist law constitute another binding source of law in the socialist systems. For example, Article 12, paragraph 3 of the Fundamental Principles of Civil Procedure of the USSR and the Union Republics stipulates that "In the absence of a law regulating a relation in dispute, the court shall apply the law regulating similar relations, and in the absence of such a law, the court shall proceed from the general principles and meaning of Soviet legislation." But nowhere are these "general principles" of socialist law listed. It is presumed that the term "general principles" of socialist law is a reference to those fundamental (preeminent) principles that permeate the entire fabric of socialist law. Generally speaking, these general principles of socialist law are tantamount to the principles of socialist equity.

Treaties and conventions are specifically recognized as sources of law. For example, Article 129 of the Fundamental Principles of Civil Legislation of the USSR and the Union Republics states: "If other rules have been established by an international treaty or international agreement in which the USSR participates than those which are contained in Soviet civil legislation, the rules of the international treaty or international agreement shall be applied." International treaty law usually is received into socialist law through an act incorporating it. Whether a separate act of incorporation is required to merge international treaty law into domestic law, or whether the act of ratification or signature of the international instrument in question per se constitutes its incorporation, is an unsettled issue in some of the socialist countries. But where the rules of an international treaty have been received into domestic law, such rules are directly applicable only if they are self-executing.

Foreign law is recognized as a source of law for the socialist domestic courts in numerous conflict of laws provisions. The references to foreign law in the respective choice of law provisions of the relevant socialist legislation are to all sources of law recognized in the relevant foreign law, including legislation, subordinate legislation, case law, custom, and, where applicable, the general principles of that foreign law. However, the application of foreign law in socialist courts is subject to the limitations that may be imposed by the individual state's public policy. Typically, socialist public policy stipulates that foreign law shall not be applied if its application would be contrary to the bases of the individual country's legal system.

There is unanimity among socialist and Western commentators on the binding nature of the sources of law discussed in the foregoing paragraphs. The sharpest disagreement among commentators involves the nature and role of judicial decisions in socialist lawmaking. Socialist courts typically hand down two types of judicial acts, decisions in individual cases and interpretive or explanatory rulings. The latter are issued by the respective supreme courts outside the context of any specific litigation and they are intended to guide the lower courts in their general application of the laws to concrete cases before them. Soviet scholars, for example, are unanimous in their assertion that neither the decision rendered by a chamber of the USSR Supreme Court in an individual case nor the guiding interpretations handed down by the plenum (en banc session) of the USSR Supreme Court constitute a binding source of Soviet law. In their view these judicial acts, especially the latter, play a major role in the systematization of Soviet law, but they do not embody binding rules of general or particular applicability.

On this same question there are two schools of thought in the Western literature. The thrust of the majority school is that decisions of the USSR Supreme

Court in individual cases are generally followed by the lower courts as a matter of course; guiding interpretations rendered by the plenum of the USSR Supreme Court are generally binding on the lower courts; consequently both of these judicial acts rank as binding sources of Soviet law; and when a Soviet court finds a gap in the law it fills the gap by engaging in interstitial legislation. The minority school agrees with the majority position that the enactment of a civil code is only a beginning, the judge and jurist must make the system function. If the situation is clearly one which should be regulated by law, but is not, then the Soviet courts will show little hesitation in stepping into the gap.

Unlike the majority school, however, the minority school is of the view that when a Soviet court fills a gap in the law it is not engaging in interstitial legislation as its common law counterpart does, simply because, unlike the situation under the common law system, under socialist law judicial decisions in concrete cases do not constitute law for a subsequent case. A socialist court, especially a lower court, does in fact follow the decisions of another court, especially those of the supreme court. In practice, socialist courts, probably consciously, follow the interpretation of an applicable law as set out in a prior decision. The fact of the matter, however, is that the court does not have to follow such interpretation. When it decides to follow a prior judicial interpretation it does not do so out of a feeling of compulsion. Furthermore, when a lower court decides to follow prior case law it does not cite the previous decision as the authority for its decision. In fact, a socialist court typically is precluded by law from citing a previous decision as the basis for its decision. In short, case law lacks the requisite element of *opinio juris* that would transform it into a source of law *stricto sensu*. We subscribe to the latter school.

Doctrinal writings have never been treated as binding sources of socialist law either by socialist writers or by Western commentators. But this is not the same as saying that doctrine has not played any major role in the development of socialist law. Historically, legal scholarship has had a profound effect on the development of individual socialist legal systems, especially during the early years of codification. But this historical effect of doctrine on lawmaking was catalytic rather than constitutive. Modern commentaries by leading socialist scholars serve as compelling evidence of the law. These writings are never cited by the courts in their decisions. But this is not because the courts do not derive any insight from them. They all do periodically. Rather, socialist courts decline to cite legal scholarship in support of their decisions because the law requires them to cite nothing but a binding rule as the basis for their decision. In a way, legal scholarship occupies the same position in the workings of socialist courts as does case law. Both are non-binding, but are compelling evidence of the applicable law in the respective socialist courts.

SELECTED BIBLIOGRAPHY

H. Berman, *Justice in the USSR: An Interpretation of Soviet Law* (Harvard Univ. Press; Cambridge, Mass.) (1966).

V. Chkhikvadze (ed.), *The Soviet State and Law* (Progress Publishers, Moscow) (1969).

L. Grigorian and Iu. Dolgopolov, *Fundamentals of Soviet State Law* (Progress Publishers, Moscow) (1971).

J. Hazard, *Communists and Their Law: A Search for the Common Core of the Legal Systems of the Marxian Socialist States* (The Univ. of Chicago Press, Chicago) (1969).

V. Li, *Law Without Lawyers: A Comparative View of Law in China and the United States* (Westview Press; Boulder, Colorado) (1978).

A. Makhnenko, *The State Law of the Socialist Countries* (Progress Publishers, Moscow) (1976).

C. Osakwe, *The Common Law of the Constitutions of the Communist-Party States*, 3 Review of Socialist Law 155–217 (1977).

I. Szabó and Z. Péteri, *A Socialist Approach to Comparative Law* (Sijthoff, Leyden) (1977).

*

INDEX

References are to Pages

[*387*]

INDEX

INDEX

References are to Pages

INDEX

References are to Pages

INDEX

References are to Pages

INDEX

References are to Pages

[*393*]

INDEX

INDEX

References are to Pages

INDEX

INDEX

†

HIEBERT LIBRARY

3 6877 00205 7346

K
560
.G43
1982